LOGISTICS
IN
WORLD WAR II

**FINAL REPORT OF THE
ARMY SERVICE FORCES**

Contents

	Page
INTRODUCTION	VII
CHAPTER 1. PREPARATIONS PRIOR TO PEARL HARBOR	1
The Peacetime Army	1
Early Expansion of the Army	2
Development of Weapons	3
Industrial Mobilization	4
Construction	7
Effect of Lend Lease on Preparedness	7
Oversea Bases	8
Service Troops	9
CHAPTER 2. STATE OF READINESS, DECEMBER 1941	10
CHAPTER 3. THE ARMY SERVICE FORCES	22
CHAPTER 4. INFLUENCE OF LOGISTICS ON STRATEGY	32
North African Campaign	35
Sicilian Campaign	38
Italian Campaign	39
European Theater of Operations	40
Persian Gulf Command	44
China, Burma, India	45
Aleutians Campaign	48
Early Pacific Campaigns	48
The Philippines	51
Preparation for the Final Assault on Japan	53
Redeployment	54
CHAPTER 5. SUPPLY	56
Requirements	57
Research and Development	62
Production	65
Purchasing	70
Storage	74
Packaging and Packing	77
Distribution	78

CHAPTER 5. SUPPLY—Continued

	Page
Lend-Lease Distribution	84
Civilian Supply in Occupied and Liberated Areas	85
Maintenance	88
Combat Vehicles	91
Motor Transport Vehicles	93
Artillery and Ammunition	94
Small Arms	97
Clothing and Equipage	99
Subsistence	101
Engineer Equipment	103
Communications Equipment	104
Chemical Warfare Supplies	106

CHAPTER 6. SERVICES

	107
Military Personnel Administration	107
Civilian Employees	112
Military Training	113
Information and Education	118
Special Services	119
Chaplains	120
Medical Services	121
Military Justice	127
Military Police	128
Construction and Real Estate	130
Communications	139
Transportation	140
Finance	149
Printing	152
Photography	153
Maps	154
Post Management and Housekeeping	154

CHAPTER 7. LOGISTICS IN THEATERS OF OPERATIONS

158

CHAPTER 8. MANAGEMENT

	171
Organization	171
Supervisory Personnel	173
Policies	174
Planning	175
Procedures	175
Work Simplification	182
Work Measurement	183
Service Control	187
Management Ideas from Within the Organization	187

CHAPTER 8. MANAGEMENT—Continued

	Page
Statistical Reporting	190
Reports Control	191
Personnel Control	191
Control Units	193

CHAPTER 9. ARMY SERVICE FORCES RELATIONSHIPS ... 194

Within the War Department	195
With the Navy	198
With the Combined and Joint Chiefs of Staff	200
With Civilian War Agencies	202

CHAPTER 10. THE TRANSITION TO PEACE ... 214

Demobilization Planning	214
Demobilization of Personnel	216
Matériel Demobilization	219
Property Disposition	224
Disposal Agency Backlogs	226
Direct Disposition by the War Department	228
Disposition of Army Service Forces Property Overseas	229
Assisting the Civilian Economy	230
Demobilization of Installations	232
Transportation	233
Civilian Supply	234
Food Conservation	238
Repatriation of United States Dead	238
Dissolution of the Army Service Forces	239

CHAPTER 11. LOGISTIC LESSONS OF WORLD WAR II. 244

Summary	252

APPENDIX I. List of Important Management Improvements Achieved in ASF to 11 June 1946 ... 253

APPENDIX II. Key Personnel ... 271

Illustrations

Chart No.		Pages
1.	Logistic Activities	x
2.	Logistic Situation, December 1941	16
3.	Organization, Army Service Forces, 1945	20
4.	Work of the Army Service Forces	---
5.	ASF Activities to End of Hostilities, World War II	25
6.	U. S. Army Supply Lines, World War II	---
7.	Supply Control	60
8.	ASF Procurement Deliveries	64
9.	ASF Index of Contract Price Changes	71
10.	Technical Service Procurement District	72
11.	Storage Depots—Army Service Forces	76
12.	Oversea Supply	82
13.	ASF Lend-Lease Shipments	86
14.	Types of Military Personnel Processing Centers	117
15.	General and Regional Hospitals	122
16.	Army Construction in Continental U. S.	133
17.	Army Communications Network, World War II	---
18.	Merchant Ship Tonnage Available, United Nations	141
19.	Ports of Embarkation and Theaters Supplied	142
20.	Army Cargo Shipped Overseas	145
21.	Embarkations for Overseas	148
22.	Army Service Forces Installations	156
23.	Typical ASF Installations in a Camp	---
24.	European Theater of Operations	---
25.	Southwest Pacific Area	166
26.	Quartermaster Local Purchase Procedure Before Standardization	176
27.	Local Purchase Procedure After Standardization	178
28.	Examples of Annual Savings from Procedural Simplifications	180
29.	Work Simplification Process and Layout Charts	184
30.	Work Simplification—Gang Process Charts	186
31.	Work Simplification Operation and Layout Study	187
32.	Work Measurement	188
33.	Examples of Service Improvements in ASF	189
34.	ASF Activity and Personnel Indexes	192
35.	Committees of the Combined and Joint Chiefs of Staff with ASF Representation	203
36.	Principal Civilian Agencies with which the ASF had Dealings	204
37.	Returns to Civilian Life	218
38.	ASF Procurement Deliveries	221
39.	ASF Termination Settlements	223
40.	Measures of Selected ASF Activities through 31 May 1946	242

INTRODUCTION

On 2 September 1945 in Tokyo Bay, the United States and its Allies concluded the greatest war in history. World War II was the most important armed conflict in which the United States ever engaged, whether measured by the size of the forces employed, the vast dispersal of the battlefields, or its tremendous impact upon national life. Between 1942 and 1945 we maintained the largest and the best equipped and supplied Army in our history. The logistic requirements of this undertaking made transcendent demands upon the resources, energies, and ingenuity of our Nation.

The word "logistics" has been given many different shades of meaning. A common definition is: "That branch of military art which embraces the details of the transport, quartering, and supply of troops in military operations." As the word is used in the following pages, its meaning is even broader. It embraces all military activities not included in the terms "strategy" and "tactics." In this sense, logistics includes procurement, storage, and distribution of equipment and supplies; transport of troops and cargo by land, sea, and air; construction and maintenance of facilities; communication by wire, radio, and the mails; care of the sick and wounded; and the induction, classification, assignment, welfare, and separation of personnel.

World War II was a logistician's war. Its outstanding characteristics were the totality with which manpower and resources were mobilized and the vigor with which the belligerents attempted to destroy each other's material resources for war. Fabrication and assembly plants, refineries, laboratories, rail and highway networks, ports and canals, oil fields, and power-generating installations, because of their logistic importance, were primary objects of offensive action. Developments in mechanized, aerial, and amphibious warfare made the logistic support of armed forces vastly more complicated and extensive. The emphasis placed upon logistics in this report is not intended to detract from the importance of strategy and tactics, the limitless gallantry and courage of the combat forces, nor the imagination and professional skill of combat commanders. The combat forces won the war by providing the guts, manpower, and skills with which our superior weight in matériel was applied in destroying the enemy. Our cause would have been lost without the magnificent logistic support by our entire Nation. Logistics provided the tools with which our air, ground, and sea forces fashioned victory.

The Army Service Forces engaged in a vast logistic undertaking. Its responsibilities were twofold: operational in the Zone of the Interior, technical throughout the world. The logistic tasks and problems that confronted the Army Service Forces were larger and more complex than any previously encountered in our history. The memory is still vivid of what was done, how it was done, the problems and their solutions, and the successes and failures of the past five years, yet sufficient time has passed to provide the perspective requisite in summarizing the logistic lessons of the war.

This report reviews the logistic preparations for national defense during the years prior to Pearl Harbor. It summarizes what was accomplished during the period of hostilities, points out difficulties encountered in each major field, delineates the influence of logistics on strategy, describes the supply and service operations in active Theaters, and outlines the problems of demobilization. It attempts to indicate the more important logistic lessons of the recent war and suggests some of their future applications.

It is necessary to reorganize our military establishment for national security. It is hoped that this report records experience which will assist and guide those whose duty it becomes to plan and provide for our Nation's future security.

CHART 1. LOGISTIC ACTIVITIES

DEVELOPMENT OF EQUIPMENT
    Scientific research
    Military characteristics
    Technical intelligence
    Design
    Specifications
    Pilot models
    Proving and testing
    Standardization

SUPPLY
    Determination of quantitive requirements for equipment and supplies
    Procurement of munitions
        Purchasing policies
        Contract provisions and forms
        Price analysis
        Contract negotiations
        Contract renegotiations
        Contract termination and settlement
        Procurement objectives
        Determination of raw material and component requirements
        Allocation and control of raw materials and components
        Facilities selection and allocation
        Requirements, allocation, and control of machine tools
        Production engineering
        Production scheduling
        Production expediting
        Conservation of critical materials
        Labor supply and industrial relations
        Inspection and acceptance
    Distribution
        Stock control
        Requisitioning
        Allocation and control of critical items
        Issue
        Marking for shipment
        Redistribution of excesses
        Disposal of surpluses
    Storage
        Receiving and shipping
        Warehousing

SUPPLY—Continued
- Storage—Continued
  - Materials handling
  - Packing and packaging
- Maintenance and repair of equipment and supplies
  - Preventive maintenance
  - Maintenance engineering
  - Shop operations
- Salvage and disposal of scrap

TRANSPORTATION of troops and cargo by air, rail, road, and water
- Port operations
- Stowage
- Traffic control
- Staging areas
- Freight consolidation
- Preparations for domestic and overseas movement
- Shipping documentation

FACILITIES
- Design, construction, repair, and maintenance of—
  - Troop housing
  - Training centers
  - Airfields
  - Ports
  - Depots
  - Roads
  - Railroads
  - Hospitals
  - Communication facilities
  - Manufacturing and assembly plants
  - Power plants
  - Water and sewage systems
- Utilities service
  - Light
  - Heat
  - Power
  - Sewage disposal
  - Refuse disposal
  - Water supply
- Acquisition and leasing of real estate
- Disposal of surplus real property
- Surveying and reproduction and supply of maps

COMMUNICATIONS
- Telephone
- Radio

COMMUNICATIONS—Continued
    Telegraph
    Postal service

MEDICAL SERVICE
    Evacuation
    Hospitalization
    Preventive medicine
    Out-patient service
    Dental service
    Veterinary service
    Convalescence and rehabilitation
    Research and development for medical treatment
    Sanitation

PERSONNEL SERVICES
    Recruitment, induction, and reception
    Classification, assignment, and separation
    Personnel requirements and availabilities
    Personnel records
    Casualties
    Prisoners of war
    Military Police
    Spiritual welfare
    Legal assistance
    Care of personal effects
    Counseling on personal affairs
    Recreation facilities
        Exchanges
        Motion pictures
        Libraries
        Shows
        Athletics
        Radio
        Newspapers and magazines

FINANCE
    Budgeting
    Accounting
    Disbursing
    Auditing
    Advanced payments
    Guaranteed loans
    Payment of personnel
    Allotments and benefits
    Transfer of funds

FINANCE—Continued
>Foreign exchange
>Deposit accounts
>Banking facilities
>Insurance

LEGAL
>Military justice
>Claims
>Litigation
>General legal counsel

SERVICE TROOPS
>Requirements
>Individual specialist and unit training
>Activation and de-activation

Chapter 1

PREPARATIONS PRIOR TO PEARL HARBOR

The logistic ability of a nation to wage modern war lies fundamentally in its resources of raw materials, industrial capacity, transport, scientific knowledge, and manpower. These are only potentials. For combat, they must be translated into fully equipped and trained forces at the strategic points. Although we possessed the necessary resources, we were unprepared for immediate military action on a large scale when the Japanese struck Pearl Harbor. Fortunately, some preparations that were of incalculable value had been made in the preceding two years.

The Peacetime Army

In mid-1939 we had 174,000 men in the Regular Army. Its three and one-half square divisions were at half strength and scattered in 130 posts across the country. Scarce motor transportation made divisional training impracticable. There were virtually no corps or army troops nor specialized service troops. The Air Corps consisted of 62 tactical squadrons. Training funds were less than five percent of annual War Department appropriations. We possessed the peacetime Army of a third-rate military power.

In 1937 the War Department had proposed the expenditure of a modest sum on industrial preparations for the production of up-to-date weapons. Congress rejected this. Attempts to provide a small reserve of modern arms and special equipment were unsuccessful. The first substantial ordnance program, instituted in the spring of 1939, was projected over three years with first deliveries beginning in September 1940. The National Guard maneuvered with stovepipe "mortars" and with dumptrucks labeled "tank." New tables of organization carried modern weapons which for months were only names to National Guard troops.

Early Expansion of the Army

The outbreak of the European war in September 1939 was the first of a series of shocks that forced the United States to face the need for preparedness. Unfortunately, the actions taken were a compromise between the distasteful reality of danger and the pleasant illusion of security. The President's proclamation of a state of limited emergency in September 1939 authorized a Regular Army of 227,000 and a National Guard of 235,000. This expansion permitted the transformation of the three and one-half square divisions into five modern triangular divisions. Early the next year, however, we could put no more than 75,000 troops into the field in a crisis, with only 15 of the 1,420, 37 mm guns that had been ordered, only 140 modern 75's of the 1,430 on order.

The year of Dunkirk, the railway car at Compiegne, and the Swastika on the Eiffel Tower, 1940, brought peacetime military conscription to the United States for the first time in our history. On 16 September 1940, spurred by the fall of France, Congress passed the Selective Service Act. It provided for an Army of 1.4 million, consisting of regulars, National Guard, and selectees. A month later, in schools and other public buildings throughout the country, men from 21 through 35 started registering under the new law. Between 16 October 1940 and the following July, more than 17 million registered. Of these millions, the act only allowed 900,000 to be inducted for service in the Army, with appropriations up to August 1941. A few weeks before Pearl Harbor, Congress renewed the Selective Service Act by a margin of only one vote in the House of Representatives.

It was one thing to register our manpower and to induct the selected into the Army; it was quite another to provide equipment and munitions to match those of our potential enemy. Before 1939, munitions appropriations were a mere trickle. Two years before the European war began, only 50 million dollars was appropriated, 20 million for armament and equipment and 30 million for war reserves. "Peace in our time" at Munich in September 1938 was followed by an authorization of 100 million dollars for the following year. A year later, upon the outbreak of war, an alarmed Congress increased this figure seven-fold.

The rush of events in the following fateful year revealed these efforts to be puny. France capitulated on 22 June 1940, and on the last day of the month, following the recommendations of a special committee appointed by the President, the War Department submitted a new munitions program to Congress under the Protective Mobilization Plan. This program was designed to equip an Army of one million men, provide reserves of critical items for an Army of two million, and build up industrial capacity for an Army of four million. We set an annual goal of 18,000 aircraft, an unheard-of figure in those days. The cost of the program was estimated at 5.9 billion dollars, of which Congress appropriated almost four billion in September 1940.

These were sizable sums, yet the armament and the four-million-man Army they represented existed only on paper. Only the barest beginning toward translating appropriations and plans into the grim tangibles of war could be made in the year before we had to face the test of survival. As the threat to American security increased between June 1940 and Pearl Harbor, the War Department successively developed five supply programs. Each program reflected an increase in the authorized strength of the Army and included requirements for initial equipment and combat maintenance for one year, the period considered necessary for building up production to offset wartime consumption. Our supply program at the time of Pearl Harbor totaled 11.6 billion dollars.

On 22 June 1941, the Wehrmacht plunged across the Russian frontier. Less than three weeks later, the President directed the Secretary of War to explore the "over-all production requirements to defeat our potential enemies." In response, the War Department General Staff prepared a troop basis indicating the size and composition of the force considered necessary to defeat Germany, Italy, and Japan. This was the basis upon which quantitative requirements were determined for weapons, vehicles, uniforms, and all the hundreds of thousands of items necessary to equip and maintain the required force. The computation of requirements for munitions was completed in October 1941. This was the Victory Program with which we embarked upon the struggle two months later. It was the first program that gave realistic consideration to the productive resources of the country.

Development of Weapons

Research and the development of new and improved weapons and other military equipment before June 1940 were restricted because of lack of funds. The average annual expenditure from 1925 to 1940 was less than 2.5 million dollars, of which 1.5 million went to the Ordnance Department. The Medical Department and the Quartermaster Corps were limited to less than $20,000 a year. In 1937 the Quartermaster General had requested $123,000 for the development of clothing, equipage, and military motor vehicles, but Congress appropriated only $2,000.

After the German victories in the spring of 1940, research and development appropriations leaped from 3.5 million dollars for the current year to 20 million dollars for the year ending 30 June 1941. Some of the technical lessons of the European War could be exploited. The M-1 rifle, the .50 caliber machine gun, the Browning automatic rifle, and the Thompson submachine gun were all in quantity production by the fall of 1941. Most of the medium and heavy field artillery weapons that were put into production before Pearl Harbor remained standard equipment, with modifications and improvements, throughout the war. The same was true of practically all the famous truck models which distinguished themselves on battlefields from Tunisia to Saipan, the ubiquitous ¼-ton "jeep," the ¾-ton weapons carrier, and the 1½-ton, 2½-ton, and 4-ton cargo trucks. The fall of 1941 also saw the standardization of the M-4 medium tank, mainstay of our armored divisions until the introduction of the heavier M-26 during the Rhineland campaign.

In order better to utilize the talents of inventors and scientists, the President established the National Defense Research Committee on 15 June 1940. A month later the National Inventors' Council was set up in the Department of Commerce to appraise inventions submitted by civilians for national defense purposes. The President took another important step in the same direction in June 1941 by organizing the Office of Scientific Research and Development, giving it authority to coordinate the research programs of the National Advisory Committee for Aeronautics, the National Academy of Sciences, the National Research Council, and the Committee on Medical Research.

Industrial Mobilization

As early as 1922, the Navy joined the War Department in planning for industrial mobilization through the medium of the Army and Navy Munitions Board. Industrial Mobilization Plans published in 1931, 1933, 1936, and 1939 emphasized the need for extensive Government control over the entire economy in any future war.

The War and Navy Departments next worked out individual detailed plans. The departments identified the critical materials which would cause difficulty in the event of total mobilization and advocated stockpiling in the United States. This was begun on a limited scale in 1940 under the sponsorship of civilian agencies.

The Army and Navy Munitions Board gave attention to the facilities available for the output of finished munitions. It devised an elaborate allocations plan for assigning industrial facilities among the various procuring agencies, and hoped thereby to prevent the type of competition which had characterized 1917 procurement. The War Department had advocated a program of educational orders and had worked out the necessary details prior to 1940. These orders were intended to give some experience to manufacturers in the production of war matériel. The educational-order program began formally in 1939, but failed to accomplish much because of the inadequate funds. After September 1940, educational orders were swallowed up by increasing demands for the delivery of munitions, in quantity, to build up our defenses.

The plan for allocating facilities was never put into effect. The period from July 1940 to 7 December 1941 was not a period of total mobilization, but rather of defensive preparations. Each procuring agency let contracts independently, on the basis of informal bids or industrial commitments conveyed to the War Department directly or through the Office of Production Management.

The Industrial Mobilization Plan contemplated the participation of Federal civilian agencies in war mobilization. The civilian agencies were to mobilize and control manpower and materials, while the Army and Navy directly procured their supplies and services. The essentials of this scheme were followed during the period before Pearl Harbor.

As the war in Europe progressed, many governmental agencies were created for the purpose of directing various phases of our defense program. The functions of these agencies covered a vast field of activities without very precise delineation of respective responsibilities. In August 1939 the President had appointed the War Resources Board for the purpose of making an exhaustive examination of the Industrial Mobilization Plan. Although the Board's report was generally favorable, the Board was dissolved in November 1939, and the plan was disregarded as an organizational blueprint, probably for the following reasons: the plan was unacceptable to civilian agencies because it had been prepared by the military; no organizational nucleus susceptible of rapid expansion in time of emergency was in existence; a full understanding of the plan and its details had not been achieved by industry or the public. This was unfortunate, as many subsequent difficulties could have been avoided or minimized by utilizing the plan in the months before Pearl Harbor for readying the Nation more effectively for war. Until 7 December 1941, however, defense efforts were controlled by the uncertainties of public opinion, and vigorous, positive administration was not possible so long as public policy was confused and objectives were not clearly understood.

As the European War became more critical, the President named an Advisory Commission to the Council of National Defense on 29 May 1940, for the purpose of coordinating national defense programs. As defense requirements expanded, however, the activities of the Commission were absorbed by operating agencies, such as the Office of Defense Transportation. During this preparatory period national resources were generally adequate for the limited military program, and the Advisory Commission did not play as important a role as its successors.

The President created the Priorities Board in October 1940 as the impact upon industrial facilities began to be felt. This Board, like the Advisory Commission, did not assume major importance because critical shortages had not yet developed, and it was not able to formulate in advance a workable system of controls.

The Office of Production Management was established in January 1941 for the purpose of stimulating production and coordinating the activities of other agencies that affected national defense. It absorbed most of the functions of the Advisory Commission and the Priorities Board. On paper, the Office of Production Management represented the most forward step toward the mobilization of our resources yet taken. It was not fully effective in actual operation, chiefly because of deficiencies in its internal organization and the lack of a firm national policy. It was superseded in August 1941 by the Supply Priorities and Allocations Board, which in turn was superseded by the War Production Board in January 1942. The latter became the major coordinator of industry for the national defense program.

During this period the civilian agencies took many important steps directing the American economy into military production. Priorities administration which gave preference to military orders was begun in February 1941. Preference orders covering the elements of production, such as machine tools, aluminum, copper, and steel, were instituted the following spring. The Federal Reserve Board restricted consumer credit and installment purchasing in August. On the twenty-first of that same month the Office of Production Management announced that automobile production for civilian use would be cut $26\frac{1}{2}$ percent by 30 November 1941, and 50 percent by July 1942. The Supply Priorities and Allocations Board restricted nonessential building and other construction in October 1941. Civilian refrigerator production was virtually halted that same month, and copper was eliminated from practically all civilian products. Because of the need to pool and control oil supplies, the President in May 1941 set up the Office of the Petroleum Coordinator for War under the Secretary of the Interior. This office coordinated all Federal activities affecting the production, refining, transport, and marketing of petroleum. The Office of Scientific Research and Development, created in June 1941 in order to mobilize the Nation's scientific resources, was of invaluable aid to the War Department from the outset in encouraging and financing fundamental research by universities and industry, and in coordinating this work with that carried on in the War Department.

Construction

As the Army grew in numbers and acquired new equipment, it required an enormous expansion in its physical plant. Except for off-continent bases and airfield construction, which were assigned to the Corps of Engineers, the Quartermaster General carried out the military construction program before Pearl Harbor. Cantonment construction was a major phase of the program and had to keep pace with and in advance of the increasing strength of the Army. The need for large, sparsely-populated maneuver areas made unprecedented demands for land, new roads, and new facilities. The few cantonments retained after World War I were of use, but were completely inadequate. By November 1941, new housing and training facilities for 1.3 million troops, and 10 general hospitals having a capacity of 10,400 beds, had been completed.

The building of suitable Army supply depots and manufacturing plants in preparation for a global war was also necessary. The Quartermaster Corps began the construction of 17 new supply depots within the Zone of the Interior and our oversea possessions, in addition to expanding existing storage facilities. The building of 42 new Ordnance Department plants was undertaken for the manufacture of TNT and DNT, small arms, smokeless powder, ammonia, toluol, tanks, armor plate, nitrate, oleum, and ammonium picrate, all materials for which private plants were inadequate for a sizable munitions program. The construction of several plants for the Chemical Warfare Service was also begun. These facilities programs were 57 percent completed by the time of Pearl Harbor. Four of the 61 ordnance plants were finished, and another 23 were in partial operation.

While the Quartermaster Corps was transforming the country into a vast training and cantonment area, the Corps of Engineers rushed the construction of airfields and the development of our oversea bases. By 7 December 1941, 21 air-base projects within the continental United States had been completed, and 163 additional projects were under construction. In addition to major projects in Trinidad, Bermuda, and Newfoundland, and the improvement of facilities in the older oversea bases, such as Panama, Puerto Rico, and Hawaii, the construction of airfields in Latin America, for an air-ferry route in the South Pacific, of pipe lines, repair shops, and depots in North Africa, and the improvement of the trans-Iranian railroad had been started.

Effect of Lend-Lease on Preparedness

The most important factor in our strategy was that time was afforded to bring our potential military power into operation. Lend-lease bolstered the resistance of our future Allies and served to stimulate our industrial expansion when orders for munitions for our own forces still were relatively small.

In September 1939, our small munitions industry could not meet the sudden demands of the western European powers. Almost immediately, however, the British and French Governments began, through contracts for war materials and through subsidies for plant construction, to stimulate the conversion and expansion of our civilian plants for war production. By the end of 1940 the dollar resources of these countries were exhausted, and it appeared that the flow of munitions would be curtailed. We averted this danger in March 1941 by passing the Lend-Lease Act, which eventually became the keystone of our aid to our Allies. Lend-lease requirements were ordinarily approved only if the requirements were for standard United States Army items or items that could be easily modified for our use. We gained the resultant plant expansion in this manner and also a means of testing our equipment in actual combat.

Additional benefits were derived from the reciprocal aid agreements made with the United Kingdom, Australia, and New Zealand in September 1941. Transfers were made to us of British antiaircraft and coast defense weapons for the defense of the Panama Canal. We also received a number of installations and quantities of supplies from the British when we occupied bases in Iceland and the Caribbean in the same year.

Oversea Bases

Our principal oversea bases before Pearl Harbor were the Philippines, Hawaii, Panama, and Puerto Rico. In the 20 years prior to 1940, these commands had become settled outposts with tiny garrisons rhythmically changing their personnel under a system of rotating tours of duty. The supply of these bases presented few problems. Garrisons relied heavily upon local resources, and shipments from the United States were small. The latter were shipped automatically within the broad limits of prior budget justifications. Supplies and equipment over and above routine needs required special funds; improvement and expansion of our oversea defenses were dependent upon congressional appropriations.

The outbreak of the European war shifted part of our defensive effort from the Pacific to the Atlantic. From 1935 on, Hawaii had received most of the meager flow of supplies and equipment. In 1940 we traded 50 over-age destroyers for long-term leases on several British bases in the Atlantic and Caribbean, and in the next year we stationed troops in Iceland, Newfoundland, and Bermuda. Increased appropriations in 1940 made it possible to begin to build up our strength in all oversea bases, but the delays in mobilizing the production of munitions made this progress almost inconsequential. Modern matériel did not begin to arrive in Hawaii and the Philippines until 1941. Troop reinforcement was hampered by legal restrictions upon the employment of inductees and reservists. The centralized supply machinery, designed to fulfill the relatively small needs of the peacetime Army, began in 1941 to creak and groan under the growing burden.

Service Troops

Service troops are to our military machine what factory workers, technicians, and administrators are to the civilian economy. The logistic potential of our forces can be measured in terms of the size and efficiency of the supply and service establishment. By this standard our Army in 1939 was even weaker than its size would indicate. Service troops, as we later knew them, were almost nonexistent. In June 1940, under the Protective Mobilization Plan, there were only 64,000 service troops of all categories in the Army. There was no integrated organization of supply and services, and no over-all logistic plan. The Protective Mobilization Plan included service units under such anomalous designations as "army troops for two armies" or "GHQ reserve units." Further, the concept of protective mobilization for the defense of United States territory gave the combat arms priority in personnel procurement.

There was considerable expansion in service organization during the two years prior to Pearl Harbor. The 1,650,000 men in the Army in November 1941 included 453,000 service troops. But mere quantity could not solve the organizational problems nor anticipate the technical lessons in the employment of service troops which only war experience could teach. There were few engineer service units as late as July 1940; the good roads, bridges, and railroads used in peacetime maneuvers had offered little useful experience in the problems which would face engineer units in war. Not until the autumn of 1941 did American signal officers go to England for training and operational duty with British forces in the radar-location system used against the German Air Force and undersea craft. Lacking operational data on modern warfare, the Army relied on the experience of World War I. Subsequent events proved that modern warfare required trained service troops in numbers very much larger than visualized by the War Department General Staff.

Chapter 2

STATE OF READINESS, DECEMBER 1941

The Army's state of readiness for war on 7 December 1941, Pearl Harbor, is revealed by the measurement of various logistic factors: How many trained and equipped troops did we have? How fast could they be deployed? What were our stocks of guns, ammunition, and other military equipment? The answer to these questions, impressive in some cases, insignificant in others, were not comforting after the sudden attack of the Japanese. The plain fact was that, in spite of the efforts of the preceding two years, Pearl Harbor found us still woefully weak for immediate defense and counterattack. Pearl Harbor caught us in the midst of what was at best only a partial mobilization.

By December 1941 the Army had reached a strength of 1,640,000, consisting of 29 partly equipped infantry divisions, five new armored divisions, two cavalry divisions, and upwards of 200 incomplete air squadrons. Fair progress in training had been made during 1941. That summer and fall large maneuvers were held involving some 900,000 troops.

Of the 1,640,000 troops, only 165,000 were deployed outside the continental limits of the United States. Only seven of the 34 divisions in the United States could be equipped for immediate dispatch to the battle zones. Even if all troops had been ready, they could not have been sent; large numbers were needed in the United States to raise and train additional forces, and sufficient shipping was not available. In December 1941 there were only 12 million deadweight tons of ocean shipping under the United States flag, and 10 million deadweight tons of shipping being constructed in yards.

We were also seriously hampered by lack of modern matériel. Wake Island, for example, was defended by a dozen 3-inch antiaircraft guns, six 5-inch guns dating from World War I, and 12 fighter planes. Canton Island, a tiny atoll but vital to our supply route to the South

Pacific, was manned by a platoon of soldiers armed with rifles and pistols. As for the Philippines, we could not send modern matériel until July 1941. The first flying fortresses were dispatched late in August. In order to avoid the Japanese-controlled areas, they flew far to the south through Rabaul, Port Moresby, and thence north to Luzon. Thirty-five of them had arrived by December. There were only 250 aircraft of all types in the Philippines on 7 December. Our strength in the Philippines consisted of 19,000 troops of the United States Army, 12,000 Philippine Scouts, and about 100,000 of the newly mobilized, partly trained, and poorly equipped Philippine Army. One hundred light tanks and 50 self-propelled guns had been delivered during 1941. On the day Japan struck, six troop ships and nine cargo vessels were at sea bound for the Philippines. None of these ships reached its original destination, although the enemy intercepted only one cargo vessel. Because of the lack of naval and air protection, they were diverted to New Caledonia and Australia.

In September 1941 the War Department requested Congress to authorize 52 million dollars for airfield construction in the Philippines, which the Congress ultimately refused. While the matter was being debated, 25 million dollars was obtained from the President's emergency fund and other sources. The Third Supplemental National Defense Appropriation Act of 1942, which was approved on 17 December, 10 days after Pearl Harbor, provided 269 million dollars for the Philippine Army.

The occupation of bases in the Atlantic was a relatively small-scale operation prior to Pearl Harbor. A total of some 16,000 soldiers was scattered through the North Atlantic as far south as Bermuda. The Caribbean Defense Command, including the Panama Canal, numbered only 66,000 troops in December 1941. In large part, these troops were engaged in the development of air and other facilities required to support larger defense forces at a later date. They had no equipment for a major defensive operation. The defense was at first dependent upon naval strength and later upon air power.

The supply situation at the time of Pearl Harbor was a varied one. Sufficient supplies of clothing, individual equipage, and housekeeping items had been obtained to equip the existing Army of 1,640,000 men. The rate of procurement of these civilian-type items was such as to maintain that Army and provide for some expansion. On the other hand, the stocks of purely military-type items, guns, and ammunition, were not sufficient to equip completely the existing troops and meet their training needs fully, much less to provide for the expansion and reinforcement of oversea bases. Only 16,000 tons of bombs were on hand; only 2,000 tanks; only 450 million rounds of small arms ammunition, less than the amount later expended in two months by the infantry alone in France. Less than 500 radar sets were available. The Engineers had no stocks of tractors nor of airplane landing mats. Our depots contained practically no stocks of Chemical Warfare Service or Transportation Corps supplies. Weapons carried over from World War I were unsatisfactory for use, except a few which had been modified, such as 75 mm howitzers and 155 mm guns.

The two years prior to 7 December 1941 were spent in preparation for production rather than in the actual production of war matériel. The procurement goal was set at supply for a force of 1.2 million men by 31 December 1941. For certain types of equipment, such as combat vehicles and small arms, the ojective was to provide for the needs of a force of two million men. Production targets for the 105 mm howitzer and the 155 mm gun were 2,700 and 300, respectively. Actual deliveries in the calendar year 1941 were 600 howitzers and 60 guns. The production of 1,460 medium tanks had exceeded the schedule of 1,030. Only 504 out of 835, 37 mm anti-aicraft guns had been delivered. Ammunition production was under way, but only negligible quantities were available to meet the requirements of a two front war. The same was true of gas masks, 60-inch searchlights, assault boats, and quartermaster and medical supplies. In December 1941 munitions production, exclusive of aircraft, amounted to 450 million dollars for the month.

Even before 7 December 1941, it was obvious that the rate of peacetime mobilization had been painfully slow. The ammunition, arms, and equipment just beginning to come off the production lines in quantity were the fruits of appropriations made one to two years earlier. The mobilization and expansion of the National Guard and the passage of the Selective Service Act had begun to provide manpower on a large scale, but the extent of the training required to produce modern fighting divisions, corps, and armies precluded their effective utilization for many months. Whenever a piece of equipment emerged from a factory, the War Department had to decide whether to give it to a soldier in training or to a soldier in an oversea garrison. Usually the need of the latter was more pressing, and this further postponed the day when the soldier in training would be ready to fight.

Fortunately, when the Japanese struck, the physical facilities, cantonments, training areas, hospitals, and storage depots for raising, training, and equipping our forces had been provided or were well under way as a result of the construction accomplished by the Quartermaster Corps and the Corps of Engineers.

Our potential resources compared favorably with those of our enemies; on this rested our prewar illusion of security. The effectiveness of Japan's opening attack was not measured by our direct losses; it lay rather in the ratio between those losses and the strength which we could immediately and effectively deploy against the enemy. In proportion to our total potential resources, our initial losses were very small; in terms of the strength available for immediate defense of our Pacific outposts, the losses were disastrous. In retrospect it is clear that our most tragic handicap in the prewar period was public unawareness of the difference between developed and undeveloped military strength in the face of sudden attack. This unawareness was shared by some of our responsible leaders, but it was the general complacency of our people that limited the over-all extent of our defense preparations and contributed largely to our vulnerability in December 1941. Deluded by the sense of security, we had ignored the time and space factors of logistics.

Our industrial position, partly because of the stimulus of Lend-lease orders, was further advanced than the actual expansion of the Armed Forces. Nevertheless, the production of munitions was far short of the tempo required for a two-front war. Industrial preparations had two major aspects: the enlargement of our basic industrial production and an increase in the facilities fashioning war matériel. Aluminum production in 1939, for example, had been 327 million pounds. In 1941 this had been increased to 618 million pounds. Yet this was only a beginning. In 1943 aluminum production totalled more than 1.8 billion pounds. Steel ingot production in 1939 was just under 53 million short tons. In 1941 it was nearly 83 million tons. In 1944 it was to increase to almost 90 million tons. Copper production expanded from 705,000 short tons in 1939 to 979,000 short tons in 1941, and then to 1.1 million short tons in 1943. In 1939 machine tool production in the United States was valued at just under 200 million dollars. By 1941 this had been increased nearly four times to 772 million dollars, and by 1942 machine tool production was valued at more than 1.3 billion dollars. Our stockpile of crude rubber at the time of Pearl Harbor was 531,000 long tons, while actual consumption during 1941 was 775,000 tons. The Japanese deprived us of our principal source of crude rubber. In 1941, plants in the United States produced 8,380 long tons of all types of synthetic rubber. In 1944, production was 797,000 long tons. Ship construction in October 1939 amounted to 20,000 deadweight tons. In December 1941 it was 92,000 deadweight tons. Peak construction in December 1943, however, was to reach 1,990,000 deadweight tons. Petroleum production had been 3.9 million barrels per day, on the average, in 1941. At its peak in May 1945, petroleum production amounted to over 4,860,000 barrels per day.

The expansion of basic industries had its counterpart in the expansion of facilities fashioning the weapons of war. Conversions from peacetime to wartime production were financed to a considerable extent by private capital. In the period before Pearl Harbor the War Department had received some 4,000 applications for Certificates of Necessity, entitling a manufacturer to amortize the cost of a capital improvement for war purposes over a 5-year period, of which nearly 2,000 had been issued. These figures indicate considerable private plant expansion of conversion. The War Department itself had initiated an industrial facilities program, costing 1.2 billion dollars, which was well under way at the time of Pearl Harbor. Some 57 percent was then complete. Twenty-seven ordnance industrial plants were already in operation, of which seven were arsenals, four small arms plants, 14 ammunition plants, and two tank automotive plants. In addition, the War Department sponsored the construction by the Defense Plant Corporation of some 80 plants. These facilities had a value of nearly 500 million dollars. The plant for the Nation's defense was being provided at the time of Pearl Harbor, but it was not yet completed nor in full operation.

Time was desperately needed to complete our mobilization and develop our military strength. We had to induct more men, train more troops, expand productive capacity and output, increase our ocean shipping, and enlarge our military facilities and services. After we had developed our strength, months would be required to deploy it effectively against our enemies. We had to build up large numbers of troops and vast quantities of supplies in oversea areas. We had to choose between concentrating in Europe against Germany and Italy or in the Pacific against Japan. Secondly, we had to take such immediate action as was possible to meet the conditions of the two-front war suddenly thrust upon us. Our defensive potential in the Pacific had been seriously weakened by the Japanese blow at Pearl Harbor. Our west coast was open to attack. The immediate task was to use available men and matériel where they would do the most good.

The Army made strenuous efforts to resupply its forces in the Philippines in order to enable them to resist as long as possible. Agents of the War Department were given complete authority to hire blockade runners to carry supplies to the Philippines, at least fifteen of which were sunk. Our Navy could not break the Japanese blockade of the area. A few American submarines managed to reach Bataan and Corregidor. Only one surface craft reached the Philippines, and this ship got only as far as Cebu.

In the meantime, a new line of communications to the Pacific had to be established as fast as possible. In January an air-ferry route to Australia was completed via Christmas, Canton, and the Fiji Islands, and New Caledonia. This last base was secured by a narrow margin. Such supplies as were available were loaded into ships to strengthen the garrisons occupying these strategic outposts in the Pacific.

Australia was to be the base from which the Japanese attack from the north was to be halted in Papua at the southern end of New Guinea. New Caledonia was to be the base from which the Japanese drive to cut our line of communications was to be halted on Guadalcanal. We rushed troops and supplies to Australia and New Caledonia as fast as they and the required shipping became available. Service troops were sent in order to build up unloading capacity and to prepare for the handling of larger quantities of supplies.

The Army faced other pressing demands in the Pacific. The losses in Hawaii had to be replaced and the garrison increased. The defenses in the North Pacific had to be strengthened; other reenforcements sent to Midway and Panama. Forty-five thousand men were embarked for the Pacific in January 1942, and 26,000 in February. Fifty-six thousand of these were destined for Australia; the others were sent to Alaska, the Central Pacific, and to the islands guarding the Australian route. In addition, two full divisions were concentrated on the Pacific coast of the United States for use in repelling any attempted attack on our mainland.

At the same time we began gradually to increase our strength in the Atlantic. Here the immediate need was less urgent than in the Pacific. Sixteen thousand men were embarked for Atlantic destinations in January 1942, and 22,000 in February. Of these, 20,000 were sent to the United Kingdom. The first troops landed in North Ireland on 26 January. Seventeen thousand men were sent into the Caribbean, and 1,000 to the Atlantic bases. These were only stop-gap measures, while we undertook complete mobilization to carry out long-range strategic plans to defeat the enemy.

CHART 2. LOGISTIC SITUATION, DECEMBER 1941

STRENGTH OF THE ARMY

Total strength.	1,686,000
Service troops.	450,000
Oversea strength.	165,000
Inductions and enlistments, monthly rate.	88,500
Divisions activated.	36
Infantry 29	
Armored 5	
Cavalry 2	

Of these divisions, two were outside the continental United States. All of the 34 divisions in this country were short critical items of equipment. From a training standpoint, 17 were ready for combat (1 year or more training and maneuvers) and 16 more were almost ready (9 mos. training or more). Had all the critical items been pooled, 5 infantry and 2 armored divisions could have been fully equipped for combat.

FACILITIES

Troop housing capacity.	1,600,000
Hospital beds.	78,700
Continental U. S. 75,000	
Oversea 3,700	

An industrial facilities program of $1,240,000,000 had been authorized for construction of which 57 percent was in place. A storage facilities program of $228,000,000 was 60 percent in place. There were in process of construction 184 air bases of which 21 had been completed. The total air base construction program authorized was $630,000,000 of which 62 percent was in place.

Ordnance industrial plants in operation.	27
Arsenals. 7	
Small arms plants. 4	
Ammunition plants. 14	
Tank-automotive plants. 2	
Ports in operation.	5
Staging area capacity (men). 16,000	
Storage depots.	45
Covered storage space (sq. ft.). 50,000,000	

EQUIPMENT AND SUPPLIES ON HAND

Ordnance Department (includes quantities in hands of troops)

Rifles	2,100,000
Sub-machine guns	28,000
Pistols	322,000
Revolvers	184,000
Shotguns	31,000
Machine guns	78,000
Aircraft cannon	94
Anti-aircraft guns	1,100
Field guns and howitzers	9,410
Mortars	8,300
Tanks	2,000
Trucks	202,000
Small arms ammunition (rounds)	453,000,000
Artillery ammunition (rounds)	5,770,000
Aircraft bombs (tons)	16,000

Quartermaster Corps

Approximately 1,000,000 additional men could have been initially equipped from depot stocks of clothing based upon Tables of Equipment in effect at that time. About 300,000 of these men would have been lacking overcoats, however, although otherwise they would have been fully equipped with clothing.

Corps of Engineers

Engineers supplies and equipment available in depots were valued at $110,000,000 but included no crawler tractors, airplane landing mats, or portable barracks.

Signal Corps

There were less than 10,000 usable ground and vehicular radio sets, less than 6,000 aircraft radio sets, and less than 500 radar sets available.

Transportation Corps

There was virtually no Transportation Corps equipment on hand in depots.

Chemical Warfare Service

There was virtually no Chemical Warfare Service equipment on hand in depots.

Medical Department

The value of medical supplies and equipment available in depots was only $50,000,000.

TROOP AND SUPPLY MOVEMENTS

Ships in Army service (ship tons)	1,000,000
Oversea troop embarkations, monthly rate	29,800

TROOP AND SUPPLY MOVEMENTS—Continued

Cargo shipments to oversea theaters, monthly rate (ship tons).................................... 284,000
ASF Lend Lease shipments, monthly rate........... $13,500,000

PROCUREMENT, MONTHLY RATE (Exclusive of aircraft) $360,000,000

INDUSTRIAL PRODUCTION

Aluminum
    1941 production (lbs.)....................... 618,000,000
    1941 monthly rate as percent of subsequent peak monthly rate, October 1943 (percent) 27.4

Copper
    1941 total new supply (short tons).......... 1,640,000
    1941 monthly rate as percent of subsequent peak monthly rate, August 1943 (percent). 77.9
    Stocks 31 December 1941 (short tons)...... 140,000
    December 1941 stocks as percent 1941 domestic consumption (percent).......... 8.3

Steel
    1941 ingot production (short tons).......... 82,700,000
    1941 monthly rate as percent of subsequent peak monthly rate, October 1943 (percent). 88.0

Crude Oil
    1941 runs to refineries (bbls. per day)........ 3,900,000
    1941 monthly rate as percent of subsequent peak monthly rate, May 1945 (percent)... 80.4

Lumber
    1941 production (bd. ft).................... 37,900,000,000
    1941 monthly rate as percent of subsequent peak monthly rate, July 1942 (percent).... 92.4

Rubber
    1941 total new supply, natural and synthetic (long tons).............................. 1,310,000
    Stocks, natural—31 December 1941 (long tons)................................... 531,000
    31 December 1941 natural rubber stocks as percent of 1941 consumption (percent).. 68.6
    1941 synthetic rubber production (long tons).. 8,400
    1941 monthly rate of synthetic rubber production as percent of subsequent peak monthly rate, May 1945 (percent)........ 0.8

Machine tools
    1941 production value.................... $772,000,000

INDUSTRIAL PRODUCTION—Continued

1941 monthly rate as percent of subsequent peak monthly rate, December 1942 (percent)	48.7
Dry cargo vessels	
Completed in December 1941 (deadwt. tons)	79,000
December 1941 rate as percent of subsequent peak monthly rate, December 1943 (percent)	5.3
Tankers	
Completed in December 1941 (deadwt. tons)	13,000
December 1941 rate as percent of subsequent peak monthly rate, December 1943 (percent)	2.5

Chapter 3

THE ARMY SERVICE FORCES

At the time of Pearl Harbor, the internal organization of the War Department was antiquated and cumbersome. Its form was not suited for the waging of a major war. Thoughtful military men knew this and for years had worried about it.

The structure was loose and overlapping below the level of the War Department General Staff. A wide variety of independent agencies, including the Arms and Services, oversea forces, ground and air forces, and the Corps Areas, reported directly to the Chief of Staff. Thus decisions, great and small, had to be made at the top. All operating policies funnelled through the General Staff. It was impossible even in peacetime for the General Staff to give the necessary thoughtful attention to over-all planning. They were too much immersed in a thousand and one daily details.

Logistic activities were especially diffused and uncoordinated. They were spread through six Supply and eight Administrative Services. These agencies reported to the Chief of Staff on military matters and to the Under Secretary of War on procurement matters. They operated independently of one another and not without considerable rivalry. This inadequate system sufficed in peacetime when the demands upon it were small, and there were enough manpower and raw materials to go around.

The attack on Pearl Harbor altered the situation. It became immediately apparent that the Nation faced a period of shortages. The peacetime systems of military procurement could not possibly arm the country for war. The Chief of Staff and his General Staff, no matter how brilliant, how experienced, or how zealous, could not manage the vast new Army without delegating authority and responsibility to others.

To meet this situation, the President by Executive Order reorganized the War Department on 9 March 1942 into a General Staff, three major commands (air, ground, and service), Defense Commands and oversea forces. The Army Ground Forces was given the responsibility for training ground troops for combat; the Army Air Forces for training and preparing the air arm. Under the general plan, oversea theaters and bases were set up under commanders reporting directly to the Chief of Staff. In addition, four Defense Commands were created for the defense of the continental United States. The Army Service Forces, at first called the Services of Supply, was made responsible for administrative, supply (including procurement), and service activities for the War Department as a whole.

One important effect of this reorganization was the grouping of the great majority of the logistic activities of the Army under a single Command. Previously, a large staff in the Office of the Under Secretary of War had been supervising procurement, and another large staff in the Supply Division, War Department General Staff, had been supervising the determination of requirements and the distribution phases of supply. The relationship between the two had been tenuous. There had been little coordination of programs or balancing of requirements and resources. The newly created Army Service Forces [1] combined these staffs under The Commanding General, who was responsible to the Under Secretary of War on procurement, and to the Chief of Staff on other matters.

This change greatly facilitated the solution of production and distribution problems and quickly served to establish coordination among the Technical Services.[2] It made possible the prompt adjustments in supply programs required by the changing needs and the availability of materials, facilities, and manpower, and prevented rival bidding for such resources among the Technical Services. It put the logistics of the Army on what promised to be a businesslike footing. By introducing a new command echelon in the War Department, it greatly reduced the burden on the Chief of Staff and his assistants.

The Army Service Forces assumed authority over six Technical Services, eight Administrative Services, nine Corps Areas (later known as Service Commands), six Ports of Embarkation, and nine General Depots, all of which had been reporting independently to the Chief of Staff. The Army Service Forces was responsible for coordinating the work of all these agencies in order to insure that troops in training and in the oversea commands received the supplies

---

[1] This term will be used hereafter in place of "Services of Supply" to avoid confusion. The name "Services of Supply" was changed to "Army Service Forces" by War Department General Order No. 14, 12 March 1943.

[2] Known as Supply Services until May 1943; redesignated "Technical Services" by ASF Circular No. 30, 15 May 1943.

and services they required. For the first time, there was a full recognition of the importance of logistics to the Army and the advantage of concentrating logistic operations in a single Command.

At once a twofold urgency faced the Army Service Forces. The first embraced the immediate necessity for expanding all its activities many fold, at a rate at least equal to and generally faster than that at which the Army as a whole was growing. Equipment and facilities had to be obtained prior to the induction of troops. The production and delivery of supplies had to be accelerated. More and more men had to be inducted into the service at a faster and faster rate. Preparations to process, house, clothe, and feed them had to be made. The military transportation system had to be expanded many times. Army communications had to be extended with speed, sureness, and secrecy. All of this had to be done on a scale and at a tempo never before attempted.

The second task was primarily one of organization. The agencies included in the Army Service Forces had to be welded into an effective team capable of meeting the demands made upon it. Coordination between the various programs had to be obtained. Simple and speedy systems for conducting the varied and detailed activities inherent in logistics had to be developed and installed. The whole complex and widespread structure, embracing nearly every field of human endeavor, had to be made effective. The new Command faced the paradoxical situation in which it had to apply tried business methods to a task so complex that no known business structure could possibly embrace it.

The test of how well the Army Service Forces accomplished its mission lies in the results. World War II was the first war in our history in which there were no major failures in supply. Our troops and their equipment were successfully transported to all corners of the globe, were well-equipped and maintained, and received good service in every respect. No battle, no campaign was lost nor substantially impeded by a logistic failure. American soldiers were better supported than those of any other army ever in the field. The results attest to the wisdom of the decision to concentrate logistic activities in a single Command.

While the broad picture was one of superb accomplishment, many difficulties arose; not all were satisfactorily solved. The task of insuring logistic success was enormous and almost beyond the comprehension even of many of those engaged in it.

CHART 5.   ASF ACTIVITIES TO END OF HOSTILITIES, WORLD

PROCUREMENT OF MUNITIONS

    ASF Total................................. $68,450,000,000
        Ordnance Department........... 34,084,000,000
        Quartermaster Corps............ 21,140,000,000
        Corps of Engineers............. 4,809,000,000
        Signal Corps................... 3,941,000,000
        Transportation Corps........... 2,023,000,000
        Chemical Warfare Service....... 1,693,000,000
        Medical Department............ 760,000,000

    More than 600,000 major prime contracts were awarded.

PRODUCTION OF MAJOR ITEMS

Ordnance Department	
Carbines	6,100,000
Rifles	7,000,000
Sub-machine guns	2,000,000
Pistols	1,950,000
Revolvers	882,000
Shotguns	438,000
Small arms ammunition (rounds)	39,000,000,000
.30 caliber (rounds)	25,000,000,000
.45 caliber (rounds)	4,070,000,000
.50 caliber (rounds)	10,000,000,000
Rocket launchers	691,000
Machine guns	2,700,000
Aircraft cannon	182,000
Antiaircraft guns	46,700
Field Guns and howitzers	61,700
Light, 37 mm to 105 mm	53,900
Heavy, over 105 mm	7,800
Mortars	102,000
Recoilless rifles, 57 mm and 75 mm	1,450
Tanks	96,000
Light	28,800
Medium	65,400
Heavy	1,800

PRODUCTION OF MAJOR ITEMS—Continued

Ordnance Department—Continued

Trucks	2,350,000
¼ ton	645,000
Light, ¼ to ½ ton	759,000
Medium, 2½ ton	795,000
Heavy, over 2½ ton	148,000
Artillery ammunition (rounds)	1,000,000,000
For guns and howitzers (rounds)	889,000,000
20 mm to 105 mm (rounds)	855,000,000
Over 105 mm (rounds)	34,000,000
For mortars (rounds)	89,000,000
For rockets (rounds)	25,000,000
Aircraft bombs (short tons)	6,860,000

Quartermaster Corps

Combat service boots (pairs)	28,700,000
Cotton khaki shirts	69,300,000
Cotton khaki trousers	67,900,000
Flannel shirts	73,700,000
Lightweight ponchos	5,110,000
Raincoats	28,300,000
Shoes—service (pairs)	79,900,000
Shoe-pacs (pairs)	4,350,000
Tents	30,500,000
Blankets	57,000,000
Sleeping bags	10,000,000
Field jackets	49,000,000
Field trousers	68,000,000
Socks	505,000,000

Subsistence

Canned and fresh meat (lbs.)	12,900,000,000
Canned, dehydrated and fresh vegetables (lbs.)	17,100,000,000
Fruit juices (lbs.)	1,700,000,000
Flour (lbs.)	7,840,000,000
Coffee (lbs.)	1,440,000,000
Granulated sugar (lbs.)	2,420,000,000

Corps of Engineers

Crawler tractors	78,000

PRODUCTION OF MAJOR ITEMS—Continued

Corps of Engineers—Continued

Cranes and shovels	15,100
Airplane landing mats (sq. ft.)	883,000,000
Portable barracks, 20 by 48 ft	35,000
Water storage tanks (gal. capacity)	146,000,000

Signal Corps

Radio sets	1,200,000
Handie-talkies	207,000
Radar sets	20,100
Field telephones	1,330,000
Portable field switchboards	85,500
Communication wire (miles)	4,580,000
Portable metallic mine detectors	146,000

Transportation Corps

Steam locomotives	7,070
Diesel locomotives	1,000
Railway cars	98,000
Tugs	729
Barges	6,150

Chemical Warfare Service

Incendiary bombs (lbs.)	1,750,000,000
Flame throwers	40,800
Chemical mortar shells, 4.2"	11,000,000
Chemical mortars, 4.2"	6,080
Gas masks	35,600,000

Medical Department

Atabrine (tablets)	4,600,000,000
Penicillin, 100,000 oxford units	24,200,000
Dried plasma, 500 cc packages	4,570,000
First aid packets	31,500,000
Sulfadiazine (tablets)	216,000,000
X-Ray machines	9,000
Dental chairs	7,000
Operating tables	23,000
Surgical instruments	10,000,000

RESEARCH AND DEVELOPMENT

Number of research projects (exclusive of atomic bomb)	7,500
Expenditures on these projects	$567,000,000

FISCAL SERVICES

War Department appropriations		$240,000,000,000
War Department expenditures		$176,000,000,000
Procurement	$116,000,000,000	
Pay of the Army	$34,600,000,000	
Rail transportation	$5,300,000,000	
Other non-procurement	$20,500,000,000	
Bank disbursements under guaranteed loan program		$8,900,000,000
Contract advance payments		$6,900,000,000
Gross refunds from statutory renegotiation		$3,160,000,000
Personal funds transferred from oversea		$1,100,000,000
War Bonds issued		$1,900,000,000
Family allowances paid		$6,500,000,000
Family allowance accounts (accounts)		4,500,000
Voluntary allotments of pay (accounts)		3,780,000
Death gratuities paid		260,000
Administrative claims processed		125,000

CONSTRUCTION AND REAL ESTATE

Value of construction in U. S.		$10,700,000,000
Air installations	$3,150,000,000	
Ground installations	$2,820,000,000	
Industrial installations	$3,200,000,000	
Storage and shipping	$1,040,000,000	
Miscellaneous	$460,000,000	
Construction jobs completed		23,200
Construction employment (peak)		1,000,000
Real estate leases		33,000
Annual rental of leases (peak)		$57,800,000
Land brought under Army control (acres)		44,000,000

TRANSPORTATION

Cargo capacity of ships in Army service (peak) (measurement tons)		17,700,000
Cargo shipped oversea (measurement tons)		127,000,000
Atlantic Theaters (measurement tons)	78,000,000	
Pacific Theaters (measurement tons)	49,000,000	
High explosives shipped overseas (short tons)		11,500,000
Cargo received from overseas (measurement tons)		8,140,000

TRANSPORTATION—Continued

Passenger capacity of ships in Army service (peak)....		666,000
Troops and other passengers embarked for overseas...............................		7,300,000
Atlantic Theaters.............	4,600,000	
Pacific Theaters...............	2,700,000	
Troops and other passengers debarked from overseas..		3,100,000
Patients debarked from overseas...............		568,000
Rail freight (ton-miles).......................		214,000,000,000
Tonnage handled by Army-Navy consolidated car service (short tons)............................		2,260,000
Troops moved in organized groups by rail............		32,900,000

STORAGE AND ISSUE

Total storage space occupied (peak) (sq. ft.)......		149,000,000
Warehouse and shed space occupied (peak) (sq. ft.)......	65,600,000	
Open-hardstanding space occupied (peak) (sq. ft.)..........	57,200,000	
Igloo and magazine space occupied (peak) (sq. ft.)..........	26,100,000	
Depot receipts (short tons).......................		83,200,000
Depot shipments (short tons).......................		68,300,000
Requisition line items shipped from depots..........		110,000,000
Lend-Lease transfers to all countries............		$14,600,000,000
Civilian supply shipments (peak) (short tons).....		7,490,000
Value of equipment repaired (peak)............		$476,000,000

PERSONNEL

Army strength served (peak)....................		8,290,000
Service troops (peak)..........	1,720,000	
ASF operating personnel (peak) (June 1943)....		1,569,000
Military (peak) (July 1943)....	554,000	
Civilian (peak) (June 1943)....	1,023,000	
Personnel processed at reception centers........		8,500,000
Personnel processed at replacement depots......		278,000
Personnel processed at reception stations.......		1,900,000
Personnel processed at redistribution stations....		240,000
Enemy prisoners of war in U. S. (peak).........		425,000
General prisoners in confinement (peak)........		33,600
General prisoners received at Rehabilitation Centers.....................................		34,300
General prisoners restored to duty.............		16,500

PERSONNEL—Continued

Loyalty investigation cases processed	2,350,000
Auxiliary plant guards (peak)	251,000

MILITARY TRAINING

ASF trainee strength (peak)	700,000
Individuals trained at ASF training centers	1,300,000
Graduates of ASF officer candidate schools	133,000
Graduates of ASF service schools	1,000,000
Trainees in Army Specialized Training Program	216,000
Trainees in special training units	295,000
ASF trained units shipped overseas	6,000
Strength of ASF units shipped overseas	1,000,000
Training film produced	1,050
Instruction manuals published	3,260
Schools operated (peak)	433
Training centers operated (peak)	38

PERSONNEL SERVICES

V-Mail letters sent overseas		643,000,000
V-Mail letters received from overseas		608,000,000
Air mail sent overseas (lbs.)		39,200,000
Ordinary mail sent overseas (lbs.)		38,500,000
Parcel post sent overseas (lbs.)		640,000,000
Requests received by personal affairs officers		5,200,000
Services conducted by chaplains		5,400,000
Attendance at religious services		328,000,000
Sales at Army Exchanges		$3,050,000,000
Continental U. S.	$2,480,000,000	
Overseas	$573,000,000	
Copies of "Yank" distributed		175,000,000
Copies of "Newsmap" distributed		25,000,000
Attendance at war information films		48,000,000
U. S. Armed Forces Institute enrollment		1,000,000

MEDICAL SERVICE

Hospitals in U. S. (peak)		460
Bed capacity of hospitals in U. S. (peak)		382,000
Beds occupied in hospitals in U. S. (peak)		240,000
Patients admitted to hospitals, total		14,700,000
In U. S.	9,000,000	
Overseas	5,700,000	

MEDICAL SERVICE—Continued

Patients evacuated from overseas		568,000
Battle casualties	194,000	
Disease and non-battle injury	374,000	
Dental treatments		105,000,000
Physical examinations given in connection with inductions		18,000,000
Veterinary operations, weight of meat, food, and dairy products inspected (lbs.)		110,000,000,000

Chapter 4

Influence of Logistics on Strategy

World War II was a war of logistics. Never before had war been waged on such varied, widespread fronts. Never had one involved so many men, so much matériel, nor such great distances. Never had combat operations so directly affected whole industrial systems and populations. Consequently, past experience provided little indication of the tremendous influence of logistics on strategy and operations, and little or no guidance on the techniques of broad scale logistic planning. Of necessity, these techniques were developed largely during the war. Logistics influenced, and in many cases dictated, considerations of strategy, whether the grand strategy of the United Nations or the strategy of a single campaign.

From the over-all standpoint, the major logistic problem of the war was the utilization of national resources in meeting the needs of the strategic plans formulated by the Combined Chiefs of Staff (United States-United Kingdom) for the complete defeat of Germany and Japan. These plans had to be translated into requirements for hundreds of thousands of items of equipment and supplies, in terms of specifications, time, and quantities. In turn, the latter had to be translated into terms of raw materials, manpower, and facilities and checked against available and prospective resources. The logistic practicabilities of the strategic plans thus were determined and adjustments made on the basis of capabilities. With limited raw materials and productive capacity, a proper balance was necessary between the various programs that included the building of cargo ships, aircraft, landing boats, naval vessels, and ground equipment, and the production of high octane gasoline. The grand strategy of the war was also dependent upon production schedules and shipping possibilities. Production programs were constantly adjusted and coordinated to conform to changing strategic priorities and operational needs.

The adjustment of strategy to logistics was not confined to United States forces alone. The United States provided extensive logistic support through Lend Lease to all the United Nations. The assignment of finished munitions was governed by projected operational plans. The resources of the United States and Great Britain in munitions and shipping were largely considered as a pool for the support of the two nations. Just as strategic plans were combined, so also were some phases of the logistic activities in support of those plans.

Throughout the war the Army Service Forces was the direct source of logistic information and guidance for the Joint Chiefs of Staff and for the Strategy and Policy Group, Operations Division, War Department General Staff. In the fall of 1943, the Joint Logistics Committee was organized as an agency of the Joint Chiefs of Staff. The Army Service Forces provided one member of this committee. A permanent committee, the Joint Logistics Plans Committee, was organized as the working agency of the Joint Logistics Committee; the Planning Division, ASF, furnished two permanent members of the former. Associate members from the War and Navy Departments, the Army Air Forces, the Staff Divisions, ASF, and the Technical Services prepared detailed studies for each specific problem studied by the Joint Logistics Plans Committee. The Army Service Forces furnished logistic information and guidance to the Strategy and Policy Group, Operations Division, WDGS, both independently and supplementary to that provided by the Joint Logistics Plans Committee.

The global nature of World War II, and the fact that the initiative was with the enemy through 1942 in the Pacific and well into 1943 in Europe, necessitated the preparation of detailed logistic studies for operations in almost every part of the world. Many of these studies served a negative purpose, either to indicate the logistic impracticability of operations in certain areas, or to show that expected results might be indecisive or incompatible with the cost in men and matériel.

No strategic plan could be drafted without a determination and evaluation of the major logistic factors: Were we able to assemble the necessary men, equipment, and supplies? Could we do this in time for movement to the initial assault? Could we continue our support of the operation? At what rate could men and supplies be placed in the target area? At what rate could the enemy move to counterattack? The answers to these questions involved detailed consideration of the availability of proper types of shipping; port clearance (as determined by port and beach capacities and the capacities of road and rail nets); the availability of suitable sites for rapid airfield construction; the availability of local resources, such as water, fuel, labor, and food; the availability of facilities, such as harbors, docks, warehouses, and power plants; and, finally, an assessment of the enemy's ability to place physical obstacles in our way, and of our ability to overcome them. The logistic effect of the proposed operation on campaigns in other Theaters also had to be determined. The timing of various operations was a major consideration. Alternative lines of action had to be considered in each logistic analysis in order to balance the many factors involved, and to determine the most desirable course of action as well as its feasibility.

Each logistic study developed one or more "bottlenecks" that were decisive factors limiting the capabilities of our forces. The problem was then to devise ways and means for eliminating the bottlenecks or to redesign the operation to fit the limiting factors. It was the function of the logistic planners to discover any limitations, to ferret out the ways and means to overcome them, and to furnish the strategic planners with advice respecting feasibility and requirements. The logistic and operational aspects were complementary in the development of a plan of operations. A plan of operations was proposed. Logistic scrutiny revealed a limitation. The plan was amended. Further scrutiny of our ability to provide detailed support revealed additional limitations. The plan was further amended, until ultimately it was impossible to determine which of the logistic factors had the most decisive influence upon the final plan. The art of logistic planning involved the ability to determine accurately in advance the effect of time and space factors on an operational concept, thus insuring the practicability of final plans.

Strategically, it was essential to strike an early blow against Germany in order to relieve the pressure on Russia and Great Britain. Available resources were inadequate for full-scale, simultaneous operations against the Japanese and the European Axis. The shorter lines of communications in the Atlantic permitted the build-up of adequate forces for a decisive blow in the European Theater in much less time than that required in the Pacific. Time was also necessary for rebuilding the United States Navy in order to insure freedom of action in the Pacific. British and American naval forces were available for convoy purposes in the Atlantic where the threat of major naval engagements was more remote. The Combined Chiefs of Staff, therefore, decided that United States forces would be built up in the British Isles as rapidly as possible, the build-up to be followed by a combined assault across the Channel. The build-up was named Operation BOLERO; the assault and invasion, Operation OVERLORD. The United States meanwhile would assume the strategic defensive in the Pacific, using available resources to stem the Japanese advance and to prepare bases from which to launch the Pacific counteroffensive.

North African Campaign

Early in 1942 the position of the United Nations was precarious. The British, while regaining control of the air over England, were being forced to retreat toward El Alamein in Egypt. The advance of the Afrika Korps threatened the Suez Canal and also the air transport route to Russia and Asia. British losses in equipment were large and serious. It was necessary to withdraw some 300 tanks and 100 self-propelled guns from United States units in training for rush shipment to the British on the El Alamein line. The Army Service Forces shipped a total of some 38,000 tons of equipment in July 1942 "around the Cape" to Suez. Because one ship of this convoy was torpedoed, an additional 75 tanks and self-propelled weapons with a total of some 10,000 tons of equipment were dispatched. These items of equipment contributed materially to British success in holding and later breaking through the line in the desert—which marked the turn of the tide against the German Army in Africa.

The Russians, long on manpower but short on equipment and supplies, were reeling under German blows. It was imperative to keep Russia in the war and actively fighting the bulk of the German land forces. This required the shipment of badly needed trucks, tanks, and guns at the expense of United States forces in training. The urgency of the situation made necessary the use of the costly northern convoy route and the establishment of the long and arduous supply line through the Persian Gulf.

An early operation by British and United States forces designed to relieve the pressure on the Russian front was most desirable. It would take more than a year to concentrate the necessary forces and equipment for a cross-channel assault. We could, however, take advantage of Axis weakness in French North Africa, and could concentrate forces there more rapidly than the Germans. This would draw sizable German forces from Europe, thereby affording some relief to Russia. Furthermore, it would provide bases for air cover for the vital Mediterranean supply route and would threaten the rear of the German Army in the desert. The Combined Chiefs of Staff decided that an attack would be made in North Africa in late 1942 and postponed the planned cross-channel assault.

The United States was already well embarked on BOLERO, and was committed to the shipment of available troops and supplies to the United Kingdom. The early concept of TORCH, the North African operation, envisaged a joint British-American task force to be mounted from the United Kingdom. Considerations influencing the early plan were the availability of troops in Britain, the short line of communications from England to North Africa, the corresponding saving in shipping, and the reduction in vulnerability to the submarine menace. The plan's logistic disadvantages soon became apparent. Sufficient stocks of supplies were not on hand in the United Kingdom to mount completely the American portion of the force. The supplies that were available were not so warehoused as to be fully useful. There were not enough service troops for depot operations in sustained support of North Africa from the United Kingdom. Preference had been given to the shipment of combat troops, construction troops, and antiaircraft units to England. It was not possible to unload the required supporting supplies from the United States, to segregate and store them, and to outload them for Africa.

Detailed plans for TORCH were late in being developed. The British wanted a concentrated attack in the Mediterranean, whereas we favored a simultaneous assault on the West and North African coasts in order to insure a line of communications independent of the Strait of Gibraltar. The resolution of this difference occupied most of the month of August. The decision was to risk splitting the forces in favor of the more positive supply line. Since time was vital, the Army Service Forces had developed a provisional troop basis and proceeded to equip the troops to be mounted from the United States. In late August, when outline plans finally became available, units that were to be equipped by early September were still being activated. Time and space factors dictated a change in target date from October first to early November. The execution of plans proceeded along with and sometimes even in advance of the full development of plans.

The receiving capabilities of the North African ports and beaches were found to be adequate for the forces which could be employed. The inability of the Navy to provide escorts for cargo convoys constituted a limitation which required a change in the operational plan. On 27 September 1942 the Army Service Forces presented to the Commanding General, United States Army Forces in the British Isles, two alternatives: reduce the size of the Western Task Force from 167,000 to 100,000 and provide full equipment and reserve supplies for all forces; or, employ the original number of men and reduce the equipment for the United States Task Forces by approximately 50 percent, mainly in general purpose vehicles. Since our mission was conceived to be primarily occupational, the second alternative was accepted.

Troops in the United Kingdom meanwhile were completing their training, receiving their equipment, and moving to ports for embarkation. However, much of the equipment that had been shipped for these units could not be readily located in the British Isles because of the inability properly to identify and store it, and duplicate shipments from the United States were required. Here again the shortage of service troops for depot operations took its toll. Some items were actually delivered to units after they had boarded transports. It must be recalled that the Theater had only recently been activated, that an extensive program of antiaircraft defense and airbase construction was under way, and that, in spite of the recommendations of the Army Service Forces, an insufficient number of service units experienced in depot operations had been sent to the Theater. On 9 September 1942 a radiogram was received listing items of equipment essential to the units in the assault forces to be mounted from the United Kingdom. A total of 131,000 ship tons of cargo was delivered to the United Kingdom between 16 and 25 October for loading in the assault convoy. In addition, eight fully loaded cargo ships were dispatched from the United States and arrived in the United Kingdom before November to join convoys from the British Isles.

The Army Service Forces also became involved in the loading of the Western Task Force. The Third Army was combat-loaded in the United States at Norfolk and Newport News. It was difficult for members of the Third Army Staff to visualize the complexities of combat-loading and the obstacles encountered by the Technical Services in getting equipment and supplies properly packaged, code-marked, and shipped in time to the Norfolk area. The names of the ships in the expedition were obliterated, and ships were known by code numbers or code names. Each piece of equipment had to be marked with corresponding code names or numbers, together with the code names or numbers of the various sections of the pier to which the supplies were moved. All of this marking work had to be done at depots in the Zone of the Interior. The Staff of the Third Army had not developed advance combat loading plans, and it became necessary for the Staff of the Army Service Forces to assist the Third Army when an absolute deadline had to be made. A valuable lesson was learned when it became generally understood that supplies and equipment must be put aboard ships in accordance with code markings and a loading plan that insured the unloading of supplies in order of need at the point of destination.

After capturing initial objectives on the North African coast, the British Task Force turned east toward Tunisia. Because of the lack of rail and highway transportation, it quickly outraced its supply support. The rapid build-up of Axis forces in Tunisia and eastern Algeria forced the British to halt, consolidate their supporting supplies, and await reinforcements. Railroads were single track and had little usable rolling stock. The decision to leave vehicles in the United States, based on an assumed occupational role, reacted unfavorably when it became a campaign of movement. In order to expand the line of communications to support the final assault on Tunisia, the Army Service Forces made a rush shipment of 222,000 ship tons of equipment, including over 5,000 vehicles, to North Africa. This equipment was assembled, loaded, and dispatched within 21 days in a special convoy of 23 ships.

The North African campaign clearly proved that combat forces depend directly upon the capacity of their lines of communications. Early emphasis upon maximum quantities of combat troops and equipment at the expense of service troops and equipment had been faulty. Only after correcting this fault could the campaign be pressed to its successful conclusion. The campaign was the first major large-scale assault for which the Army Service Forces provided support. From it were derived invaluable lessons and experience. The successful procedures developed were standardized and used in subsequent operations.

Sicilian Campaign

The natural sequel to the eviction of the Axis from Africa was the establishment of bases dominating the life-line to Suez. The Allies decided at Casablanca in January 1943 to occupy Sicily. This decision was made only after considering the effect of this campaign upon others then projected. OVERLORD was still to be the major strategic effort, although sufficient men, matériel, and ships could not be made available for Sicily without deferring the build-up of BOLERO, as well as further restricting the already meager shipments to the Pacific. A further logistic implication of an assault upon Sicily was that, if successful, it would undoubtedly lead to an assault against Italy, an area of great defensive strength where strong Allied forces could be checked by weaker Axis forces. In the pursuit of such a campaign, we might waste men, matériel, and shipping without striking a decisive blow. A continued commitment of resources to the Mediterranean would necessarily detract from the major cross-channel blow of OVERLORD.

With the decision made to undertake the Sicilian campaign, the preparation of plans, both operational and logistic, became a Theater responsibility. The mission of the Army Service Forces was the full support of the plans of the Theater Commander. Several major difficulties were encountered. Theater stock control procedures were in their infancy. The ability of the Theater to re-equip troops being made ready for the campaign was doubtful, therefore emergency requisitions were sent to the United States. The 45th Division was combat-loaded from the United States, because time and the status of preparation of the division did not permit shipment to the Theater for combat-loading there. The congestion of internal communications in North Africa was such that, although supplies and equipment were available there for the continued support of HUSKY, the Sicilian operation, it was impossible, with the service troops and facilities available, to insure this support. The Army Service Forces maintained HUSKY by automatic shipments of supplies from the United States throughout the course of the operation.

Once begun, the campaign progressed rapidly and without serious logistic difficulties. Its spectacular progress, without major losses of matériel, left considerable excess equipment in North Africa and Sicily. This was later used in Italy and Southern France, but it pinned down service units in Africa and was used to advantage only because of strenuous efforts by the Theater.

Italian Campaign

Studies of possible operations in the Mediterranean followed the occupation of Sicily ranged from France to Greece. Allied operations in Yugoslavia, Greece, and the islands of the Eastern Mediterranean would have assisted in some degree the Russian campaigns on the eastern front. Logistically, it would have been possible to mount and support operations with limited objectives in any of these areas. Consideration of port capacities and inland lines of communications indicated that only in southern France could adequate forces be built up for a decisive blow against the Germans from the Mediterranean.

An operation in southern France taken by itself would have been a gamble on our ability to reduce greatly the effectiveness of the German line of communications. The Army Service Forces therefore recommended that all available resources support the build-up for OVERLORD, with southern France as the only subsidiary operation in the Mediterranean.

Studies of civil relief in an Italian campaign indicated that Italy would not be self-supporting at any time during Allied occupation. Considerable shipments of coal, food, clothing, and medical supplies would be needed to prevent unrest and epidemics. The Allies made preparations to assume this logistic responsibility before the invasion.

The probability of a favorable political upheaval, the value of air bases closer to the heart of Germany, the strategic advantage of keeping the initiative in the Mediterranean, and above all the desirability of relieving German pressure on the Russian front dictated the assault on the Italian peninsula. The occupation of the toe of Italy met little opposition, but the defensive strength of the peninsula prevented continued rapid advance. Expansion and exploitation of the beachhead at Salerno was strongly contested, and a war of attrition resulted. The air bases at Foggia and Bari, however, secured as a result of the invasion of Italy, proved of incalculable value. They placed the industrial area of Austria and the oilfields of Rumania within range of our heavy bombers, and provided additional bases for shuttle-bombing in conjunction with bases in the Ukraine. Regensburg, Schweinfurt, and Ploesti, which had cost the Eighth Air Force so heavily, became regular targets for the Fifteenth Air Force.

In the Pacific we advanced by isolating Japanese garrisons and concentrating superior forces at critical points; on the narrow Italian peninsula this was not possible. The disruption of enemy logistic capabilities was not so complete, and limited approaches made impossible the concentration of superior Allied forces. Logistically, the enemy and ourselves were on a par, until bombing had greatly reduced the capability of the Germans to resist further pressure.

As in the case of Sicily, the maintenance of forces in Italy could be more efficiently carried out by direct supply from the United States after the assault had been mounted.

There were not enough troops, equipment, or shipping to accelerate the OVERLORD build-up, supply the minimum needs of the Pacific, and support an overwhelming force in Italy. Because of the limited possibilities of a strategic decision in Italy, some forces were withdrawn for employment in the invasions of France. This strongly influenced the operational capabilities of the Mediterranean theater and resulted in the drawn-out campaign which ended only in May 1945.

European Theater of Operations

The campaign in northern Europe that began with the invasion of Normandy had its logistic beginning immediately after Pearl Harbor, when it was decided to strike first in Europe and to maintain a strategic defense in the Pacific. The water distance from America to Europe was approximately half that to combat areas of the Pacific, so that available shipping would permit a much more rapid build-up of adequate forces for a decisive blow. The United Kingdom provided a ready-made base of operations with modern transport and cargo facilities only a few miles from the enemy. The war-making capacity of the United Kingdom was vital to the Allies and could best be employed against Germany. Furthermore, the build-up of troops would provide an early and effective safeguard against any German invasion of England.

Plans for the build-up in the United Kingdom, Operation BOLERO, included the construction of airfields from which to launch an all-out American bomber offensive beginning in the fall of 1942, a small emergency ground force for employment by September 1942 if necessary, and a force of at least 750,000 troops to participate in a combined cross-channel offensive in the spring of 1943. The air assault was assigned first priority.

Calculations made by the Army Service Forces in the spring of 1942 indicated that the capacities of British ports would have to be materially increased. Investigations further revealed that insufficient British labor was available for constructing necessary airfields and housing and for handling supplies. The BOLERO troop basis of 750,000 prepared in May 1942 indicated a requirement of 175,000 service troops. Cargo lift available for June, July, and August totaled more than four million measurement tons. Although this was within the capacity of British ports, it far exceeded the capacity of the United States service troops in the United Kingdom to receive, segregate, and warehouse. Since it was obvious that cargo-shipping capacity would be the ultimate bottleneck in BOLERO, it was decided to store the supplies in British or makeshift United States depots pending the arrival of adequate service troops.

In May 1942, the Services of Supply, European Theater of Operations, was organized in the United Kingdom. By the end of July, the movement of troops was in full swing. This new command, handicapped by shortages of service troops, was organizing the construction forces and building the first of the tremendous system of airfields which was to blanket East Anglia and, to a lesser degree, other areas of England and North Ireland. Gradually depots were developed and American transportation service was integrated with the British system, but the few service units were fighting a losing battle against the mounting piles of supplies and equipment.

The North African operation threw an even heavier burden upon the Services of Supply, ETO. Service units urgently required to handle supplies and construction units for building airfields in the Mediterranean area were sent to the new theater. The cross-channel invasion was postponed until 1944 in favor of TORCH, but the air assault upon Fortress Europe was never relaxed.

By May 1943 service troops in the United Kingdom totaled 37,500, and 90,500 troops had been moved in for the Eighth Air Force. Meanwhile, planning for the invasion of the continent proceeded. American forces in the British Isles were arriving slowly as a result of the large diversions to the Mediterranean and the shortage of all types of ready units in the United States. The prospect for an increase in the rate of movement was not promising until the late fall of 1943, when troops would become available both in the United States and North Africa, and the minimum commitments to the Pacific would have been met. Until the spring of 1943, it was customary to ship troops and equipment simultaneously. The port capacity of the United Kingdom would not be utilized completely, because of the small shipments of troops during the summer and early fall. If the practice of simultaneous shipment of troops and equipment continued, the ports of Britain would be unable to discharge all cargo when the tremendous influx of troops began in the late fall. Consequently, the Army Service Forces initiated the practice known as "preshipment." Organizational equipment was shipped in bulk in advance of the troops on a predetermined troop basis.

By utilizing the preshipment system from May 1943 to May 1944, the capacity of British ports absorbed the full load. The preshipment procedure was the only method capable of overcoming the bottleneck of port-clearance capacity. A total of 5,530,000 measurement tons of supplies and equipment were shipped in advance of troop units from the United States to the United Kingdom during the year preceding the invasion. One million six hundred thousand men were moved into the United Kingdom during the same period.

The special Combined Staff in London had primary responsibility for OVERLORD planning. Simultaneous studies on the broader strategic aspects of OVERLORD in conjunction with those of other operations were carried on continuously in Washington. Although the effective range of fighter support from the British Isles limited the number of possible assault areas, all areas were studied for possible follow-up or contingent operations.

Studies prepared by the Army Service Forces showed that special measures would have to be employed in order to provide adequate port and beach capacities in the selected target area. The assault and follow-up forces were initially estimated at five divisions simultaneously afloat in landing craft, plus two follow-up divisions and two airborne divisions, with a subsequent build-up to at least 20 divisions. The movement of even the minimum tonnage of supplies and equipment for the assault force across the beach was a task that previously had been considered impossible. A plan for two artificial harbors was conceived in London as a practical means of developing the required beach capacities. One of these harbors was destroyed by storms and was of little value in the operation. However, the use of amphibious trucks and cargo-handling equipment on the beaches, the splendid organization of operations on the beaches themselves, the beach clearance facilities, and the superbly trained and led service troops yielded results far beyond expectations, and made success possible in the selected target area. The Germans had concluded that the support of forces through this area was impossible, and as a result were out of position at the time of the assault.

The original plan called for the prompt seizure of western French ports in order to provide the required port capacity. The tactical success achieved after the St. Lo breakthrough prompted a departure from this plan in favor of a pursuit which might quickly destroy the German armies in France. This logistic gamble almost succeeded. However, the line of communications stretched beyond its capacity and halted the Allied forces. The capture of the port of Antwerp and its rapid rehabilitation made possible the accumulation of supplies and equipment for the advance across the Rhine and the complete defeat of Germany.

Because of the U-boat menace, the Theater had originally planned to support Continental operations entirely from the United Kingdom until submarine bases could be neutralized by land assault. The success of the antisubmarine campaign in 1943, however, permitted a change of plan. Computations made by the Army Service Forces in the winter of 1943-44 indicated that requirements for landing our troops and supplies over the beaches would saturate the capacity of the ports of the United Kingdom and exceed the capabilities of available service troops. Plans were made, therefore, to provide for the direct shipment of supplies and equipment from the United States to the French coast beginning D-day plus 15. At the request of the Theater, the New York Port of Embarkation worked out a plan for "commodity loaded" ships that primarily carried one class of supplies. During the period between 6 June and 30 September 1944, 1,050,000 long tons of supplies and equipment were shipped directly to France from the United States. During the same period, 1,680,000 long tons were transshipped from the United Kingdom to France for American forces, and 501,000 long tons from the Mediterranean. The bad weather in the fall of 1944 hampered beach operations, and tenacious German defense of the port areas seriously affected the build-up in France of reserve supplies and equipment. This forced the Theater to utilize the specially loaded ships from the United States as floating warehouses and to call forward only the supplies most vitally needed in support of the operations. Until the port of Antwerp was finally captured, the Theater retained a large pool of shipping in European waters. This floating reserve amounted to 244 ships in October 1944.

The Commanding General, ASF, presented a plan at the Teheran Conference in December 1943 that was adopted as a subsidiary operation in support of the cross-channel assault. This was one of the many studies of alternative or subsidiary operations in Europe prepared by the Army Service Forces. This study, developed in the spring of 1943, proposed operations in the south of France involving an assault force of five divisions, one of them airborne and one armored, mounted from North Africa and Italy. Beach and port capacities were considered adequate for this force in establishing a bridgehead. Computation of port development capabilities and the line of communications indicated at the maximum, capacity for a force of two million men by D plus 365 days. The plan envisaged the use of ports from Sete to Toulon. The study concluded that such an operation could be mounted and supported with available bases and shipping, provided that the efficiency of the enemy line of communications could be reduced by 60 to 75 percent.

This highly successful assault on southern France followed the Normandy landings by approximately two months. The rapid progress of our forces up the Rhone Valley contributed materially to the speedy clearing of the German armies from western France. Furthermore, it contributed greatly to the solution of the difficult logistic problem in northern France. The opening of the ports of Marseille and Toulon relieved some pressure on the Channel ports and beaches during the critical period just prior to the opening of Antwerp, also making possible the reequipping of the French Army and the provision of essential civilian-relief supplies. Throughout the winter, the Rhone Valley line of communications reduced railway congestion in western and northern France and the Low Countries.

Economic and political studies of the occupation of Europe were initiated in the fall of 1942 in order to determine the availability of local resources and the probable demands upon the United Nations for shipping, food, fuel, and textiles in case of sudden German collapse. The scope of these studies varied from the occupation of France to the occupation of all Europe as far as the Vistula. The reports proposed a number of occupational zones for Germany to the Joint Logistics Committee of the Joint Chiefs of Staff. They developed the advantages and disadvantages of each and the lines of communications required to support them. They indicated that support of United States occupational forces through France and Belgium would overtax communications networks. The Army Service Forces therefore recommended that the United States reserve the ports of Bremen and Bremerhaven, and that rail access through the British zone be provided. This was the action subsequently taken.

Persian Gulf Command

The Red Army in 1942 was in very dire straits. It had been pushed back to the gates of Leningrad and Moscow. Tula and Stalingrad were all but surrounded, and the Crimea had been overrun by the Germans. The Russians had lost a major portion of their industrial capacity and production in their newly established factories in the Urals and in eastern Siberia was not yet under way. They needed equipment and they needed raw materials. Tanks, airplanes, small arms and cannon, gasoline, aluminum and steel, machine tools, clothing, and foodstuffs were required in tremendous quantities. A trickle of supplies and equipment was moving over the northern convoy route at heavy cost in lives and ships. To swell this trickle to a flood, it was necessary to establish the long and difficult supply line through the Persian Corridor.

The United States Army started the establishment of a full-fledged supply route in the Persian Corridor in September 1942. The mission of the Persian Gulf Command was the movement of supplies and equipment from deep-water ports in the Persian Gulf to Soviet transfer points in northern Iran. American troops moving into Iran in the fall of 1942 took over the operation of the Iranian State Railway and the existing truck assembly and port facilities. They constructed docks and warehouses, and plane and truck assembly plants. They built highways and organized a motor-transport service. They put Diesel locomotives and modern rolling stock on the railroad and assembled trucks and planes on a production line basis. They unloaded ships with the temperature at 120° in Khorramshahr, and moved supplies through mountain passes where the temperature was 18° below zero.

American troops, totaling up to 29,500, were supplemented by employing as many as 44,000 local laborers. The greatest monthly movement of supplies to Russia through the Persian Corridor was attained in July 1944, when 289,000 long tons were delivered to the Soviet. Of this total, 171,000 tons were moved by rail, 98,000 tons by truck, 1,170 tons by air, and 17,600 tons by the United Kingdom Commercial Corporation, a quasi-official British company. During the entire period of active operations, commencing in late December 1942 and terminating in the midsummer of 1945, a total of 5,560,000 long tons of Lend-lease cargo was moved through the Persian Corridor to Russia. These supplies played a vital part in the Russian offensives that culminated in the capture of Berlin.

China, Burma, India

Japanese strategy from 1932 onward was aimed at denying the Chinese armies the support of the industrial areas, first of Manchuria and later of China itself, and at cutting off Chinese agricultural resources. The latter was accomplished either by outright seizure of the major agricultural areas or by periodic forays in strength for the purpose of seizing and destroying the harvests.

After the Japanese closed the south China ports in December 1941 and January 1942, the Chinese armies were denied aid from America except by way of the Burma Road. Although this road never delivered more than 18,000 short tons of supplies per month, the psychological effect of its operation was of vital importance to the Chinese war effort. In March 1942, the Japanese capture of Rangoon blocked this route.

The loss of the south China ports confined the Chinese armies to the waging of guerrilla warfare because of the lack of military supplies. The closing of the Burma Road shut off even its trickle of support. The large, poorly trained and equipped Chinese forces, nevertheless, were forcing the Japanese to keep large ground forces in China.

A primary objective of United Nations strategy was to keep China actively in the war. Implementation of this strategy was a matter of logistics. No line of communications by way of the China ports was possible without control of the South China Sea. Reopening the old Burma Road would have required a major campaign in Burma. Liberation of south Burma and Malaya would have required large amphibious operations for which troops, landing craft, and other equipment could not be spared from other operations, and at best would have provided only an indirect source of aid to China. Limited resources in Asia in 1942 prevented the mounting of a major campaign against the Japanese. The Combined Chiefs of Staff decided to give first priority to the provision of direct aid to China through the use of all available resources in north Burma.

Supplies and equipment could be delivered to China at that time only by air over the Himalayas (the "Hump"). Air delivery of heavy construction equipment, machinery, and heavy organizational equipment to Chinese troops was impossible, hence the opening of an overland line of communications was imperative. The Japanese held all of north Burma. The terrain from Ledo in Assam to the old Burma Road at Wanting on the Burma-China border, a point within the offensive capabilities of the Chinese forces, is an almost trackless waste of mountains, canyons, and broad, swampy valleys. The Himalayas are probably the wildest and most rugged mountains in the world, and the Assam-Burma foothills are covered with dense and steaming jungles. This locality is recognized as one of the most pestilential regions in the world, with malaria, dysentery, and typhus predominating. During the monsoon season the rainfall ranges from 150 to 175 inches, with as much as 14 inches falling in 24 hours. In addition to the natural obstacles, it was necessary to drive the Japanese from the trace of the road as construction proceeded. To many, the difficulties appeared insuperable. The land route was vital, however, to the Chinese.

Simultaneously with the construction of the Ledo Road it was necessary to expand the long and unsatisfactory line of communications from Calcutta which served the Assam area. The latter consisted of the Bengal-Assam Railroad, which was operated by the Indian Civil Service, and the Brahmaputra barge line, which was operated by a number of independent British commercial companies. Construction of the airfields in upper Assam and operations over the Himalayas were requiring heavy tonnages of supplies and equipment. In addition, considerable quantities of supplies and equipment were used to maintain and operate the Ramgarh Training Center in Assam, whose function it was to train and equip Chinese forces for use in securing the land route from Ledo to Kunming. Throughout 1942 and 1943 the China-Burma-India Theater devoted its efforts to expanding the port of Calcutta, accelerating the operation of the Bengal-Assam Railway by providing operational and maintenance personnel, building airfields in Assam, laying pipe lines from Calcutta and Chittagong to Upper Assam, and constructing the Ledo Road and its paralleling pipe lines.

Progress in north Burma depended upon the rate of construction of the Ledo Road, because the road was essential for the support of combat troops. Lack of railroads and highways during this entire period limited other land operations in Burma to raids by specially trained commando and long-range penetration groups supported almost entirely by air. These units harassed Japanese forces in Burma and prevented their mounting an offensive against Bengal.

The desperate plight of the Chinese Army in the fall of 1943 prompted an urgent request at the Cairo Conference that United States forces be sent to China in order to bolster the morale of the people and to assist Chinese combat forces. It was evident, however, that the support of sizable ground forces over the Burma line of communications would be entirely impracticable. Amphibious operations against the south China coast would require even greater resources than those that had been required for the North African operation. Such a commitment was out of the question in view of the impending assault on Europe.

After the Japanese had been pushed out of north Burma and the road and pipe lines extended to Mogaung and Myitkyina, a strong thrust to the south was made by Chinese and American troops which threw the Japanese off balance and facilitated the movement of the main Allied force from southeast India into Burma. After Chinese troops trained at Ramgarh drove the Japanese from southwest China and northern Burma, the land line of communications into southwest China progressed rapidly, culminating in the opening of the Stilwell Road (the combined Ledo and Burma Roads) in January 1945 and the completion of the pipe line to Kunming on 7 July 1945. The support that the road and pipe lines provided for an intermediate air transport refueling base was particularly important. Without this base, no large increase in air lift over the Himalayas would have been possible.

Although substantial tonnage was being flown into China, extensive operations would not be possible without the land line by which large quantities of wheeled vehicles, and other heavy material not transportable by air, were delivered. Such a line would open the possibility of large-scale offensive operations against the Japanese. The American Theater Commander, jointly with the Chinese, prepared a plan for a Chinese offensive with American air support to open the ports of Canton and Hongkong. But the importance of increasing the flow of supplies by way of the Stilwell Road and pipe lines had to be balanced against the importance of immediately employing the available resources of men and equipment to support an early Chinese offensive designed to capture the Canton-Knowlton port area. The Combined Chiefs of Staff decided that the advantage of such an offensive would be minimized if it were delayed by work designed to increase the capacity of the road, so the latter was deferred. The end of the war found the Chinese ready to strike toward the south coast.

Aleutians Campaign

At the Casablanca Conference in January 1943 it was decided that it was imperative to drive the Japanese from the bases they had seized in the Aleutian Islands. The campaign to accomplish this was planned and executed by the Western Defense Command. The scope of the operations was limited to that which could be supported by resources available to the Western Defense Command and the Alaskan Department, augmented by some special items provided by the Army Service Forces. Shortages of service units rendered the support of this operation difficult. However, the logistic implications were comparatively minor, because the forces involved were small.

The Aleutians campaign provided logistic information concerning operations in cold and arctic climates which was subsequently used in determining the feasibility of and estimating requirements for similar operations. The campaign added emphasis to lessons then being learned in the Pacific: Amphibious operations, regardless of size, cannot succeed without trained and adequate service organizations.

Early Pacific Campaigns

The decision to undertake a strategic defense in the Pacific committed us to a program of developing bases from which to launch our eventual counteroffensive. First, however, it was necessary to halt the Japanese conquest and to secure the few major-base areas remaining. We needed time in which to defeat the European Axis, time in which to rebuild the fleet, time in which to train men, and time in which to manufacture supplies and equipment. The heroic defense of the Philippines gave us a few precious months in which to move forces to Australia, New Zealand, New Caledonia, and the New Hebrides. The battles of the Coral Sea in May and Midway in June 1942 checked the Japanese advance. From then on the war in the Pacific became a series of operations for the successive seizure of areas that were to be developed for air cover and the logistic support of subsequent advances. The objective of the 1942 campaign in New Guinea was to shorten supply lines by establishing major bases along the New Guinea coast for the support of future operations. The primary objective of the assault on Guadalcanal was to seize a forward air base in order to cover further operations from the South Pacific.

Because of the distances in the Pacific, tremendous quantities of shipping were required for relatively small forces. The shortage of shipping and of service troops came perilously close to costing us the Guadalcanal victory. The campaign across the Owen-Stanley mountain range to Buna Mission was painfully slow. The work of the Army Service Forces in support of these campaigns involved a careful weighing of the requirements of the North African campaign and BOLERO against the critical requirements of the Central, South, and Southwest Pacific Theaters.

During 1942 the bulk of available shipping was utilized in the Atlantic. Only minimum requirements were allotted for the occupation and build-up of Pacific bases. Difficulties arising from the shortage of shipping in the Pacific were aggravated by difficulties in the assignment of shipping priorities between the Army and Navy and by a lack of coordination in the development of bases in the Pacific areas. Critically needed shipping was tied up for long periods in oversea ports, particularly Noumea, Caledonia, while the inadequate cargo-handling facilities were occupied with shuttling vessels for piecemeal unloading. It was necessary to dock vessels, search them for urgently needed items, and then replace them with other ships for the same type of selective unloading, in order to make available even the minimum essentials. The Director of Operations of the Army Service Forces went to the Pacific for the purpose of investigating this problem. His recommendations resulted in the establishment of a Joint Logistic Staff and phased shipping to the South Pacific Theater. This scheme was adopted later in the Pacific Ocean Areas.

The Joint Logistics Board formed by the commander of the South Pacific was a local agency operating under the area command. It established shipping priorities and priorities in the use of local facilities. It was successful in that no further major difficulties of this sort developed during its existence. The Joint Staff for the Pacific Ocean Areas, which was organized approximately a year later, absorbed the

South Pacific Joint Board and functioned for the entire Pacific. This staff was superimposed upon Army and Navy staffs already in existence. It exercised control over all shipping in the Pacific Ocean Areas and prepared or reviewed logistic plans. Since the various base commands retained their direct channels to the Ports of Embarkation, however, the potentialities of the Joint Staff were never fully realized. Separate channels for routine supply requisitions for Army and Navy continued to be used. Duplication of requirements and dual standards of living, which might well have been eliminated by this Joint Staff, continued in varying degrees throughout the war.

In the summer of 1942 the Army Service Forces made long-range estimates for the production of critical items for the Pacific campaigns. For example, the vital communications plan for the Southwest Pacific was the first for which procurement was made. The plan provided for a complete communications network from Australia and the Solomons through New Guinea, Borneo, and the Philippines. Developed by the Signal Corps, it was an outstanding achievement in procurement planning.

The build-up of supplies in New Caledonia, Espiritu Santo, and Guadalcanal, took more than a year. Not until June 1943 could the South Pacific Theater mount further assaults in the Solomons. Landings on New Georgia in June were followed by the seizure of Vella Lavella and Treasury Islands and the establishment of the Bougainville beachhead. The Theater developed these areas as air bases for an eventual assault on Rabaul and further operations on Bougainville. As operations progressed in the southeastern New Guinea area, bases were developed in Milne Bay and Finschafen, and heavy concentrations of supplies were built up.

Operations in the Southwest Pacific were characterized by swift shore-to-shore amphibious operations designed to bypass pockets of resistance and establish forward bases from which further "end runs" could be mounted. Such operations were dependent for their success upon immediate logistic support and the rapid build-up of supplies and equipment in the new areas. Almost without exception these areas were trackless jungles, and all facilities, including roads, trails, and airfields, had to be constructed. An Engineer Amphibian Brigade, organized and trained by the Army Services Forces, operated some of the landing craft for these shore-to-shore operations, moved supplies and equipment for the combat elements and the construction forces, and established supply installations concurrently with the clearing of the beaches. These highly trained and specialized units made the type of operations required in the Southwest Pacific possible.

By the summer of 1943 the development of base facilities in Hawaii and the ship-construction program had progressed to the point where the Joint Chiefs of Staff could consider the mounting of a major offensive in the Central Pacific. In July 1943 the Navy and the Army Service Forces collaborated in preparing a joint logistic plan for operations against the Gilberts and Marshalls. Specific assignments of logistic responsibility were worked out. The plan was presented by the Joint Chiefs of Staff, and accepted, at the Quebec conference. Conferences with representatives of the Theater followed, and the required supplementary supplies and equipment were concentrated along the west coast of the United States. The need to load the task force from Oahu, Hawaii, together with the usual shortage of service troops, required the direct movement of maintenance supplies and equipment from the United States.

Meanwhile studies of future operations against Truk, the Palaus, and the Marianas were progressing. Each area was studied in detail for the purpose of determining the requirements for assault, consolidation, airfield construction, and base development. Accelerated ship construction and the stabilizing of campaigns in the Mediterranean to some extent relieved the critical Pacific shipping situation.

Although service units were still a major shortage, certain combat units, notably the First Cavalry Division, became available to the Southwest Pacific Theater. New Britain and New Ireland were bypassed, and the Admiralties were occupied. This maneuver made Rabaul useless to the Japanese and gave the Navy a major base at Manus in the Western Pacific.

The Japanese garrisons in the bypassed areas, cut off by our submarine, surface, and air blockade, rapidly lost their potentialities as combat forces. With their air forces eliminated, they ceased to threaten our line of communications. Without supplies and reinforcements, they withered on the vine and became a liability to the Japanese.

The improved shipping position and our base in the Admiralties permitted the Navy to bypass Truk and Ponape and to attack the Marianas in June 1944. There service troops constructed air bases for the B-29's that later attacked Japan. In September our forces bypassed Halmahera and seized the Palaus and Morotai. These moves provided the air bases used in completing the preliminary phases of the Pacific campaign.

The Philippines

Logistic studies of the Philippine area were begun in 1942 by the Army Service Forces, looking toward the conversion of the islands into bases for operations against Japan or the China coast. Early plans called for the development of Mindanao as a staging area and air base for the seizure of Luzon, which in turn would be the base for operations against China, Formosa, and the Japanese home islands. These studies furnished the basis for procurement, priorities, and distribution plans.

In May 1944 the Joint Strategic Survey Committee suggested that an operation against Formosa, rather than the Philippines, might hasten victory. There were not enough service troops to permit operations against Formosa and Luzon simultaneously. The Army Service Forces reviewed the two plans and concluded that Luzon was the better target. The ports of Formosa were limited in capacity and were susceptible of easy blocking. Larger airfield capacity and a better road network were available on Luzon. The greater land mass of Luzon provided opportunity for fuller use of available assault shipping. The island's occupation could be covered by land-based aircraft. Labor and material were more abundant on Luzon. The Joint Chiefs of Staff withheld decision pending an analysis by the Joint Logistics Committee of the availability of resources and other logistic factors. Representatives of the Army Service Forces contributed largely to this study. The Joint Chiefs of Staff in October 1944 directed the seizure and occupation of Luzon.

The offensive power of the Navy and the Air Forces made the reoccupation of the Philippines possible. Operating from forward bases captured from the Japanese and, in the case of the Navy, from tremendous trains of auxiliary ships, the two arms destroyed the Japanese air forces, and restricted the movements of Japanese troops and denied them reinforcements and supplies.

Logistically, the Philippine campaign presented no new problems. The Leyte operation was a part the opportunistic diversion of a task force en route to Yap. The assault at Lingayen Gulf was a normal ship-to-shore amphibious operation. Except for special attacks on fortified islands, operations employing the Engineer Amphibian Brigade were the type used along the coast of New Guinea.

The securing of Pacific supply lines and the success of the cargo-ship construction program made possible direct shipments from the Zone of the Interior, hence the vast quantities of supplies stored in New Guinea became less vital to operations. Sufficient service troops were not generally available for loading from one set of bases simultaneously with the establishment of new forward bases. As a result of these two factors, the rear-base stockpiles were reduced slowly, and weather and storage conditions prevailing in the tropics caused excessive wastage.

In the develpment of the Philippine base, the provision of suficent service troops was again a major logistic problem. Theater plans and those of the Army Service Forces had borne fruit in a flood of supplies and equipment. Japanese devastation imposed heavy demands upon construction troops. The civilian population was destitute. These latter two factors increased the already heavy demands for service troops to receive, unload, and distribute supplies; to construct depots, ports, and airfields; and to maintain the combat forces that were mopping up the Archipelago. Additional service troops could only be obtained by redeploying them from Europe.

Port capacity in the Philippines depended on the service troops' ability to clear the docks of incoming-cargo shipments. Meanwhile, it was necessary to make plans for the outloading of the forces to be used against Kyushu and Honshu, because service troops from Europe would arrive too late to take part in this phase of projected operations. Relying upon redeployed units in the target areas, therefore, all available units had to be used for base development.

Preparation for the Final Assault on Japan

In the fall of 1944 the war was progressing rapidly, and it was apparent that the invasion of the main islands of Japan could be accomplished. The invasion of Luzon had been planned for the end of the year. The use of the Philippines as a base for continued operations was definitely planned, although the extent of their development for this purpose was not yet decided. The Joint Chiefs of Staff had directed that operations against Iwo Jima and the Ryukyu be undertaken in the spring of 1945. The war in China continued to be subordinated. The war in Europe had not yet ended, although every effort was being made to end the European phase as rapidly as possible. The war in the Pacific had to continue, for the moment, with shortages of both equipment and troops.

All supplies and equipment possible, however, were made ready for the final effort against the home islands of Japan. The War Department General Staff and the Joint Chiefs of Staff indicated the probable course of operations against Japan. Definite details of the final operations were not available at this time, although tentative dates had been established for planning purposes.

To assure supplies and equipment for the duration of the war, whether on a one-front or a two-front basis, the Army Service Forces coordinated the procurement planning of the Technical Services on a long-range basis. To this end, in December 1944 the Army Service Forces prepared logistic studies for the prospective operations against Kyushu and Honshu. These contained target dates; troop bases showing major units, phasing of troops, and supplies; supply levels; and proposed construction projects. Procurement was adjusted on the basis of these studies early in 1945. The studies and projects were then forwarded to the War Department General Staff and to the Theater. Theater planning for the operation against Kyushu had progressed to such a point that the Army Service Forces plans could not be used intact by the Theater in their determination of requirements. However, the two plans, Theater and Army Service Forces, compared favorably, and only minor changes in procurement were necessary.

The Theater used the Army Service Forces' logistic plans for the operation against Honshu as a guide in their planning for that operation. Logistic factors determined the choice of target dates and the size of forces. The target dates depended on the ability to deploy supplies, equipment, and troops and to construct the necessary bases. Assault shipping, availability of troops from the United States or Europe prior to the operations, and the capacity of landing areas supporting the forces ashore limited the size of forces. The logistic preparations for supporting assault operations against Japan, including plans for the tailored packing and loading of 482 ships for the Kyushu operation and some 700 for Honshu, were well under way when hostilities came to an end, and 135 of the specially-loaded vessels were used to support the occupational forces.

Redeployment

Redeployment was a clear-cut example of the influence of logistics upon grand strategy in the Pacific. Operations had been limited to those areas where an initial superiority of forces could be achieved and maintained. The transfer of men and matériel from Europe made possible the concentration of forces necessary for the support of an invasion of Japan proper.

Planning for the continuation of operations in the Pacific after the capture of the Philippines was based upon the time required for redeploying from Europe the additional service troops and supplies necessary for the construction of bases in the Pacific and for the equipping of assault forces. Redeployment involved the moving of 1.2 million men from Europe, 400,000 directly and 800,000 by way of the United States. It also involved moving five million tons of equipment and supplies from Europe directly to the Pacific, and returning five million tons to the United States. This operation proved to be the most difficult that had confronted the logistic organizations in Europe, the Pacific, and the United States. The service organization in Europe had been designed for the receipt of supplies and their processing and delivery to consumers at the front. The end of hostilities and redeployment to the Pacific necessitated a complete reversal of the process. The service troops needed in Europe for preparing shipments were the same troops required in the Pacific for receiving, warehousing, and issuing matériel on a scale never before reached in that area. The previous operations in the Pacific were minor compared to the final assault envisaged against Japan. The construction of major bases, adequate for the support of more than a million men in combat, were now required in the Pacific.

Vast distances were involved in the transfer of men and supplies from Europe to the Pacific, either directly or by way of the United States. Service forces in the European theater had to be trained in the methods of screening requisitions, packaging, documentation, and shipment, because their previous experience had been confined to the receipt of matériel. The time consumed in shipping supplies from Europe was so great that the service organizations in the United States and the Pacific had to advance their target dates by several months. The task of coordinating movements, of training key personnel and staffs in Europe for the task of outshipping, of accepting supplies returned to the United States, and of repairing, warehousing, and re-issuing them fell to the Army Service Forces. Redeployment was a triangular operation, whereas earlier operations had involved the direct flow of supplies. The final assault against Japan was dependent for its success upon the orderly flow of men and supplies from both the United States and Europe. Only if redeployment were on schedule would operations take place on schedule. The war came to an end before the redeployment operation could be fully tested.

Chapter 5

SUPPLY

The major task of the Army Service Forces was to provide supplies and equipment for the Army at the place and time and in the quantities required by strategic and operational plans. If the Service Forces failed, the most brilliant plans would come to naught, and the best trained troops would be helpless. The supply of the Army would have been a colossal task even with unlimited resources. Shortages of raw materials, industrial facilities, manpower, and transportation influenced the conduct of the war and constituted the most serious problems of the Army Service Forces.

Initially, strategic plans were made and requirements were computed for accomplishing the plans. When it was found that the requirements could not be met because of shortages and the competing demands of other claimants, the plans were adjusted and new calculations of requirements were provided. As critical shortages developed in particular items, and as new or unforeseen contingencies arose in oversea commands, additional adjustments were necessary. Consequently, plans were constantly changing, and each such change brought major alterations throughout the complex machinery engaged in procurement, distribution, storage, and transportation. Planning was continuous and never final. Changes and unexpected developments are, of course, the very essence of war, but their impact is tremendous in that phase of logistics which is related to the mass production of countless thousands of items.

The job of the Army Service Forces in the field of supply was to determine detailed requirements; translate them into production factors; secure raw materials, industrial facilities, and manpower; see that the end items were produced in accordance with schedules; store the items where they would be readily accessible without waste; and, finally, to deliver them to all parts of the world in the right quantities and at the right time.

Requirements

Because of the desperate urgency of war, the impossibility of accurate forecasting, and the unexpected shifts in operational demands, the Army Service Forces was guided by the maxim that it was better to have too much than too little. Because of an incomplete public understanding of the problems involved, this was criticized on the ground that requirements were overstated, and that methods of determining them were inadequate. Every effort was made to determine Army requirements carefully and accurately. The record must speak for itself.

Before Pearl Harbor, the G-4 Division of the War Department General Staff had prepared equipment expenditure programs that merely indicated quantities procurable under different appropriations. Because these programs were limited in scope and did not provide schedules, they were inadequate as a basis for production planning or for informing the War Production Board of the Army's needs in terms of raw materials and industrial facilities. A phased program of long-range estimates of military needs, which would cover all items of supply, and which could be translated into terms of raw materials and facilities, was required.

A comprehensive Army Supply Program designed to meet these needs was planned late in 1941. It first appeared in April 1942 and was issued periodically throughout the war. The first Army Supply Program set forth the procurement objectives of the several Technical Services for the calendar years 1942 and 1943 in terms of end items. Each Technical Service prepared requirements for its supplies and equipment in accordance with standard instructions. The computations, which were based upon troop bases, tables of equipment and allowances, replacement factors, and data furnished by the War Department General Staff, were so extensive and complex that they required the use of electrical tabulating machinery. Unfortunately, a continual source of difficulty in the preparation of the Army Supply Program was that the War Department General Staff was unable to provide consistent and timely information upon which to base the Program. As a result, the computation of requirements was not as realistic as it might have been.

When the initial Army Supply Program had been converted into terms of raw materials and facilities, the War Production Board, after taking into account other programs contributing to the war effort, determined that it was unrealizable, because of the limited supply of raw materials and the inadequacy of our productive capacity. Accordingly, the Joint Chiefs of Staff revised the strategic plans to which the Program had been geared, and ordered a reduction that was reflected in the Army Supply Program of November 1942. This adjustment also made larger quantities of raw materials and more facilities available for the production of aircraft and merchant shipping.

As the needs of the Army in Europe and the Pacific increased in relation to other demands, this was reflected in the Army Supply Programs of 1944 and 1945. The Army Service Forces continuously revised the Army Supply Program as operational demands shifted or as shortages in raw materials or manpower became critical. Thus it served to coordinate strategy, requirements, and resources.

The first phase of the procurement program was designed to provide the initial equipment of a rapidly expanding Army. The requirements for this purpose were determined by using authorized tables of equipment. When the program for initial equipment had been rounded out after the first two years of war, the primary job became one of determining the amount of replacement equipment needed. It was clear that experience would be the best guide in establishing such requirements. Teams of officers were sent overseas for the purpose of studying and revising replacement factors in the light of operations. This was not enough, however, and closer control and coordination of inventories, requirements, and procurement were necessary.

The Supply Control System, which was established in March 1944 and subsequently improved, brought together on one form all pertinent data for each item required, for review, critical analysis, and proper control. Such data included past issue experience, stocks on hand, anticipated deliveries, and estimated future demands for all purposes. Monthly computations were made for the 1,900 principal items that made up 80 percent of the dollar value of procurement. Demands for these items were phased by months or quarters, instead of on an annual basis as was done in the Army Supply Program. The same procedure, although in less detail, was applied to the 850,000 secondary items making up the balance of Army Service Forces procurement. As the operation of the system became routine, the more important of the secondary items were segregated, and a careful analysis was made of them.

As differentiated from initial and maintenance supplies, the determination of requirements for operational projects presented great difficulties, because each operation required equipment and materials for and peculiar to a given campaign. Requirements for such projects included landing craft, port rehabilitation equipment, construction materials, airplane landing mat, railroad equipment, bridging equipment, cranes, boats, barges, and tugs. During the early stages of the war, the Army Service Forces had little or no guidance from the War Department General Staff or Theater Commanders in computing these requirements. This was understandable because the strategic plans being considered at the highest Government levels were constantly changing. Theater Commanders and their newly formed staffs were primarily concerned with organizing and training their commands. In order to meet the situation, the Army Service Forces prepared logistic plans that were believed to be logical and in consonance with plans under consideration by the Joint and Combined Chiefs of Staff. The plans developed by the Army Service Forces formed the basis for computing operational requirements for the first 18 months of the war. Had this not been done, later campaigns would have found Allied forces short of essential equipment. By June 1943 the Theater Commanders and their staffs had begun to accumulate field experience, and the Army Service Forces initiated action requiring them to submit their estimates of operational requirements well in advance of their campaigns. For example, the European Theater submitted requests for equipment and materials for the reconstruction of Cherbourg in August 1943, eight months before the landing in Normandy. Procurement directives for this project were issued the same month. Later the Army Service Forces attempted to project its planning even further, and in 1944 detailed requirements for Pacific operations were formulated and sent to Theater Commanders for comment even before the governing strategic decisions had been reached.

Lend-lease also presented problems in determining requirements. Although the assignment of finished munitions was on a current basis, procurement plans had to be made far in advance. An official protocol set forth Russian needs on a yearly basis. The British restricted their demands so that they were in accord with our military requirements and productive capacity. Other Lend-lease requests were anticipated as far in advance as was possible. Nevertheless, from the standpoint of procurement, there was considerable uncertainty and incompleteness in statements of Lend-lease requirements. For example, the necessity to rearm the French in 1943 and 1944 was not anticipated. Only the 10-division strategic reserve included in the Army Supply Program made this possible.

The Army policy of encouraging Lend-lease nations to use standard American military equipment simplified procurement and production. It permitted diversion to American military use when required. Another advantage of this policy and Lend-lease operations in general was that our Allies' estimates of replacement needs were available for our guidance. Often their combat experience was used in making

CHART 7. SUPPLY CONTROL

ITEM: Rifle, U.S., cal., .30, M1
ITEM NUMBER:
UNIT: Each
UNIT COST: $50.00
STANDARD DOLLAR WEIGHT: $50.00
SUBSTITUTES FOR THIS ITEM ARE: None
THIS ITEM SUBSTITUTES FOR: Carbine, cal., .30, M2 — CLASSIFICATION I [X] CONTROLLED [X] NONCONTROLLED
DATE OF REPORT: 28 FEBRUARY 1945

L N E	FACTOR	CURRENT UNFILLED DEMAND	ACTUAL 1945 JAN.	FEB.	1 Jan. thru 28 Feb.	MAR.	APRIL	MAY	JUNE	3RD QTR.	4TH QTR.	YEAR 1945	L N E
	ISSUES AND ISSUE DEMAND												
	U.S. ARMY		60,495	19,067	79,562	34,457	24,842	25,561	25,400	73,238	74,600	296,942	1
	ZONE OF THE INTERIOR	48,363	157,073	111,074	268,147	85,661	75,081	78,296	61,278	238,802	221,551	907,815	2
	THEATERS, OPERATIONAL PROJECTS	62,123	0	13,330	13,330	11,661	0	0	0	0	0	0	3
	OPERATIONAL PROJECTS	0	900	0	900	0	0	0	0	0	0	0	4
	ASSEMBLY, CONVERSION, MODIFICATION	0	79	97	167	190	191	190	190	181	181	1,005	5
	OTHER												
	TOTAL U.S. ARMY	110,687	218,538	143,568	362,106	135,969	100,914	104,047	106,868	312,221	296,132	1,205,762	6
	NAVY	0	30,000	10,000	40,000	20,000	10,000	5,000	5,000	15,000	10,000	50,000	7
	INTERNATIONAL AID	0	0	0	0	0	5,000	5,000	5,000	0	0	7,500	8
	OTHER													9
	STOCK ADJUSTMENT - DECREASE		53	13,960	14,013								10
	TOTAL ISSUES AND ISSUE DEMAND	110,687	248,591	167,528	416,119	155,969	115,914	114,047	116,868	327,221	306,132	1,263,262	11
		110,687				282,632	342,570	393,617	433,485	540,706	1,246,838	1,510,100	
	LEVELS												
	EQUIPMENT RESERVE		120,005			119,203	119,203	119,203	119,203	119,203	119,203	119,203	12
	STOCK LEVEL (84.5% 60 DAYS)		141,037	94,556		204,580	210,535	210,691	208,026	397,300	200,793	200,793	13
	PRODUCTION RESERVE													14
	TOTAL DEMAND (11 thru 14)					509,439	712,308	826,511	940,714	1,257,209	1,566,634	2,830,096	15
	SUPPLY READY FOR ISSUE (EX PROC. & ASSEMBLY)												
	STOCK ON HAND READY FOR ISSUE		430,886	298,579	430,886	279,776	0	0	0	0	0	0	16
	RETURNED STOCK - SERVICEABLE WITHOUT REPAIR		14,546	8,292	9,838	30,000	53,376	26,720	22,862	66,058	65,814	286,208	17
	RETURNED STOCK - AFTER REPAIR		18,340	58,081	76,421								18
	OTHER													19
	STOCK ADJUSTMENT - INCREASE		108	268	376								20
	RENOVED FROM STOCK (NOT ISSUED)													21
	TOTAL SUPPLY READY FOR ISSUE (SS PROCUREMENT)		450,880	365,620	517,521	309,776	53,376	26,720	22,862	66,058	65,814	286,208	22
						309,776	363,152	389,872	412,734	478,792	544,606	830,814	
	COMPUTED PROC. REQ. (ex. subs)(15 - 22)					280,663	349,156	436,639	527,980	778,417	1,021,228	1,999,282	23
	DEMAND AS A SUBSTITUTE					0	0	0	0	0	31,772	42,718	24
	SUPPLY FROM SUBSTITUTES												
	COMPUTED PROC. REQ. (add. for subs.)(23+24)					280,663	349,156	436,639	527,980	778,417	1,053,000	2,042,000	25
	RECEIPTS FROM PROC. & ASSEMBLY					97,000	208,000	313,000	419,000	737,000	1,053,000	2,042,000	26
	FROM PROCUREMENT, READY FOR ISSUE		96,690	81,684	178,374	97,000	111,000	105,000	106,000	318,000	318,000	987,000	27

60

		FROM ASSEMBLY OF COMPONENTS								
		SUPPLY BALANCE								
										28
		TOTAL SUPPLY LESS ISSUE DEMAND (22+26/4-11)	EP	140,120	188,582	206,255	218,249	275,066	319,996	29
		TOTAL SUPPLY LESS TOTAL DEMAND (22+24-14-18)	EP	-181,663	-141,156	-121,639	-108,980	-41,617	0	30
		MEMORANDA		ON HAND PCES						
92,000	81,000	STOCK RETURNED FOR REPAIR	A	23,276	22,142	22,862	22,700	65,098	66,200	264,142	31
120,443	109,256	PROCUREMENT DELIVERIES A SCHEDULE	P	97,000	111,000	105,000	106,000	318,000	318,000	987,000	32
0	50	TOTAL CURRENT UNFILLED DEMAND	BP								33
70	47	O.S.S.	P	190	190	190	190	180	180	1,000	34
		FACILITIES	P	0	0	0	0	1	1	5	35
											36
											37
37,863	42,826	ORDNANCE REPAIR SCHEDULE	P	30,000	53,376	26,780	22,560	66,098	65,814	286,208	38
											39
											40
											41
											42
											43

| | | STOCK STATUS (END OF PERIOD) | | FACTOR | L | R | NO. | | | |

								PROGRAM COMPARISONS			
									1945 AS COMPUTED AT END OF		1946 AS COMPUTED AT END OF
								2ND MONTH PRECEDING	1ST MONTH PRECEDING	CURRENT MONTH	PROPOSED	2ND MONTH PRECEDING	1ST MONTH PRECEDING	CURRENT MONTH	PROPOSED
241,150	224,172	AVAILABLE													44
57,629	55,604	OBLIGATED													45
		HELD UP EQUIPMENT RESERVE													46
		OTHER													47
298,979	279,776	TOTAL - READY FOR ISSUE		TOTAL DEMAND			58	MPR-20	MPR-20K	MPR-20X		MPR-20	MPR-20X		
92,031	64,578	AWAIT REPAIR & IN PROCESS						1,180,306	1,337,706	1,982,953		637,444	580,376	1,263,262	
		AWAITING ASSEMBLY		SUPPLY LESS DEMAND			59	0	0	0		0	411,452	0	
		OTHER													50
391,010	344,354	TOTAL STOCK ON HAND		COMPUTED PROC. REQUIREMENT			60	1,232,924	1,232,924	1,233,774		987,310	248,548	987,000	51
				PROCUREMENT OBJECTIVE			61	1,232,924	1,232,924		1,232,934	987,310	248,548		
		DISPOSAL COMPUTATION		PROGRAMMED PROCUREMENT			62	1,232,924	1,232,924	1,233,774	1,232,934	987,310	660,000R	987,310	
		DISPOSAL LEVEL		EST. PROC. AND ASSEMBLY			63	1,232,924	1,232,924			987,310	660,000	987,000	
		WAR RESERVE													
		AVAILABLE AS SURPLUS													
		REQUIRED TO DISPOSAL AGENCY													

REMARKS

a/ For analysis see lines 34 and 35

b/ Production reserve as authorized for planning purposes, subject to approval of Headquarters Board.

P - PERIOD	BP - BEGINNING OF PERIOD	A - MINIMUM REQUIRED TO TERMINATE PROCUREMENT	TECHNICAL SERVICE
C - CUMULATIVE	EP - END OF PERIOD	P - ADVANCE PROCUREMENT AUTHORIZED	
* - DATA NOT AVAILABLE	R - REVISED	K - LIMITED BY PROC. CIRCUMSTANCES	ORDNANCE
		R - PRODUCTION RESERVE AUTHORIZED	

WD AGO FORM 0470 THIS FORM SUPERSEDES WD AGO FORM 0470 DATED 1 DECEMBER 1944
1 FEBRUARY 1946 WHICH WILL NOT BE USED AFTER RECEIPT OF THIS REVISION.

adjustments in replacement factors rates for the United States Army. This was true in the case of medium tanks and led to an increase in the production program that subsequently made it possible to meet most of the Army's demands. Similarly, an analysis of the experience of the United Kingdom led to a complete revision of the methods of calculating United States requirements for tires and tubes, thereby effecting a considerable saving in production and a decrease in the planned expansion of facilities.

Research and Development

The military characteristics and the specifications of all items in the Army Supply Program must be established before production can be initiated. The search for new weapons and equipment and the improvement of existing ones are always vital military activities.

Before the outbreak of war in Europe, the War Department obtained little money which could be devoted to research and development. Many of the Army's weapons and much of its equipment were obsolete and ill-adapted to total, mechanized war. From 1939 until Pearl Harbor, strenuous efforts were made to catch up on research, and a great number of projects in different fields were undertaken in order to improve the tools of war. In this period the British, and to some extent the Russians, made their military experience available. However, research and development are time-consuming, and the United States was well behind in the reasearch race when the Japs attacked.

When we entered the war, the immediate task was to provide an effective fighting force to help stop the enemy's advance. Research and development activities entered an intensive phase in a number of fields with a view to improving existing weapons. Enough general work had been done to guide our efforts into lines that would rapidly yield tangible results. Only with such results could we hope to meet the immediate crisis.

The battle experience of our own forces demonstrated the need for many new types of equipment, and this soon became the guiding factor in research and development. For example, there were demands for improved clothing, ammunition with greater penetrating power, new demolition charges, more powerful anti-aircraft weapons, better protection for personnel exposed to enemy fire, and improved communications facilities. The Army Service Forces continuously sought to develop this improved equipment and get it into production, to bridge the gap between the producer and the user, and to meet the desires of the user insofar as it was possible. Exclusive of the atomic bomb, the number of research projects reached a peak of 2,000 in January 1945 and involved a monthly expenditure of 15 million dollars.

The Technical Services utilized every possible facility in carrying on research work. The Office of Scientific Research and Development coordinated projects involving fundamental research, whereas the War Department concentrated upon applied research. Occasionally, the line between the two was difficult to draw. When projects were turned over to the Office of Scientific Research and Development, it mobilized all possible research facilities in the search for a solution. These scientific projects frequently produced suggestions that proved invaluable to the Army. For example, the variable time (VT) fuze was originated by the Office of Scientific Research and Development. The National Inventors Council also screened many ideas, of which a small proportion was found to be useful. Coordination of research was also worked out with the Navy in some fields, such as armor plate, radar, and rockets. Headquarters, ASF, coordinated the research and development work of the Technical Services. This centralized control brought together the common interests of the several Technical Services in particular pieces of equipment. Thus, the problem of vehicular communications was worked out between the Ordnance Department and the Signal Corps. The work on boron was centralized in the Quartermaster Corps, with ballistics testing being done in cooperation with the Ordnance Department. Central direction by the Research and Development Division, ASF, made possible the assignment of primary responsibility to the most appropriate agency, which received all necessary assistance from the other Services.

A major recurring problem in research and development activities was that of providing full information to field commanders on the latest improvements in weapons. Demonstration teams were set up in order to show new equipment to Theater Commanders and to bring back additional ideas for improvement based upon combat experience. The mere shipping of equipment with instructions respecting its operation was found to be inadequate, as oversea troop commanders needed to see first-hand how a piece of equipment would perform when properly utilized. Frequently new equipment was demonstrated overseas before it was in full production, and such demonstrations created demands which could not be immediately met. As a further method of keeping various commands informed of developments, the Army Service Forces circulated two monthly publications, one secret and one confidential, reviewing the characteristics of items newly classified as standard.

The research and development program was climaxed by the production of the atomic bomb. Responsibility for the atomic program was turned over to the War Department when the President decided, upon the advice of scientists, that there was a definite possibility of creating

CHART 8. ASF PROCUREMENT DELIVERIES

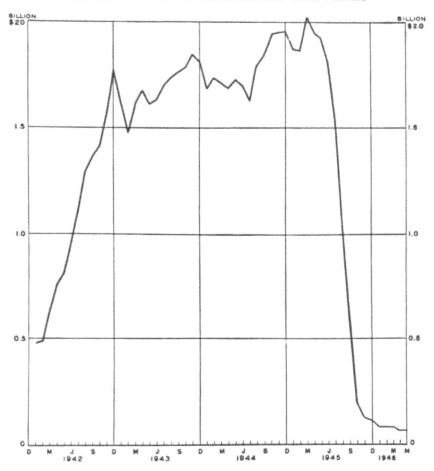

an explosive weapon based upon atomic fission. Apart from the need for secrecy, the Army Service Forces faced many problems in this program. There was still a great deal of fundamental research to be done. This aspect of the project was continued by scientists who previously had been selected for the work by the Office of Scientific Research and Development. The Army Service Forces facilitated their research in every possible way, and productive effort was closely geared to research findings. The peculiarities of the elements in which atomic fission could occur, with consequent terrific destructive force, made it necessary to construct gigantic plants in order to separate and produce the desired constituents. For this reason the administration of the program was assigned to a separate command, the Manhattan

District, under which several great engineering works were constructed, among them one at Oak Ridge, Tenn., and one at Hanford, Wash. Many new types of equipment were designed; many new processes developed and tested. Research scientists, engineers, and industrialists worked together in separating isotopes of uranium and producing a new element, plutonium. Many other problems were encountered in fashioning these elements into a practical weapon.

The work on the atomic bomb was a departure from past military research and development practices. In general, the Army had confined research to those fields in which the fundamental questions had already been answered. In the case of the atomic bomb, although the fundamental principles were already recognized, there was considerable question as to whether these principles could be applied to military use. This experience indicates that in the future the Armed Forces must maintain closer contacts with basic scientific activities and devote more attention to the exploration of new areas of scientific knowledge.

Production

The production of matériel, an enormously intricate process, consisted of bringing together the requisite raw materials, industrial facilities, and manpower, and the manufacture of the end items, at the times, and in the quantities needed.

A severe machine tool bottleneck developed as production changed from a preparation for defense to the meeting of requirements for active warfare. The Office of Production Management had sponsored considerable expansion of machine tool production during 1941. Some additional expansions were made in 1942. The immediate task of the Army Service Forces was to assist prime contractors and operators of Government-owned plants in obtaining the machine tools needed for expanding production lines. The War Production Board maintained control over the production and distribution of machine tools, and the Army Service Forces worked closely with the Board in establishing priorities.

In the summer of 1942 the War Production Board became concerned over the failure of industry to use machine tools to full capacity, and the Army Service Forces began a drive promoting the efficient use of machine tools. Utilization for 24 hours a day was considered full capacity, but this was at best a very rough measure. Frequently production lines were not operated more than 16 or 18 hours a day, the remaining time being spent for maintenance operations. In many production lines a single machine tool might be required only a fraction of the day in the productive process.

American production, for the most part, was based upon special purpose tools, which frequently made it impossible to transfer machine tools constructed for one type of work to some other more urgent use. Of course this limitation had its compensating aspect; special purpose tools materially increased production, when lines were established and work was well under way. Where necessary and possible, Headquarters, ASF, directed shifts in machine tools from one Technical Service to another, or among the Army Service Forces and other Government agencies. Each Technical Service, in turn, shifted machine tools among its contractors when changes were made in production programs.

By the end of 1942 the shortage of machine tools had largely ceased to be a serious bottleneck. However, purchases of machine tools were made throughout the war as models were changed, new types of matériel were standardized, or new production lines were set up.

Inadequate plant capacity also hampered the large-scale output of munitions in the early days of the war. This limitation was overcome by constructing new plants and by expanding existing facilities. Army-owned facilities were provided for many noncommercial purposes, such as the manufacture of smokeless powder, and shell loading. Government-owned plants were also used in the manufacture of tanks and chemical items. Large companies provided the management personnel, under contract, for their operation in many cases. The Army thereby purchased the services of a high quality staff with experience in large-scale enterprise. For the most part, it was possible to obtain contractors for operating government-owned plants from related fields of industrial activity. On occasion, however, companies without any directly related experience were asked to operate a plant and generally did so with conspicuous success.

As far as possible, individual manufacturers were persuaded to convert their own plants to the production of munitions. This kept new construction at a minimum and lessened the difficulty of obtaining efficient management for new plants. Large silverware manufacturers produced surgical instruments; an electrical refrigerator manufacturer made machine guns; a company that had formerly turned out burial vaults manufactured 100-pound bombs; and an automobile manufacturer produced antiaircraft guns. Although such conversions sometimes required new plants and in almost all cases required new tools, it was industrial "know-how" that made it possible to produce munitions on an undreamed-of scale.

In 1942 the War Production Board warned the War Department that the Army might construct more plants than could be operated at full capacity with the available supply of raw materials. Accordingly, the Army Service Forces carefully reviewed all plant construction then in progress and curtailed the 1943 program in conformance with the limited supply of available raw materials.

The shortage of certain raw materials was encountered even before Pearl Harbor. This was an unusual experience for American industry. The priorities system, the first attempt to solve the materials problem, was designed to indicate the order in which essential military end items were to be produced. The system did not solve the problem that became a serious reality, namely, that if all high priority orders were completely filled the shortages of materials would prevent low priority orders from being filled at all. Moreover, time was required to reduce civilian inventories and to divert raw materials to war production; manufacturers of war matériel overestimated their requirements and increased their stockpiles; the Technical Services entered into long-range commitments for high priority items in order to encourage conversion. No priorities system could meet the general shortages thus generated; some method of allocation was required. The priorities system itself, however, continued to be useful, especially after the introduction of time and quantity limitations. In addition, the War Department was not, until after the adoption of the Army Supply Program, in a position to determine completely and accurately what raw materials it needed. Nor did the War Production Board have accurate data respecting the total supply. The result was that the early efforts of the War Production Board to control critical materials by means of priorities, and later through allocations to industry under the Production Requirements Plan, were unsuccessful.

The War Production Board in November 1942 adopted the Controlled Materials Plan. Its basis was the allocation to claimant agencies of specific quantities of critical raw materials, which they in turn suballotted to their contractors. Use of the Army Supply Program enabled the Army Service Forces to determine requirements with reasonable accuracy and to adjust the distribution of allocations among its contractors in accordance with need. Although many supplementary arrangements with the War Production Board were necessary on such individual items as cotton duck, leather, lumber, rubber tires, and brass, the Controlled Materials Plan provided a workable system.

Most raw materials problems had been solved in one way or another by the end of 1943. Basic fabricating facilities had been expanded, and revised strategic plans and downward adjustments in the Army Supply Program had brought military needs into line with total supply. A conservation program had resulted in the substitution of noncritical materials for critical ones in the specifications for many end items. This sacrificed quality in many military articles, but reduced the Army's needs for critical materials. The full effect of the curtailment in civilian uses of materials was felt by 1943. The Controlled Materials Plan, with effective supervision of inventory accumulations by contractors, achieved an orderly distribution of available raw materials.

In point of time, industrial labor shortages developed after the problems of raw materials and plant facilities had been largely solved. A surplus of labor existed at the time the United States started preparations for war. Normal processes of labor supply and demand took care of the initial expansion of industrial production. Manpower shortages developed and became acute in 1944 and 1945, when the efforts of the Army and Navy and industry were at their height.

Some labor difficulties were the result of inadequate national labor controls. Although the Army Service Forces worked closely with the War Production Board and the War Manpower Commission in establishing employment ceilings and in setting up priority referrals for labor, these devices were not fully effective. The Army Service Forces, in addition, appointed special teams to work in cooperation with civilian agencies in certain areas and in certain industries in order to meet manpower problems through recruiting devices, improvements in employee relations, better community facilities, and wage adjustments. The Army Service Forces, working with its contractors, also endeavored to keep requests for industrial deferments from military service to a minimum.

One of the troublesome problems that was never satisfactorily solved during the war was the determining of the labor requirements of production programs. Although end-item programs were quite accurately translated into basic materials and components, no satisfactory method was found for translating them into manpower requirements by types of skills. Both the War Production Board and the Army Service Forces attempted it, but without notable success. The lack of comprehensive data on labor needs for war purposes added to the difficulties of placing labor in essential jobs in accordance with production priorities.

One method of circumventing labor shortages was to restrict the placement of contracts in areas where shortages were acute. This was not always feasible, because production activities were necessarily confined to areas where facilities were available. As far as possible, however, it was done. In making adjustments in production, cutbacks were made first, if possible, in critical labor areas and then in those plants having a poor record of labor utilization. All of these were make-shift devices and manpower controls were never adequate. If the war had not ended in Europe when it did, the situation would have become far more serious.

Production scheduling on a month-to-month basis and the ability to shift quickly from the production of one item to another, with accompanying shifts of raw materials, were essential. Even if unchanging requirements could have been established for a year in advance and there were no shortages of materials, facilities, or manpower, scheduling on the required scale would have been enormously difficult. The very nature of war, however, made this impossible. Operating experience and unexpected strategic developments constantly required changes in items, specifications, and quantities. The time interval between the determination in the field that an increase, decrease, or change in design was desirable and the reflection of that change in production was necessarily long. Nevertheless, the Army Service Forces had to make plans months ahead of actual developments and to schedule production in accordance with the best estimates of likely contingencies.

Initially production scheduling was on a monthly basis at uniform rates, but shortages and rapidly changing demands made it necessary to gear the schedules more closely to available productive facilities, raw materials, component parts, and manpower. Whenever programs fell behind schedule or sudden increases were necessary, production was expedited or additional resources were made available by curtailing or slowing down other projects.

Under the Supply Control System, the Technical Services and Headquarters, ASF, reviewed production schedules for principal items each month in order to insure that delivery rates were consistent with supply demands. Demands in many cases varied greatly from month to month; the resulting fluctuations in production schedules were of course not compatible with production efficiency. In a few items, such as gun tubes, reserves over and above foreseeable demands were authorized because of the manufacturing difficulties and the long time required to resume production after a cut-back or termination. Judgment of a high order was required for smoothing out production schedules sufficiently to meet estimated demands without substantial excesses or shortages.

Changes in production schedules often made it necessary to curtail or terminate existing contracts and to negotiate new contracts. This led to the development of contract termination procedures that were extensively used as the war neared its end and as cut-backs increased in volume. The Army Service Forces and the War Production Board worked out methods whereby other interested agencies were immediately informed of cut-backs in order that they might make changes in the allocation of materials and in the use of labor.

Purchasing

The utilization of all manufacturers in almost every field made it necessary to discard peacetime competitive bidding as a method of placing contracts. A new method of determining fair prices was required. Its development was complicated by the fact that there was no civilian price experience for many of the items that were procured.

Cost-plus-a-fixed-fee contracts were adopted at first for items for which there was no pricing experience. These contracts were patently undesirable, if close pricing was to be achieved. Accordingly, the Army Service Forces used fixed-price contracts wherever possible, with standard clauses providing for negotiated price revisions based upon cost experience. As a means of facilitating the proper determination of fair prices, the Army Service Forces trained its procurement personnel in careful price analysis and negotiation. Although most price records had to be kept on a product basis, for a number of the larger suppliers the Army Service Forces maintained price analyses on a company-wide basis. This resulted in substantial additional savings. Although most military items were exempt from the price ceilings of the Office of Price Administration, the Army Service Forces pledged itself to a strict control of prices. A price index was kept as a means for measuring price trends. From early in 1942 through August 1945, this index declined 20 points.

The Renegotiation Act of 1943 grew out of the recognition that neither close pricing policies nor excess profits taxes would be successful in preventing war profiteering. In spite of industry's fear of delays in the settlement of accounts, the War Department completed 55,000 out of 60,000 renegotiation assignments and obtained refunds aggregating more than five billion dollars, by September 1945, without interfering with war production. Careful procedures were adopted, full negotiations were conducted, and scrupulous consideration was given to all relevant factors. The appointment of leading business and professional men to the War Department Price Adjustment Board and to the Price Adjustment Sections of the Technical Services insured a high degree of cooperation from industry.

The standardization of procurement forms and contracts improved relations with industry and increased purchase efficiency. Short form contracts were also developed which contained the minimum number of standard legal provisions. These proved to be especially useful when purchasing commercial items in small quantities. Headquarters, ASF, reviewed only the more important contracts to insure the consistent application of policies. This review and the use of standard clauses wherever possible minimized the possibility that a procurement office might offer special inducements to a contractor, or that special conces-

CHART 9. ASF INDEX OF CONTRACT PRICE CHANGES

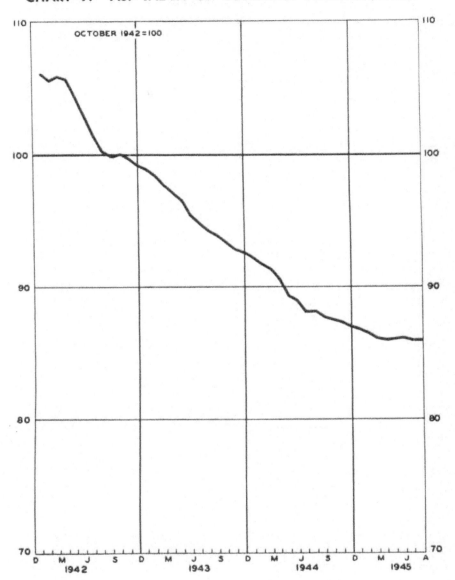

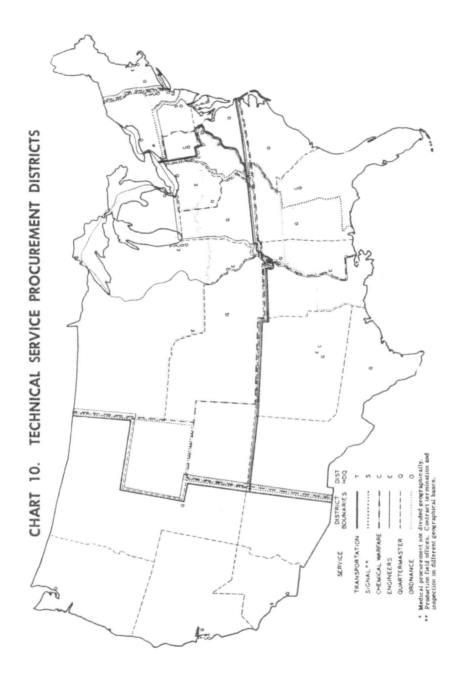

CHART 10. TECHNICAL SERVICE PROCUREMENT DISTRICTS

sions in price or contract rights might be granted. Further standardization was accomplished by issuing a comprehensive Procurement Regulation applicable to all phases of contracting and purchasing. In this way the many divergent rules and regulations of the different Technical Services were standardized in the interest of greater efficiency.

The need to participate in the war effort felt by small manufacturers was of increasing concern in 1942. The Army Service Forces and the War Production Board were interested in utilizing all productive facilities that could contribute to the output of war matériel. In the period prior to Pearl Harbor, War Department contracting operations had favored the larger manufacturing establishments, because their production costs were ordinarily lower than those of smaller plants. Moreover, large enterprises had the financial resources and the managerial capacity required for new production programs. Before the passage of the Smaller War Plants Act in 1942, the Army Service Forces had launched a program designed to broaden participation in war production. During the last year of the war, 60 percent of all contracts were awarded to plants employing under 500 wage earners. In terms of total dollar value, this was 25 percent of all contract commitments of the Army Service Forces. For civilian-type items, smaller war plants were able to handle even more than 50 percent of the dollar value. In the production of such items as heavy artillery, tanks, and ammunition, the larger plants played the more important role. All prime contractors, however, were encouraged to subcontract as widely as possible, and in this way many more small plants were brought into war production.

The procurement organization of each Technical Service was different from the others. For procurement planning purposes, in the 1920's and 1930's, each Service had established procurement planning offices scattered throughout the United States. The Ordnance Department used its 13 procurement district offices for a large proportion of its purchasing during the war. On the other hand, the Quartermaster Corps bought, not through his procurement planning district, but through depots specializing in the type of goods procured. The Boston Depot, for example, purchased shoes; the Philadelphia Depot, woolens and clothing; the Chicago Depot, foodstuffs; the Jeffersonville Depot, all cotton duck and general supplies. The Signal Corps, at the beginning of the war, had several field offices for procuring supplies, but subsequently concentrated purchasing, by commodity, in the three offices located at Fort Monmouth, Philadelphia, and Wright Field. The Medical Department originally had four offices, but at the end of the war had a single procurement office in New York City.

As the war progressed, the Ordnance Department's geographic organization for procurement was modified by the establishment of commodity offices, such as the Tank-Automotive Center in Detroit. Some Services, such as the Signal Corps and the Quartermaster Corps, established separate geographic organizations for contract inspection and production expediting. The general trend, however, was toward purchasing on a commodity basis.

Neither the geographic nor the commodity bases for procurement was exclusively satisfactory during the war. There were many common problems in purchasing which had to be solved on a geographic basis, such as the supply of labor, local community problems, the spreading of contracts among different producers, the avoidance of duplication in plant and product inspection, and the handling of accounts, financial services, and transportation. The boundaries of the procurement districts of the Technical Services, no two of which were the same, complicated the coordination of these procurement activities among the Services. On the other hand, there were decided advantages in commodity specialization, which enabled the procuring Service to deal with an entire industry, wherever located. Moreover, commodity purchasing facilitated the maintenance of records of existing and potential supplies available for military needs, the control of procurement in the light of stocks and estimated demand, and the prompt changing of procurement programs.

Storage

The storage mission of the Army Service Forces was to assure that adequate quantities of all types of supplies and equipment were readily available when needed at key points in the supply pipeline. In the performance of this mission, it was equally important that stocks be maintained at the lowest practicable levels in order to reduce the total volume in the pipeline, and that there be a constant forward flow of supplies and equipment from the manufacturer to the user. In marked contrast to the leisurely handling of storage matters in peacetime, it was bustling big business during the war. Two million people were engaged in handling more than four million tons of supplies a month at 125 large installations in the Zone of the Interior.

The three principal aspects of storage were space, mechanical equipment, and manpower. As in other fields, requirements had to be established, steps taken to fulfill them, and controls instituted to assure proper utilization.

By the end of 1942 an estimate had been made of anticipated maximum requirements for covered storage space. Substantially all needs could be supplied by using existing facilities and those under construction. Plans for additional major construction were cancelled. As a result of this early and comprehensive analysis of the maximum supply load, many millions of dollars and great amounts of manpower and materials were saved. The extensive use of open storage space also contributed to the reduction in over-all construction requirements. Centralized control of space was essential in order to avoid excesses in some installations while shortages existed elsewhere. In accomplishing this, all space was placed in a common pool for allocation and reallocation to the Technical Services. This step alone made it possible to save over 32 million dollars in the cost of new construction in the last fiscal year of the war. When the war ended, storage facilities were occupied to within 15 percent of their maximum efficient utilization. Centralized control also made possible the introduction of standardized improvements in storage procedures. Standardization of aisle width and other modern warehousing practices resulted in further reduction in space requirements.

In the field of materials handling equipment, the fork-lift truck and the palletized load, used together, provided prompt and efficient handling of stores. The use of these devices permitted the stacking of as many as 100 packages of the same commodity on a 4-foot square pallet, and the fork-lift truck displaced gangs of six to eight men using manual methods. The extensive use of materials handling equipment placed a strain upon the available supply. In the Fiscal Year ending 30 June 1944, over 45 percent of all available equipment was sent overseas, and in the next year 57 percent was also assigned to Theaters. Because of the limited supply, constant care was exercised in order to assure that equipment was placed only where it would be most fully utilized.

Many other modern practices also contributed to storage efficiency and the better use of manpower. Among them was the stock locator system, which permitted storage by lot size rather than by the wasteful numerical sequence method; and a daily car situation report, that made careful planning of loading operations possible. In spite of all efforts to achieve greater efficiency in operations and better utilization of personnel, the manpower problem was critical throughout the period of hostilities. Continuous efforts were made in order further to reduce the number of personnel required; among the most significant was the Work Simplification Program applied to materials handling. Under this program methods of doing specific operations were charted, and improved by the use of techniques familiar to industry but not heretofore used in the Army.

The proper geographic distribution of storage facilities in the Zone of the Interior had been given inadequate attention in the period prior to Pearl Harbor, when the majority of the storage depots were located and placed under construction. Each Technical Service had de-

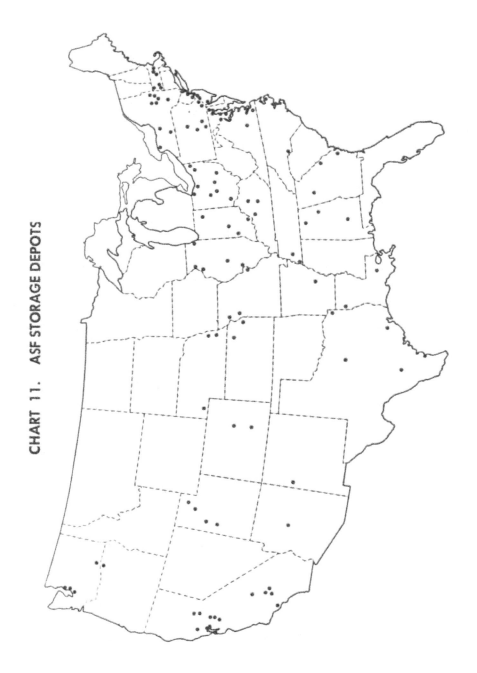

CHART 11. ASF STORAGE DEPOTS

veloped its own distribution system and storage plan independently. There was no integrated storage plan for the Army as a whole. As the war progressed, it became evident that the entire distribution system depended for its efficiency upon the location of depots. It also became apparent that the existing depot system did not meet all needs. Unfortunately, it was then too late to make the large scale changes that were desirable, and it was also impractical to redistribute the large stocks that had been developed. The difficulty consisted of reconciling such inconsistent needs as proximity to manufacturers, proximity to large military posts in the United States, and proximity to Ports of Embarkation. The solution required careful planning and such adjustments between facilities as were practicable. For example, toward the end of the war, the number of depots in the western part of the United States became inadequate for supporting the shipment of supplies through west coast ports. Depots were cleared of surplus and slow-moving stocks in order to provide space for more active commodities. After VE-day many supplies destined for the Pacific were shipped from the east coast and ports on the Gulf of Mexico.

In addition to performing its own storage function, the Army Service Forces worked with other agencies of the Government to provide storage for industrial property that became surplus when war contracts were curtailed. As part of this work, it made considerable space available to the Reconstruction Finance Corporation and other disposal agencies for the storage of surplus commodities until they could be sold.

Packaging and Packing

The packaging and packing of supplies for oversea shipment were closely related to the storage function. "Packaging" contained the product itself, and was usually performed at the production point; "packing" prepared items for transport, and was usually done at depots, or in the field in the case of organizational equipment. Packaging involved the cleaning of an item, the application of corrosion preventatives, wrapping, the use of cushioning materials, and unit containers; packing involved the shipping container, including cushioning, blocking, bracing, weatherproofing and strapping. The two operations were closely interrelated. Thus the packaging of C and K rations in individual waterproof containers made the packing less difficult. On the other hand, the packing of unpackaged ammunition was a continuing concern, whether it was done in individual or bulk lots.

Careful attention was given to packaging and packing from the beginning of the war, in order to prevent loss through breakage or deterioration. Amphibious operations in both Europe and the Pacific, rudimentary oversea dock and storage facilities, and the great humidity in the Pacific all produced an urgent need for extraordinary moistureproofing and packaging. The Army Service Forces tested many different water-proof barriers in order to find the one best adapted to the packaging of particular items. One laboratory tested approximately 1,300 different types of greaseproofing. On occasion, difficulties were encountered in persuading an industry to adopt the desired packaging and packing specifications. This was true of the antifriction bearing industry which did not desire to change the cleaning, preserving, and packing methods employed during the previous 20 years. The procurement of packaging and packing materials also became quite troublesome. Within the War Department, the Quartermaster Corps took over the direct purchasing of waterproof, greaseproof, and moisture- vapor-proof materials for the Army Air Forces and the Army Service Forces at a time when the supply of those materials was most critical. It was later found that the duplication of orders between and the separate stockpiling by the several Technical Services and the Air Forces had actually caused the shortage.

The moistureproofing and fungusproofing of communications equipment were among the noteworthy achievements of the war. Great strides were made in improving packing and crating methods in order to make better use of limited shipping space. The shipment of general purpose vehicles knocked-down, or in twin or single unit packs, was particularly useful in saving shipping space. In spite of the progress made by the end of the war, much remained to be done in improving packaging and packing practices.

Distribution

The initial equipping of units and individuals and the replenishment of supplies and equipment were the two principal phases of supply distribution in the Zone of the Interior. Supplies and equipment for newly activated units were issued on the basis of tables of equipment and allowances; replenishments were provided on the basis of requisitions. Thus, initial equipment was automatically shipped to units from central control points, whereas replenishment items were drawn by the users as needed.

In January 1942 the G-4 Division of the War Department General Staff had inaugurated a direct system of supply. Previously, Corps Area Commanders had received all requisitions from troops within their areas, and reviewed and forwarded them to depots. Under the new system, post supply officers received requisitions from troops, and either filled them from station stocks or forwarded them directly to the depots designated to supply the particular post. This had reduced the length of time required to fill requisitions.

The Technical Services prepared requisitions for newly activated units, and shipped initial equipment directly from depots or manufacturers to post supply officers. They had a better knowledge of allowances than the newly appointed troop commanders, who were thus relieved of the burden of preparing voluminous initial requisitions. The Technical Services also maintained records of selected critical items and the status of unit equipment, and could therefore closely control the issue of such items in accordance with established priorities.

In the early days of the war, the Army did not have enough guns, ammunition, and certain other items of a strictly military nature to fill all requirements simultaneously. This condition persisted for a few items to a lesser degree throughout the war. As new models came off the production lines, they were sent to Theaters first, and supplied for training purposes as they became more abundant. Transfers of equipment between units were frequent in order to insure that units going overseas carried their complete allowances and necessary replacements. In addition, weapons were sometimes withdrawn from units in the Zone of the Interior in order to replace shipments lost at sea or expended in battle.

The Technical Services, at the specific direction of Headquarters, ASF, maintained rigid distribution control over important and critical supply items, including tanks, heavy artillery, mortars, flame throwers, tires and tubes, recoilless rifles, various calibers of ammunition, dry batteries, X-ray film, field wire, various radio and radar sets, and heavy tentage. Priorities were established by Headquarters, ASF, in accordance with which newly activated units received only certain percentages of their equipment during training. Nondivisional units, for initial training purposes, received 20 percent of their allowance; divisional units received 50 percent. When a unit prepared for oversea movement, every effort was made to supply it with 100 percent of its allowances and, when this could not be done from depot stocks or from production, equipment was transferred from other units. Priority at all times was given to oversea shipments. Priorities between the several Theaters were established on the basis of strategic plans. Thus, the European and Mediterranean Theaters enjoyed first priority on most items; the Pacific Theaters were given second priority; Lend Lease needs and supply to China, India, and Burma were lower on the priority list.

The development and adoption of the Stock Control System was the most important single wartime improvement in distribution operations within the Zone of the Interior. Before 1943 each Technical

Service officer at a post followed a different supply and requisitioning procedure. Variations between posts were also numerous. No one knew how much stock of thousands of items was on hand. Some posts might have a six-month supply of a single item and others have none. The Army Service Forces recognized these deficiencies and in 1942 began studies which resulted in the establishment of a stock control system at posts in May 1943. Each post thereafter had an established supply level, which constituted the normal inventory of that post. Stocks above this level were excess and were returned to depots. Post supply officers were required to make periodic physical inventories of supplies and to adjust their stock records accordingly. They also reviewed the stock level from time to time on the basis of issue experience and anticipated needs. The using units stationed at a post and drawing their supplies from its warehouses were provided with a single form for requisitioning any type of supply. In turn, each post used standard forms in requisitioning replenishments from depots. Depots established schedules so that requisitions came from posts at definite intervals, thus avoiding peak and slack loads in depot operations. A great deal of training and readjustment was required. Technical Service depots, Service Command Headquarters, and post supply officers all cooperated in fixing stock levels for hundreds of thousands of items, and in reviewing them as troop population increased or decreased. Before the end of the war the system was operating successfully throughout the Zone of the Interior.

One of the first adjustments made for meeting the gargantuan task of supporting our oversea forces was the decentralization of the oversea supply machinery. In February 1942 the oversea supply plan and the standing operating procedure known as POM (Preparation for Oversea Movement) for equipping and moving troops overseas were prepared. In March 1942 the Army Service Forces designated a single Port of Embarkation as the main source of supply for each oversea command. Such ports served both as a springboard from which the initial operations in establishing a Theater were launched, and as the collecting and loading point for subsequent supply. An Oversea Supply Division was organized in each Port of Embarkation, which served as the control point for information and records showing the supply status of each Theater. These were supervised by the Office of the Director of Plans and Operation, Headquarters, ASF, in order that controlled items and depot operations could be properly checked.

Methods of correlating supply with demand in supporting oversea operations shifted between the alternatives of automatic supply and supply by requisition. The supply plan put into effect early in the war placed considerable emphasis on automatic supply. For established oversea bases, this method was employed for supplies such as rations and fuel that were consumed at a fairly uniform rate and for which the demand could be anticipated with reasonable accuracy. The requisition method was prescribed, however, for supplies and equipment having fluctuating consumption rates.

A somewhat different procedure was employed in supplying task forces. During the early, critical stages of an operation, and immediately following a landing or assault, commanders and their staffs had little time in which to appraise on-hand resources or to estimate their future needs. For this reason, the Army Service Forces usually supported the initial phases of an operation automatically in all classes of supply. As early as possible, reserve stocks of supplies were built up, in the areas secured by operational forces, in accordance with prescribed maximum and minimum levels designed to provide a cushion against unforeseeable contingencies. Automatic supply for all commodities then gave way to partial supply by requisition, thus adjusting the flow of supplies to fluctuating needs and permitting the readjustment of unbalanced stocks.

The progressive introduction of the requisition method in oversea supply was accompanied by a growing dependence upon another method for the supply of items that had to be apportioned among all Theaters because they were critically short. This method employed the Matériel Status Report. A similar report was used in supplying ammunition. Submitted at monthly intervals by the Theaters, these reports served in effect both as requisitions and as statements of the supply status of critical items in the Theaters. Ports of Embarkation reviewed them in order to add quantities en route and to reconcile quantities on hand in oversea areas with port records of shipments. The Technical Services then received the reports and apportioned available stocks among the Theaters.

In the fall of 1943 an amended oversea supply plan formally recognized that the method of supply for any given Theater depended on the stage of operations. Automatic supply was prescribed for the initial stages. A "semi-automatic" system, employing Matériel Status Reports, Ammunition Status Reports, and the automatic supply of rations and some fuels, was prescribed for subsequent operational phases.

The automatic and semi-automatic supply systems were never very satisfactory. Unbalanced stocks developed in the Theaters even in the case of rations, which theoretically had a highly uniform consumption rate. As much as three months elapsed from the time a Matériel Status Report left a Theater until the shipping instructions for critical items were issued in the United States. Ports and Technical Services seldom could reconcile statements of quantities on hand in the Theaters with their own records of shipment.

CHART 12.

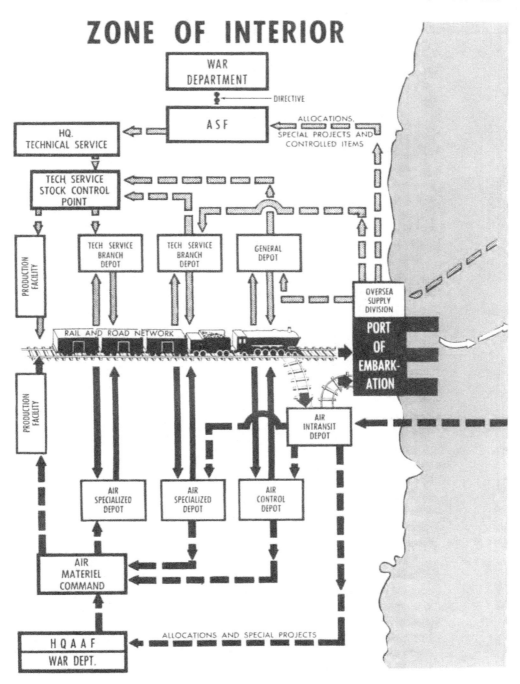

OVERSEA SUPPLY

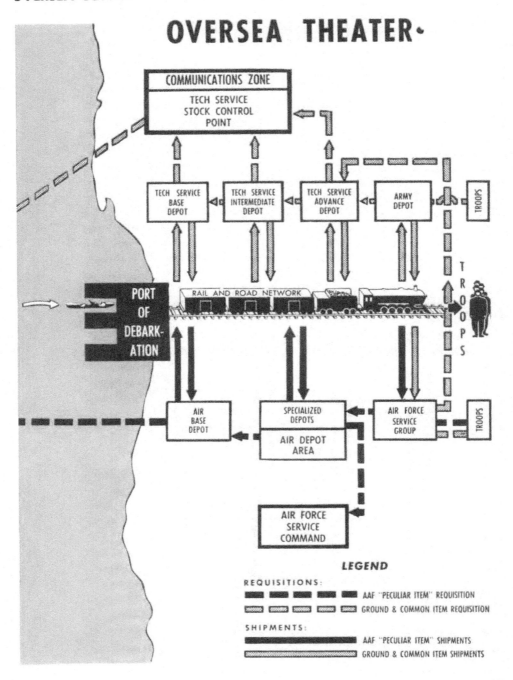

In 1945 the Matériel Status Report was superseded by the Critical Items Report, which was prepared at Ports of Embarkation. This report showed the quantities of a limited number of short supply items that had been shipped overseas, including those en route. Theaters in turn submitted monthly requisitions direct to the Technical Services for needed critical items. The Army Service Forces established a distribution plan and fixed shipping schedules on the basis of these documents. This system speeded up supply materially.

Ports of Embarkation reviewed requisitions in order to make sure that oversea commands were not overstating their needs. Actually the ports reduced very few requisitions. When a particular requisition seemed unduly large, the port called this to the attention of oversea supply officers. The requisition might then be reduced. If the Theater insisted that the full quantity was needed, usually shipment was made to the limit of available stocks in the Zone of the Interior.

The Army Service Forces made continuous efforts to improve the handling of the enormous volume of requisitions from overseas. In June 1944 a uniform, simplified procedure for handling the requisitions of all Services was installed. Direct flows of requisitions were prescribed, and multiple extracting from depot to depot was eliminated. Time limits were established for handling requisitions during the various stages of processing.

The Army Service Forces in 1942 established a marking system for both packages and shipping papers called "Identification of Separate Shipments" in order to indicate their destination and to identify them with the requisitions which they were filling. This system permitted the ready identification of the requisition, the requisitioner, the shipper, the number of shipments, and the type of items.

Lend-Lease Distribution

Soon after the creation of the Munitions Assignment Board under the Combined Chiefs of Staff in January 1942, the Munitions Assignment Committee (Ground) was established under the Board. The Chairman was the Director of the International Division, ASF. This Committee handled the actual assignment of ground equipment to Lend-lease nations in accordance with planned military operations. In order to maintain control over the use to which assigned munitions were put, the Army Service Forces recaptured any assigned supplies that were not shipped within 60 days after they were made available. Furthermore, it was arranged that no Lend-lease supplies of American origin could be retransferred by a Lend-lease recipient to a third country. If this had not been done, the whole concept of assignment in accordance with military need would have been defeated. As an additional safeguard, steps were taken to have some Lend-lease shipments made directly to the Theater Commander, permitting him to distribute them in accordance with military need. In the Pacific this proved particularly advantageous because of the great distances involved and the need for flexibility in military plans.

Lend-lease administration involved more than the task of merely assigning munitions to our Allies. It also included the delivering of assigned items to the Lend-lease countries. In general, the British were able to provide their own transportation. In order to insure the flow of supplies to the Russians, however, the Army operated the Persian Gulf Service Command for handling supplies going through the Persian Corridor. A line of communications also had to be operated from Calcutta to Assam in order to deliver supplies to China.

The Lend-lease program made possible a reciprocal aid procedure, whereby American forces overseas received logistic support from the Allied nations on a similar basis. Our Allies made a large quantity of supplies and numerous services available to our troops in Europe, and Australia and New Zealand contributed notably to the maintenance of our forces in the South and Southwest Pacific.

Civilian Supply in Occupied and Liberated Areas*

A unique problem in supply during World War II was that of maintaining a minimum standard of subsistence for the civilian populations of occupied and liberated areas. The reason for military concern with the supply of civilian populations was simply that we could not permit military operations to be jeopardized by starvation, disease, or unrest in the areas where our troops were fighting the enemy. American forces, first in North Africa and then on the Continent, won Allied territory that had previously been held by the enemy. The German policy of living off the land and of subordinating each occupied nation's economy to Germany's needs deprived many countries of their natural resources and cut them off from other normal sources of supply. Immediately following the occupation of North Africa, the Army Service Forces found it necessary to provide 30,000 tons of military shipping a month in order to meet emergency civilian requirements. Throughout the remainder of the war, the Army Service Forces handled the determination of civilian supply requirements and the procurement and shipment of such supplies, under general policies established by the Combined Chiefs of Staff.

In advance of each campaign the Combined Chiefs of Staff made a decision as to whether the United States or Great Britain would have

---
*See also page 234.

CHART 13. ASF LEND-LEASE SHIPMENTS

(EXCLUDES THEATER-TRANSFERS FROM ARMY STOCKS)

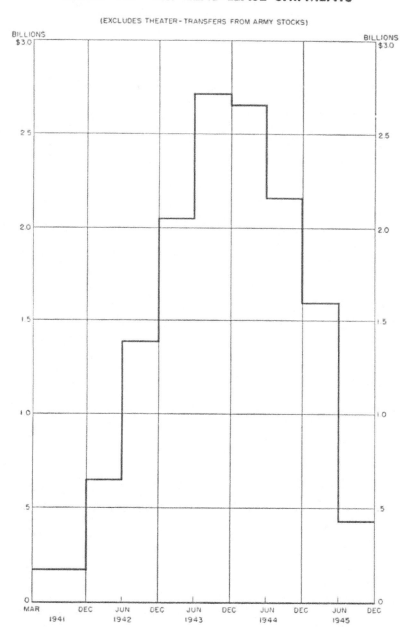

responsibility for the procurement and shipment of supplies for subsisting civilian populations. The food stockpile which had been built up in Britain to meet German submarine blockade was used for some civilian relief in Northwestern Europe. This reduced shipping requirements for civilian supplies from the United States at a time when shipping was critically short. Theater Commanders stimulated local production of essentials in order to reduce shipping requirements for civilian needs and also for some of the needs of our forces.

Since military supply procedures were not adaptable for use in civilian distribution, the Army Service Forces helped to formulate separate procedures for the distribution of civilian supplies in the Mediterranean and European Theaters. The Theater Commander was allocated specific tonnages for civilian supplies and, within these allocations, placed requisitions with the Ports of Embarkation in the United States. Supplies shipped to the Mediterranean were distributed by the Allied Control Commission in Italy; in Northern Europe supplies were distributed through Army channels. Civilian supplies from America destined for the British Zone were shipped in British vessels and distributed through British Army channels.

It was originally understood that military responsibility for civilian supply should continue only so long as active military operations required. The application of this principle, however, gave rise to numerous difficulties. The first important problem was encountered after the invasion of North Africa in November 1942. The area was, for the most part, French, and was regarded as liberated territory. Some fears were voiced that military control of civilian supply in this area indicated a desire on the part of the military to dominate civilian affairs, and for that reason a number of our civilian Government agencies became involved in economic matters in North Africa. The attempted exclusion of military interest resulted in a chaotic situation.

Sicily and Italy were at first regarded as enemy territory. The limited recognition of an Italian provisional government altered this status; nevertheless, civilian supply was handled by the Allied Control Commission under military direction. The long continued Allied operations in Italy and the importance of Naples and the area to the north as a line of communications made military control of the economic life of the country a necessity.

In France and Belgium the Supreme Allied Commander handled civilian supply in accordance with instructions from the Combined Chiefs of Staff. These liberated territories were vital to military operations. Military supply responsibility was terminated in France on 1 May 1945, except for coal and petroleum, which were not taken over by the French National Government until 1 September 1945.

The United Nations Relief and Rehabilitation Administration, an international agency for providing relief supplies for civilian populations, was by the terms of its charter concerned with assistance only to liberated areas previously occupied by Axis powers. It cooperated with Allied military forces in Northern Europe, and later it was particularly active in the Balkan countries. After April 1945 all responsibility for civilian supply in Greece and Yugoslavia was handled by the United Nations Relief and Rehabilitation Administration. In other liberated territories and Italy, military responsibility for civilian supply ended 1 September.

The American Zone in Germany was occupied enemy territory, where military responsibility for civilian supply was expected to continue until some change in the status of military government occurred.

In the Pacific the supply of civilian populations did not become a military problem until after the liberation of the Philippine Islands, and then on a smaller scale than in Africa and in Europe. Military authorities assumed full responsibility for civilian supply in the Philippines until after VJ-day. At that time civilian agencies of the Federal Government, in cooperation with the Philippine Commonwealth Government, assumed responsibility for the supply of the civilian population.

Maintenance

When the United States entered the war there were relatively small quantities of matériel in the hands of the Army. The Army Service Forces realized at the outset that a critical situation would arise in the maintenance, repair, and rehabilitation of equipment. The new types of equipment being produced would far outnumber those in use, and some of them would be of unprecedented complexity of design. Steps were promptly taken in order to determine what maintenance facilities, tools, parts, and maintenance equipment would be needed.

The study of maintenance problems quickly revealed the great importance of preventive maintenance. Proper lubrication was recognized as a matter of primary urgency. The Army Service Forces initiated a War Department lubrication order form replacing various existing forms of instructions. Original instructions were supplied commercially and were attached to items of equipment by the manufacturer. Subsequently these instructions were printed on cardboard and widely distributed by The Adjutant General's Office at a lower cost. All existing channels for the dissemination of uniform lubricating instructions were used throughout the Army.

Initially, no standard form existed for the technical literature supplied for use with Army equipment. Equipment manufacturers prepared most of the technical instructions, using various formats and dissimilar methods of presentation. The Army Service Forces established a pattern for the production of all technical manuals of instructions for operators. A system requiring routine checking of each preventive maintenance operation by using organizations was also introduced. The educational program on preventive maintenance was supplemented by distributing posters and through feature-length magazine articles. Radio time on the Armed Forces Radio Network was also used for furthering the program. One poster publicizing the War Department lubrication order resulted in a 600 percent increase in requisitions for these orders.

The direct maintenance mission involved the repair of equipment used by troops in training in the United States for return to the using organization or for return to stock for future issue. The Army Service Forces directed the expansion of the maintenance facilities of the Technical Services and Service Commands. Maintenance responsibility was assigned to the best qualified Service. A maintenance organization was set up for posts and camps, and a uniform shop-planning system was put into effect. A quota system was developed that permitted the close supervision and direction of all repair and reclamation activities. Commercial facilities were used to supplement shops operated by the Army. Schedules for future repairs became sufficiently accurate to permit a definite determination of matériel available from these sources. The load was also equalized between repair shops.

The supply and control of spare parts required constant supervision. The Army Service Forces established a system for determining the spare parts requirements of using organizations and repair shops. Provision was then made for stocking parts at maintenance shops in order to avoid delays and the repeating of requisitions. Duplications between shop stocks and station stocks also were eliminated.

A study of tool sets revealed that many identical items were being procured by different Technical Services under different nomenclature. Certain obsolete sets were still listed in catalogs. A program was designed that eliminated all obsolete tools, and standardized tool sets that could be used by more than one Service. As a result, there was a 50 percent reduction in the number of specialist tool lists. In addition, an Army Service Forces tool and tool equipments catalog provided a ready cross reference for the identification of all tools and tool equipments, and indicated interchangeability.

The Army Service Forces developed standard maintenance shop procedures for use in the Zone of the Interior. Financial reimbursement for maintenance work between Technical Services was discontinued. Each Technical Service made its shop facilities available to all other Services and also performed maintenance work for the Navy, Coast Guard, and other Government agencies as required.

The mass oversea movement of troops in 1944 left large quantities of matériel in the United States to be repaired, either for return to stock or for shipment overseas. Service Command repair shops improved the quality of their work so that equipment could be sent directly to depot stocks. Turn-in procedures were simplified. Technical Service depots worked closely with Service Command shops in determining the items needed for immediate repair and in getting them back into supply channels. A great increase in the Army Service Forces maintenance load was expected after VE-day, and detailed plans were made for handling this load. However, an early VJ-day made it unnecessary to process great quantities of equipment for use against Japan.

The securing of adequate maintenance personnel was difficult for using organizations and shops. Many were at a considerable distance from cities, and Civil Service wage rates were often lower than those offered by commercial and industrial establishments. Extensive on-the-job training programs provided a partial answer. The utilization of prisoners of war was also a saving factor; by May 1945 one-third of the personnel at fourth echelon shops was prisoners of war.

In order to satisfy the supply needs of the Army economically, all possible equipment was repaired and reissued in lieu of new items. No repairable item was disposed of unless such action was in the best interest of the Government. Uniform inspection standards insured the serviceability of repaired items of equipment. The Army Service Forces devoted much attention to the establishing of factors used in classifying matériel so that the maximum usable life, without excessive repair costs, was obtained. Standards were higher when fiixing serviceability for oversea use than for use in the Zone of the Interior. In some items, such as clothing, this differentiation proved to be unjustified and was modified.

The Army Service Forces necessarily purchased many different models of similar types of equipment from many different manufacturers. A program was launched to standardize certain items. Some 40 models of industrial air-cooled engines were replaced by 20; 91 models of liquid-cooled engines were replaced by 44; the number of models of diesel engines was reduced from 99 to 53; 37 models of compressors replaced 121; and 216 types of batteries were replaced by 67. This program greatly simplified the tasks of supplying spare parts and performing maintenance operations.

Combat Vehicles

Following World War I, the tank was considered mainly a means of supporting the advance of the foot soldier. Tank armor was provided only for protection from machine gun fire, and the tank's armament was designed only for overcoming hostile riflemen and machine gunners. It was not until after the creation of the Armored Force in June 1940 that tank design was freed from this limited concept. Based to a considerable extent upon British experience in the Battle of France, our medium tank was developed. In 1940 the medium tank weighed 21 tons and was armed with a 37-mm gun and eight .30 caliber machine guns. The next improved model, the M3 or General Grant, weighing 25 tons and armed with a 75-mm gun, was in production in 1941. The high silhouette of the tank and the limited traverse of the gun led to a redesigning which brought the M4, or General Sherman tank, into common use in 1942.

The Ordnance Department experimented with a heavy, 60-ton tank with a 3-inch, high-velocity gun during 1941. In the light of tactical forecasts on the progress of the European war, the Army Ground Forces decided that no production of this weapon should be undertaken. The German armies early in 1943, however, began to use their heavy Tiger tank. In direct tank-to-tank combat, this German model was superior to our lighter General Sherman tank. Although our tank tactics had not called for direct tank-to-tank combat, the need for a heavier tank now became apparent to troop commanders. By the spring of 1945 our General Pershing tanks, weighing 46 tons and armed with high-velocity 90-mm guns, had battered their way beyond the Rhine.

Similar improvements were made in the light tank. In 1940 the American Army had a light tank for scouting purposes weighing 14 tons and armed with a 37-mm gun and four .30 caliber machine guns. In 1945 the Army had a light tank weighing 24 tons and armed with a 75-mm gun.

The rapid production of tank equipment was an extraordinary achievement. In the whole period from 1919 to 1935, the Ordnance Department built only 33 experimental combat vehicles, and from 1935 to 1940 it procured less than a thousand tanks. By the end of the war a total of more than 96,000 tanks and 48,000 self-propelled artillery mounts and motor gun carriages had been procured.

The heaviest armor in use on combat vehicles at the beginning of the war was a 1-inch face-hardened plate. As new uses for the tank were envisaged, such as attacking fortified positions, heavier armor was built into it, so that by 1945 combat vehicle protection ranged as high as a 4-inch homogeneous armor. The use of heavier armor and the design of tanks was limited by the carrying capacity and width of the standard pontoon bridge until 1945, when a new bridge design permitted a gross weight of 50 tons and a maximum width of 142 inches. Because of early shortages of alloy elements, new armor compositions and new methods of heat-treating were developed. Homogeneous rolled and cast armor replaced face-hardened plate, and welding supplanted riveting.

Radial aircraft-type engines were modified and used in tanks. Diesel engines were also employed. It was not until a new tank engine was developed in cooperation with the Ford Motor Co., however, that a satisfactory power plant was found. It was used in conjunction with a hydramatic, or fully automatic, transmission which provided smoother operation and much easier driving, first in the light tank and later in others.

Complementing the tank was a line of motor-driven gun carriages for weapons ranging from the .50 caliber machine gun to the 8-inch howitzer. After 1940, weapons were mounted on half-tracks, trucks, and specially designed chassis. The need for a mobile artillery piece in armored divisions led to the mounting of a 105-mm howitzer on the medium tank chassis. Subsequently, a 3-inch gun was placed on a tank chassis as an antitank weapon, and finally a 155-mm gun was placed on a mobile mount. By the end of the war more and more effort was being devoted to the development of self-propelled artillery.

High-speed tractors had been developed by the Ordnance Department during the peace years. After 1940, attention centered upon their use in hauling artillery, and three new sizes of fast artillery tractors were developed and put into production. At the same time other types of tractors for use in snow and jungle operations were developed, of which one of the most successful was the cargo carrier known as the "weasel."

Combat vehicles were complex mechanisms with specialized engines, clutches, transmissions, tracks, armor, and weapons. They had no counterpart in peacetime commercial production, and new facilities were required for their manufacture. The American Car and Foundry Co. received its original order for light tanks in 1939, and British purchases in 1940 built up production facilities at three other private plants. In August 1940 the Quartermaster Corps began construction, for the Ordnance Department, of the Chrysler Detroit Tank Arsenal. Although originally intended for the production of medium tanks, this plant was subsequently used only for assembly. The major part of the manufacturing was done by privately owned plants. The Baldwin Locomotive Works, the Pullman Standard Co., and the Pressed Steel Car Co. became major tank manufacturers. The Ford Motor Co. built medium tanks in some of its existing plants and in a plant which it constructed for that purpose. The General Motors Corp., Fisher Division, assumed the management of a second Ordnance tank arsenal. Subsequently, the facilities of the Federal Machine and Welder Co. and the Pacific Car and Foundry Co. were added to those building medium tanks, M4's or Shermans, and related vehicles mounted on the same chassis.

Very few industrial firms experienced in the production of heavy steel castings had the machines for making tank hulls and tank turrets. A Government-owned plant constructed for the purpose, a combination of firms under the Standard Steel Springs Co., and others, undertook the fabrication of armor plate.

The reconditioning and rebuilding of tanks in the later stages of the war became a major production enterprise at the four Ordnance tank depots in the United States.

Motor Transport Vehicles

The procurement of trucks and other motor transport vehicles presented fewer problems than combat vehicles, because most of the equipment could be adapted from commercial designs. The major tasks were to increase the production of heavy trucks of over 2½-ton capacity and to solve the problems involving spare parts. Production difficulties were encountered in the fabrication of such components as engines, axles, and transmissions. The supply of spare parts was complicated by the use of commercial designs bearing different identification numbers. Although there was a high degree of interchangeability between the products of different manufacturers, each had its own numbering system. The correlation of the interchangeable parts from different manufacturers was a difficult task. Although considerable progress was made in the cross indexing of makers' catalog numbers during the war, the problem was not completely solved.

As a result of competitive bidding during peacetime, the Army had acquired different makes and different models of trucks. There were little standardization and little interchangeability between vehicles. The supply of spare parts and the performance of maintenance would have been greatly simplified, if standard engines and transmissions for all Army vehicles had been available. Had such action been taken during the war, however, additional new machinery and extensive retooling would have been required, and deliveries would have been reduced. The most that could be done was to identify spare parts that were interchangeable and give them common labels.

Before the war, maneuvers definitely revealed that standard commercial vehicles equipped only with rear-wheel drive were not adapted to military use. Consequently, the manufacture was initiated of wheeled vehicles that were completely new from the standpoint of usage and type, although they embodied service parts and major assemblies already in production for commercial vehicles.

The demands for vehicles were so great that many automobile manufacturers had to subcontract on a much broader scale than had ever been previously practiced in the automotive field. No particular difficulty was experienced in getting steering mechanisms, frames, or electrical systems. In the heavy truck field, assembly plants were expanded and many new facilities were utilized that had not previously manufactured automobile parts. Foundry facilities were enlarged and produced basic castings such as cylinder heads and blocks.

The scarcity of tires made it difficult to provide sufficient numbers of transport vehicles. Although tire manufacturing facilities were generally adequate, the loss of our natural rubber supply at the beginning of the war necessitated the development of synthetic rubber. This required new methods of rubber production and new machinery. In the second quarter of 1943 the consumption of rubber for ordnance was nearly 30,000 long tons, of which 83 percent was plantation crude. During the first quarter of 1945, consumption had increased to 57,000 tons, but only 20 percent was crude rubber. The rest was synthetic.

In the years from 1941 to the end of the war, over 1.3 million light and medium trucks, 741,000 light-heavy trucks, and 171,000 heavy-heavy trucks were procured, as compared with 85,000 trucks owned by the entire Army in World War I. The 2½-ton 6X6 truck was one of the most valuable pieces of military equipment used throughout the war. It was the backbone of motor transport in the Theaters of Operations. The amphibious truck, known as the DUKW, was extremely useful in landing operations and in unloading ships.

Artillery and Ammunition

Ruled by the axiom that "munitions are expendable; men are not," our Army used vastly more artillery and ammunition than was ever before conceived possible. There were 60 major types of artillery weapons above .60 caliber, from the 20 mm automatic aircraft cannon to the 16-inch coast artillery gun. Equipment included fire control instruments and carriages. Sighting devices on the guns themselves were relatively simple. The instruments controlling the fire of antiaircraft guns, however, were extremely complicated. Some of them contained as many as 25,000 precision-made parts that were expensive to produce and difficult to replace. Additional equipment included height finders, electric generators, and other equipment. Carriages had to be designed that would withstand the tremendous weight of the guns and the recoil mechanisms without sacrificing mobility and speed. For the 20 different calibers of cannon used during World War II, there were some 270 types and sizes of shells. The 105 mm howitzer alone used 25 different types of shells, from high explosive with delayed action fuzes to special concrete piercing projectiles.

There was no peacetime industry upon which to rely for the production of artillery and ammunition. Plants had to be provided and personnel trained. Firms of all sizes were pressed into service. Manufacturers of such commodities as soap, soft drinks, bed springs, toys, shirts, and microscopes participated in the artillery production program.

American experience in artillery production before the war was confined to four Government-owned arsenals, which were capable of producing pilot models. The labor force at these arsenals expanded during the war from a total of 2,600 to more than 25,000 workers. The machine tool scarcity was keenly felt in manufacturing artillery. Knowledge and available tools were pooled in order to increase production. Numerous expedients were used in meeting sudden demands. For example, when a particularly heavy demand for artillery ammunition came late in 1944, a machine tool expert in Europe found some 200 valuable lathes. These were sent to the United States and put to work. Many new production devices were found that increased the output of artillery. Breech rings, for example, were cast rather than forged, thereby saving both manpower and machine tools. Traditional methods of mixing explosive charges were revised and production was increased. New methods of loading artillery ammunition greatly simplified the entire process. A locomotive company, a steam shovel company, and a manufacturer of railway passenger cars made heavy gun carriages for the 155 mm gun. The recoil mechanisms were made by an elevator company; the larger gun tubes at Ordnance arsenals. Smaller guns were made by companies that previously had manufactured automobiles and refrigerators. At the peak of production there were 2,400 prime contractors and 20,000 subcontractors producing artillery. During the war over 600,000 complete cannon of all types and 200,000 spare tubes were procured.

Various manufacturers of war matériel were brought together in Industry Integration Committees. These Committees provided a means for exchanging information on production techniques, for developing methods of solving shortages of raw materials and machine tools, and for pooling vital skills. The technical information collected by the Committees was also used in establishing production schedules. Later, production cutbacks were discussed and arranged through these Committees. The Department of Justice, and subsequently Congress, exempted agreements reached through the Industry Integration Committees from the operation of antitrust laws, provided such agreements were approved by the War Production Board.

The shortage of brass led to the development and production of steel cartridge cases. The shortage of cotton linters for the manufacture of smokeless powder made it necessary to use sulfite wood pulp. The shortage of tin and steel made it necessary to pack ammunition in cardboard containers. A machine was developed at the Watertown Arsenal for the centrifugal casting of 155 mm. gun tubes. Extruded pipe and seamless tube proved to be satisfactory for the manufacture of barrels up to 75 mm. Welding was adopted for the manufacture of gun carriages.

The battle for Cassino indicated that more spare gun tubes were required and that larger artillery pieces were desirable. The production of spare tubes and heavy artillery was accordingly stepped up, and the mobility of the latter was improved. The standard mortars of World War I were used and greatly improved in World War II. An important change was a decrease in the weight of the 60 mm mortar, permitting it to be fired without a tripod while being held against the ground by hand. The weight of the 81 mm mortar was also reduced, improving its mobility. Experiments with larger sizes of mortars by the end of the war had introduced the 57 mm and 75 mm recoilless guns that brought artillery fire into the realm of infantry operations. In the field of airplane armament, a 75 mm gun was automatically fired from a plane in flight for the first time in July 1944, and an experimental 105 mm aircraft gun was being developed in 1945.

The extensive use of rockets was a development of World War II. Although the launchers themselves were relatively simple, rocket ammunition presented many special problems, and there was much yet to be done in this field when the war came to an end. The bazooka was among the earliest of the new developments. This was a rocket launcher for use by the infantry as an antitank weapon. It also was employed in landing operations and in assaults upon defensive positions. Paratroopers used a two-piece version.

In the field of fuzes, the activating part of all ammunition, the most important development was the VT or proximity fuze, which contained a tiny radio sending and receiving set that detonated the shell upon its approach to the target. The fuze proved equally effective against planes in the air and against vehicular concentrations and troop formations on the ground.

The wartime demands upon the chemical industry were such that its operations could not be readily converted to the output of ammunition. It was therefore necessary for the Army to construct over three billion dollars' worth of facilities for making explosives and smokeless powder, and for loading shells and bombs. Twenty-five plants were built for loading, 21 plants for making high explosives and smokeless powder, and another 12 for manufacturing the chemical components of explosives. All of these were operated under private contract. By the end of the war these plants had produced more than one billion rounds of artillery ammunition and approximately four and one-half million tons of various types of bombs.

Rapidly shifting strategic needs made it difficult to keep the operations of ammunition plants in balance and to vary production in accordance with the changing requirements. Oversea commanders did not adequately forecast their needs for the heavier calibers of artillery ammunition required in the North African campaign. When larger North African requirements became apparent, the Army Service Forces urged commanders to forecast artillery needs for the Italian campaign based upon North African experience. These efforts were fruitless. After the invasion of Italy the Army Service Forces again received requirements that increased each month. When the invasion of France was planned, an attempt was made to persuade Theater Commanders to base advance estimates for heavier caliber ammunition on past experience. Theater Commanders did not, however, include such consideration in their original long-term estimates. After D-day the estimates again mounted monthly, until they required more than the maximum production obtainable from all existing facilities. Only the expansion of industry at a cost of one billion dollars and eight months in time would have produced sufficient ammunition for the rate of fire that Theater Commanders requested. Some expansion of production facilities was initiated, but the war in Europe ended three months later, and the program was canceled. A thorough analysis of the supply of artillery ammunition made after VE-day revealed that both the European and Mediterranean Theaters had adequate stocks of all except a few types of artillery ammunition throughout the period of combat operations.

Small Arms

Both superior quality and sufficient quantity were production goals for small arms and ammunition. The basic designs for small arms weapons were available when the United States entered the war. Subsequent improvements and changes were for the most part adaptations designed to meet special needs such as street fighting or jungle warfare.

The .30 caliber Garand rifle was the most important small arms weapon of the war. Originally designed as a standard infantry rifle, it became a sniper's weapon by installing a telescopic sight. It was first put into production in the Springfield Arsenal in 1937, and an educational order was awarded to the Winchester Repeating Arms Co. in 1939. From these two sources alone nearly four million rifles were produced during the 44 months of the war, and, although some production of the Springfield rifle continued, the Garand filled the basic needs of the Army.

In order to meet infantry needs for a light rifle weighing not over five pounds, a carbine was designed and tested in 1941, and contracts were let in September of that year. The urgent demand for this weapon made it necessary to increase the delivery rate to 500,000 carbines a month at the end of 1943. In addition, the Browning Automatic Rifle of World War I was improved, and six New England manufacturing establishments pooled their resources, producing a total of 223,000 of these rifles by the end of the war.

Another outstanding development in small arms was the Thompson submachine gun. Of simple design, it was fully automatic and also could be fired single shot. Although weighing less than eight pounds, it was far more reliable than earlier models of submachine guns. The first guns came off the production lines in April 1943, only 10 months after the need for this weapon had been recognized.

When the war began, three types of the .50 caliber machine gun were already standardized. These were the watercooled, aircraft, and heavy barrelled models. Parts were interchangeable, and production could be quickly shifted to any one of the three. As the war progressed the cyclic rate of fire was doubled, and many production improvements were introduced. Two new plants were built early in the war, and productive capacity was increased to 10,000 a month. The Army Air Forces decided in July 1942 to use this gun exclusively, and by early 1944 production capacity was further raised to 45,000 a month. A total of nearly two million .50 caliber machine guns was produced during the war.

The small arms ammunition requirements of the Armed Forces reached astronomical figures during the war. American infantry in Europe expended 293 million rounds of small arms ammunition in one month. Deliveries of .30 caliber ammunition reached more than 800 billion rounds in one month. With Frankfort Arsenal as a nucleus, and the close cooperation of experienced sporting arms manufacturers, productive capacity was rapidly expanded. The Quartermaster Corps built six Government-owned plants for the Ordnance Department before the end of 1941 in order to increase capacity. Existing plants were expanded and seven additional plants were constructed in 1942, thereby increasing daily capacity to more than 71 million rounds of small arms ammunition. Selected manufacturers, not experienced necessarily in ammunition production, operated these plants.

Because oversea expenditures fluctuated widely, it was difficult to keep production and inventory in balance with demands.

Clothing and Equipage

At the beginning of the war there was no practical combat experience upon which to base military clothing design. Much research and experimentation was necessary before satisfactory items could be produced which would provide comfortable lightweight clothing for wear under all types of combat conditions. Almost all items of clothing and equipment existing before the war were found to be obsolete and unsatisfactory for combat operations. For example, a jungle uniform had been developed before 1942 to meet the needs of troops training in Panama. When this uniform was used in combat in New Guinea it proved to be too hot and too heavy. It absorbed much more than its own weight in water, and mosquitoes could penetrate the fabric. New designs and new fabrics were tried. Field tests were conducted in New Guinea. As a result, an entirely new tropical uniform was developed in order to meet the requirements of jungle warfare. Many of the items developed for use in France in World War I had been abandoned during peacetime in favor of other models more suitable for garrison wear in the United States. An outstanding example was the Army service shoe. For garrison wear a dressy, less rugged shoe than the 1918 model had been used. Its inadequacy for the combat soldier was revealed early in the war. Changes were made, and the combat boot was developed and adopted as a result of experience in North Africa.

In the absence of combat information, the Quartermaster Corps experimented with various types of clothing under all possible simulated conditions. Expeditions were sent into Canada and Alaska for testing arctic clothing and sleeping bags. The experience of the war demonstrated clearly the need for Quartermaster observers in each Theater to study the performance of clothing and equipment in actual use.

The absence of an extensive prewar research program on clothing made it extremely important to develop Quartermaster research facilities after war started, and to test clothing under combat conditions. The many improvements in clothing used in all climates during the war demonstrated the importance of such research and experience. The field uniform of 1945 contained no item that was in use in January 1942.

Field experience also dictated many improvements in other Quartermaster equipment. For example, at the beginning of the war, troop commanders wanted small field bakery units. Experience proved these units to be inefficient. Larger bakeries of a highly mobile type were developed and procured. Improvements were made and new items developed in a vast number of different types of equipment, including mobile showers, mobile shoe and textile repair units, mobile laundries, ice cream-making machines, lanterns, wire cutters, entrenching tools, and others.

The Quartermaster Corps encountered many production problems common to other Technical Services. As in the case of the others, it also had its own peculiar difficulties. One example was the procurement of cotton duck. Military requirements for tents, vehicle covers, ammunition bags, and other items far exceeded all peacetime demands upon the industry. A major program of industrial conversion was initiated early in 1942, resulting in the shift of a part of the textile industry to the cotton duck field. The production of DDT presented other special problems. In May 1943 there was less than one pound of DDT in the United States. Various chemical companies assisted in a program that provided facilities having a total production capacity of more than three million pounds a month by the end of the war. Even the manufacture of such relatively simple items as ice axes and climbing ropes involved problems in mass production. Because of the critical supply of raw materials, substantial amounts of rubber, aluminum, copper, tin, nylon, and other materials had to be eliminated from most Quartermaster equipment. The program for making all possible substitutions for these materials entailed numerous adjustments that frequently were made at the expense of having ideal equipment.

The Quartermaster Corps largely dealt with manufacturers whose peacetime business was highly competitive and sometimes devoted to a luxury market. Many suppliers were small manufacturers who were reluctant to take Army business because of their high profit margins. Some of them had unreliable standards of business ethics and little or no trained, technical personnel. These factors made inspection trying.

Some difficulty was experienced in the European Theater in the winter of 1944–45 in providing adequate quantities of heavy clothing to troops in the front lines. Subsequent investigations revealed that the Theater and the Army Service Forces shared responsibility. Requisitions were not forwarded sufficiently far in advance to permit timely supply from the United States. For example, 80 percent of the requisitions for wool drawers arrived in the United States in the months of September and October. Eighty-two percent of the wool undershirts were requisitioned after August, and 71 percent of the wool socks were scheduled for shipment to the Theater after September. In certain instances, the Theater Commander and the Quartermaster General failed to reach a common understanding on Theater requirements. The Army Service Forces was not as foresighted as it might have been in anticipating requirements. The Theater did not make a decision respecting its needs for wool field jackets and wool overcoats in sufficient time for the Quartermaster Corps to adjust its procurement program. Sizable quantities of clothing for winter use did reach the Theater, but were not promptly distributed to troops in the front lines. In the United States every effort was made to meet the requisitions as they arrived. For the most part, delay rather than a lack of supplies was the difficulty in meeting winter clothing requirements in the European Theater.

Subsistence

Much was accomplished during the war in improving the nutritive content of the Army ration, in providing balanced menus, and in providing variety in combat rations. At the time of Pearl Harbor the Army had little knowledge of the best means for meeting the characteristics required of field rations. Research previously performed by the food industry helped considerably, although this work had been concerned primarily with the distribution of food to a civilian market where turnover was rapid, storage conditions were ideal, and temperatures were easily controlled. These were different from the conditions that Army rations encountered in the field. Food for the combat soldier had to be edible and palatable after storage for as much as two years, either under arctic conditions or in the heat and moisture of the tropics. Food had to be packed securely so as to protect it against rough handling and insect infestation. It had to be palatable whether eaten hot or cold, and compact and light enough to be carried by the individual. A great deal of research was required in order to meet these standards. The Quartermaster Subsistence Research Development Laboratory in Chicago was expanded, and the facilities of universities and industry were used extensively. At the end of the war the C ration had ten different meat components. Improved types of hard biscuits had been added, and premixed cereals, jam, and a greater variety of popular beverages were included. The K ration originally designed for the use of parachute troops was extended for general combat issue. The 10-in-1 ration was developed for use by small groups isolated from company or unit kitchens. Highly specialized rations were also developed for air crews and for emergency use. In addition to, and as a part of, the different types of rations, dehydrated foods, boneless beef, and other special forms of food were developed under Army sponsorship.

Nonperishable foods were purchased through three depots. On the average, Army requirements for food amounted to some 12 percent of total food supply in the United States. For certain items the percentage was larger: 64 percent of canned fish, 56 percent of canned fruit, and 46 percent of canned vegetables. Canned foods had to be bought during the packing season in order to meet all requirements until the next harvest. Except for food purchased seasonally, the Army did not carry large stocks of food in the United States. The actual quantity on hand in the Zone of the Interior was kept within 75 days' supply for troops in the United States and 60 days' supply for troops overseas. Oversea inventories, in turn, were kept at a level of about 70 days' requirements.

The diet of soldiers stationed in the United States contained approximately 70 percent fresh or perishable subsistence, such as dairy products, fresh fruit, fresh and frozen vegetables, eggs, and similar items. As refrigerator space became available in cargo vessels and was constructed in oversea areas, greater quantities of fresh foods were sent to troops in Theaters of Operations. Most perishable subsistence was purchased at the 35 Quartermaster Market Centers scattered throughout the United States. Each center bought for the posts, camps, and stations within its area. These centers were located in the major marketing areas and in the vicinity of large troop concentrations. They did not outbid civilian purchasers of fresh foods in the open markets, nor were fresh food dealers required to sell to the Army at prices under those paid by civilian buyers. The market centers were simply a means for purchasing fresh foods in large quantities, thereby preventing competition for supplies by individual posts. By the end of the war about one-half of the money for food was spent through market centers.

In 1943 a Food Service Program was established for the purpose of improving feeding within the Army. Improved mess supervision, better training of cooks and bakers, more careful attention to menus, the avoidance of frequent servings of the same food item, and improvement in mess records were included in the program, which was designed to make Army food more attractive and palatable for soldiers. An important part of the Food Service program was to reduce food wastage. Attention was given to educating cooks in the utilization of kitchen fats. This reduced purchases of fats by 50 percent in July 1943. Troops were cautioned to take only what they could eat, and garbage was carefully inspected for indications of waste. Kitchen waste was also cut down. The savings from this program during 1944 were sufficient to feed three infantry divisions for 12 months.

Engineer Equipment

Many standard items of construction equipment used during the war were of commercial design and presented few research and development problems beyond the modifications necessary to effect an item's adaptation to military use. The procurement of slow, track-laying-type tractors, for example, was largely a matter of obtaining production facilities having an output sufficient to meet military demands. Modifications of tractors consisted of adding attachments to standard types. On other equipment, modifications were more extensive, but the availability of commercial items and the cooperation of manufacturers in changing their standard models readily met most Army needs. At the start of the war much emphasis was given to lightweight equipment in the mechanical, electrical, construction, and water supply fields. Later the emphasis was shifted back to heavier types because complaints from Theaters indicated that equipment was unable to withstand operational strains.

The difference between adapting American tactics to the jungle and adapting the jungle to American tactics was largely attributed to the bulldozer. We were able to bring our matériel resources to bear against the Japanese from the air and on the ground because of the use of the bulldozer in preparing bases and airfields. The construction feats of the Army all over the world would have been impossible without this piece of equipment. The extensive use of bulldozers in the Southwest Pacific and in Burma-India near Japanese positions resulted in high losses among operators. Armored cab kits were then developed and dispatched in a matter of weeks. The tank-dozer was the eventual outcome. It was also used with outstanding success in the Italian and European campaigns.

Mass production of airplane landing mat made it possible to construct runways and flight strips near the fighting fronts. Steel and then aluminum landing mat was made in large quantities and used extensively in all Theaters. The increase in the size of combat vehicles made necessary a pontoon bridge capable of carrying heavier loads. The floating bridge developed for this purpose was a revolutionary departure from previous military bridge designs. Among the most important developments in engineer equipment was the production of secret devices enabling American troops in the Pacific to locate Japanese troops infiltrating our lines at night. These devices, used most successfully on Okinawa, were excellent examples of scientific, industrial, and Army collaboration in meeting needs for specialized equipment.

A great variety of other engineer equipment was also produced. A mobile map reproduction plant was developed that could be transported in ten truck-mounted sections. Mobile maintenance shops for construction equipment were devised. Petroleum distribution equipment, consisting of flexible pipe lines and of pumping stations, was developed and used for the rapid distribution of petroleum products. Floating power plants, floating spare parts depots, floating maintenance shops, and improved heavy dredges were also important pieces of equipment.

Communications Equipment

The research and development budget for communications was the second largest in the Army Service Forces, and advances in this field during the course of the war were tremendous. One of the principal objectives was the development of radio equipment that was reliable in operation at all times. Front-line radio sets at the end of the war were superior to any previously available, but they still were not entirely satisfactory for field communication. The lack of camouflage features made the operator a target for enemy fire. The life and ruggedness of batteries were not fully satisfactory. When the war came to an end, efforts were being made to design radio sets that could be concealed on the person of the user. Few basic changes had to be made in vehicular and tank radio sets designed early in the war; however, noise interference was suppressed, and the sets were made lighter and more effective. Late in 1943 satisfactory communication between airplanes and ground stations was accomplished, but the technique of communication between close support aviation and ground troops had not been mastered at the end of the war. The need for long-range radio relay stations was evident by December 1942. Completely new types of equipment were built, and these proved to be of great usefulness.

Satisfactory field wire existed before the war, but, with the loss of crude rubber sources, synthetic insulation had to be provided. This required substantial changes in manufacturing techniques. The Signal Corps developed a light weight assault wire and a long-range multichannel cable that could be installed rapidly. The latter possessed transmission qualities equal to open-wire pole lines. A wide variety of weather instruments were designed that provided methods of observation not previously employed in civilian weather forecasting, including special equipment for making meteorological observations on long-range plane flights. Highly efficient radio-sound equipment which provided meteorological data from above cloud levels and beyond the visual range was produced in quantities. Prewar sound-ranging equipment was greatly improved, and sets were developed that were capable of locating enemy machine guns and artillery.

The use of crystals for frequency control on medium range radio equipment required the production of quartz crystals in immense quantities. Early in 1942 an expansion program was inaugurated that increased the number of manufacturers to over 125. The requirements for dry cell batteries, on the other hand, did not cause pressure on the industry until late in 1943. From this time on, producers constantly increased their output, which was raised from 100 million cells in the first quarter of 1943 to 623 million cells in the first quarter of 1945. The eventual designation of the Signal Corps as the central purchaser for all Army and Navy dry batteries brought to an end the troublesome competition within the Armed Forces.

For the most part, the Office of Scientific Research and Development and industrial laboratories performed basic research in radar. The Signal Corps expedited production, filled requirements, and issued approved designs. Radar equipment varied from lightweight warning ground sets to complete permanently installed systems. It also included equipment designed to neutralize enemy radar. Antiaircraft fire control sets automatically provided data for electronic directors controlling the fire of all the guns in a battery. Warning sets were developed that picked up enemy aircraft over 200 miles away, and these proved to be of great usefulness in the defense of installations in Britain against the V-1, or flying bomb.

As American offensives got under way, mobile radar equipment was developed that included devices for locating enemy mortars, moving vehicles, and other ground targets. This opened the whole field of the tactical employment of radar in ground warfare. Indeed, the whole concept of radar employment, from 1943 on, shifted rapidly from the defensive to the offensive. Radar equipment enabled our troops to deny the Germans the use of their main supply roads near the front lines at night. Radar equipment located land targets for night bombing. It was newly developed American equipment that largely prevented German radar installations from locating the Allied landings in Normandy. Even radar equipment that could distinguish friend from foe was developed.

In the radar and electronics field the major production problem was one of developing the technical capacity required to meet the exacting specifications of military equipment. No Government-owned plant was necessary, but an exchange of licenses and of technical knowledge was indispensable to the production of communications equipment. In the past, the radio field had been dominated by a few small manufacturers of high quality equipment, a large number of manufacturers of equipment of lesser quality making up the balance of the field. The entire radio and electronics industry had to be shifted to higher quality standards in order to meet military demands.

Chemical Warfare Supplies

Research and development in the field of chemical agents expanded rapidly after the beginning of the war. Supply was so accelerated, and our capacity to retaliate brought to such a high level, that an enemy equipped with huge stocks of toxic agents and enjoying ideal tactical conditions for their application refrained from using them. The failure of the Germans to use gas against our initial operations in France provided unique testimonial to the value of adequate preparedness.

The Chemical Warfare Service continuously made studies in order to determine what chemical characteristics were desirable under differing terrain, target, climate, and weather conditions. The relative effectiveness of high and low altitude sprays were determined, and two new nonpersistent chemical agents were developed and adopted for use in meeting varying strategic and tactical needs. The 4.2-inch chemical mortar became an important offensive weapon. Designed originally for firing chemical shells, its adaptation to high explosives and smoke made it extremely valuable to ground troops. A recoilless mortar was also developed, but was employed only on a limited scale. The portable flame thrower was of particular importance in meeting combat needs in the Pacific. The range and capacity of flame throwers was improved, and more effective fuels were developed and adopted. By the close of the war, flame throwers installed in tanks became a major weapon for attacking Japanese field fortifications.

Smoke also played a vital part in World War II. Mechanical smoke generators, one of the important scientific developments of the war, were capable of laying dense smoke over extensive areas. They were extremely valuable at Anzio Beach. In the Mediterranean, despite numerous attempts by the enemy, there was no instance of effective bombing of our ports when protected by smoke screens.

Incendiary bombs developed during World War II were extraordinarily effective against enemy targets during the strategic bombing of Japan. Heavy bombs, loaded with special oil fillings, were used in conjunction with lightweight incendiary chemicals. Aimable clusters made possible accurate bombing with small incendiary munitions.

Great progress was made in the defense against chemical agents. The gas mask was improved, as were methods of impregnating clothing against skin irritants. In the field of preventive and therapeutic medicine related to gas warfare, noteworthy improvements were effected in conjunction with the Medical Corps.

Chapter 6

SERVICES

Military Personnel Administration

The induction, classification, assignment, transfer, and separation of military personnel comprised one of the most complex and difficult of all the missions assigned to the Army Service Forces.

The fluctuating availability of manpower and the changes made in policy by the War Department and other agencies dealing with manpower problems caused frequent changes in standards of fitness for induction. As the war progressed, the number of physically fit personnel available sharply decreased, thereby forcing the Army progressively to reduce its physical standards. The situation was further aggravated by the demands of unit commanders for individuals of high military and physical qualifications. The War Department presented monthly quotas to the Selective Service System, showing requirements for induction into the Army. The number of inductions equaled the quotas in only 14 of the 44 months of the war. The difference between inductions and quotas was substantial in 13 months, and was as much as 100,000 persons in December 1942. This was a situation over which the Army had no control. The shortage more adversely affected logistic training activities than the training of the other two Commands, because the Army Service Forces usually had third priority on the total Selective Service call. Because of the severe shortage of manpower, illiterate and non-English-speaking individuals were inducted. The Army Service Forces established special training units to which these men were assigned for 12 weeks. This permitted the salvage of a substantial portion of them for useful work in the Army. Originally, men with venereal diseases were rejected. Arrangements were made in 1942 for inducting individuals with uncomplicated venereal diseases and for providing the necessary treatment at reception centers. Approximately 200,000 venereals were inducted between October 1942 and June 1945.

When physical standards of induction were high at the start of the war, individuals were inducted for "general service," or for "limited service" only if their defects were not likely to be aggravated by military service. It was originally intended that individuals in a limited service status would not be sent overseas, but the lack of uniformity in physicians' judgments rapidly rendered this term relatively meaningless. Also, there were many jobs in the Theaters that required no higher standards of physical fitness than those in the Zone of the Interior, and it became impossible to distinguish between personnel "qualified" or "not qualified" for oversea duty on the basis of "limited" or "general service" classification. A committee was established in the fall of 1943 to devise a more precise method of rating physical qualifications. In May 1944 this committee recommended the "physical profile" plan, which divided the medical examination into six phases and provided for the rating of selectees on six factors. Four grades were assigned for each factor: the first two grades represented standards for general service; the third, standards acceptable for service in the Zone of the Interior; and the fourth, standards below the minimum for induction. The plan was applied to inductees and personnel processed through reassignment centers and reception stations for their distribution among Army Ground, Air, and Service Forces. Later it was extended to include personnel transferred between these three major forces and for certain types of assignment within each force.

The Navy, Marine Corps, and Coast Guard were soliciting and accepting volunteers by enlistment during 1942, although the Army had abolished recruiting except for aviation cadets in certain categories of the Enlisted Reserve Corps. These Services carried on active recruiting campaigns among high-school students and other groups of eligible young men, offering various inducements. It was not uncommon for Navy recruiting parties to seek out registrants at induction stations. An Executive Order was issued in March 1943 requiring the procurement of all personnel between the ages of 18 and 38 through the Selective Service System. This to a large extent prevented the loss of potential Army inductees to the other Services.

Under the "work or fight" plan, approximately 15,000 men who had left essential employment in war industries without the consent of the employer were inducted. The plan undoubtedly kept many workers in industry, but it had an undesirable effect in stigmatizing service in the Army as a form of punishment.

It was very difficult to fit individuals with diverse educational and occupational backgrounds into a pattern for which they had no experience. Among inductees there were of course no men with civilian experience in repairing tank treads, in handling .50 caliber machine guns, or in rendering enemy booby traps harmless. The classification of the individual's skills and aptitudes was the foundation upon which assignments were made. The Army in 1940 made a listing of 300 common types of civilian jobs and 124 basic types of military jobs. No correlation, however, was established between them. The listing of military jobs was expanded in 1942 from 124 to 600, in an attempt to classify specific duty assignments. This plan was defective in that an attempt was made to distinguish between such occupations as those of tank mechanic and truck mechanic. It was not until the summer of 1944 that the Army in a series of Technical Manuals finally recognized that it was more important and useful to base classifications upon types of occupations than upon specific duty assignments.

The original distribution of enlisted men was based to a large extent upon the Army General Classification Test score. This test was originated in 1940 and was designed to measure learning ability. For the purpose of making specific assignments, it was supplemented by tests measuring the aptitudes of individuals for mechanical, clerical, and various operational jobs. Toward the end of the war, assignments were based almost entirely upon physical condition, because the Army Ground Forces so urgently needed infantry replacements that their other qualifications had to be disregarded. At the same time older men and men with various physical deficiencies were being supplied by Selective Service. Because the average age of men in combat units had increased inordinately, the upper age limit for induction had to be lowered twice in 1944.

An attempt was made in the fall of 1943 to appraise the soundness of personnel assignment within the Army Service Forces. More than 575,000 men were interviewed. It was discovered that there were important errors in the records of 57 percent of the enlisted men, and that 3½ percent were definitely misassigned. Audit teams visited Army Service Forces installations and checked on classification and assignment procedures in order to improve the techniques used.

There was an inevitable variance between the number, quality, and experience of the men supplied by Selective Service and immediate personnel needs. Original classification and assignment procedures attempted to place an individual in a specific job, making no capital of the fact that the average American can adapt himself to many different types of work, and that with a modest amount of training a single individual can be useful in a variety of jobs. For example, a current surplus of men classified as mechanics would be held in order to meet an indefinite future need, while an immediate need for truck drivers remained unfilled.

Current military needs had to be met from current inductees. The machinery necessary to relate availability to requirements for specialized military personnel did not exist. Nor was the determination of future requirements adequately controlled. Because of the unchecked "stock piling" of specialists for use as operating overhead in the Zone of the Interior, a serious situation developed in the summer of 1943 when the Army Service Forces was required to supply 76,000 enlisted men to troop units, with only 70 percent of that number actually available. In the action taken to fill all activated units to authorized strength, the practicability of converting personnel from one specialty to another in a limited period of time was demonstrated.

Although Replacement Training Centers were originally visualized as supplying oversea replacements, experience indicated the necessity for establishing east and west coast depots to furnish replacements for oversea shipment. Procedures and qualifications for replacements were compiled in a single manual known as POR (Preparation for Oversea Movement of Individual Replacements).

Originally assignments of newly trained enlisted men were governed by the number of men arriving at Reception Centers as balanced against estimates of requirements. An attempt was made in 1943 to centralize all assignment and reassignment activities in the Office of The Adjutant General which adjusted surpluses and shortages between commands. This meant that The Adjutant General's Office received reports from 1,900 different agencies and made the assignment of as many as 500,000 men a year. The paper work mounted, and delays became exasperating. At one point, 19,000 men, who had completed their training, were awaiting assignment. In order to overcome these defects, assignment authority was decentralized and a system established for the automatic flow of personnel awaiting assignment, or surplus personnel, to Army Service Forces Training Centers. Troop units and installations within the Zone of the Interior were supplied with personnel by specific Training Centers. The Service Commands and the Technical Services were charged with the responsibility of reporting their net overages or shortages to The Adjutant General, who shifted personnel in bulk in order to meet existing requirements.

Many specialized installations were used for processing personnel. Much of this specialization resulted from the need for speed. There were too many different types of processing installations and too many agencies involved in the administration of military personnel. The procedures inherited by the Army Service Forces were cumbersome and inefficient. Personnel administration suffered from inadequate advance planning and, while the decentralized assignment procedures outlined above represented a great advance toward orderly personnel management, the complete streamlining and clarification of procedures were not accomplished during the war.

The Army Specialist Corps was established in June 1942 as a noncombatant military organization in order to provide officer personnel with special technical qualifications for administrative and service duties. Originally it was planned to have members of the Army Specialist Corps work side by side with Army officers, performing duties for which they were especially fitted. Early experience, however, indicated that it was impractical to have officers of the Specialist Corps and the Army engaged in like activities. Single administration, single command, and single standards were essential. Accordingly, the Army Specialist Corps was discontinued in October 1942, and a substantial number of its members were commissioned in the Army of the United States.

All War Department agencies engaged early in the war in finding and commissioning civilians with special backgrounds or technical experience for performing the missions of these rapidly expanding agencies. The Officer Procurement Service was established in the Army Service Forces in July 1942 with an Army-wide mission of obtaining officers from civil life. Branch offices were established in large cities throughout the country, and their operation prevented competition between Army agencies for a particular individual.

The two cornerstones of military personnel administration were the Morning Report and the Service Record. Morning Reports provided daily data on the assignment, leave, or sick record of each individual in a unit. The Service Record was designed as a summary of the soldier's individual career in the Army. Substantial improvements were made during the war in summarizing Morning Reports, in putting the information on punched cards, and in providing strength data. Machine Record Units at the various echelons furnished data to the central Machine Records Unit of the Office of The Adjutant General for consolidation. The Service Record was redesigned and improved during the war. Forms were simplified, and a manual was issued explaining in detail the preparation of entries to be made in the Service Record. The number of files maintained for each individual was reduced to two: a field file and the central file in the Office of The Adjutant General. Procedures were also established for the maintenance in record depositories of necessary data on military personnel after discharge.

The reporting of casualties was a part of military record keeping. Theater Commanders originally reported casualties to the War Department by radio or cablegram. Errors in transmission were as high as 25 percent. Early in 1944 a system was established whereby Theaters prepared a punched card for each casualty. These cards, after being checked, were sent to The Adjutant General by air. This new system permitted the European Theater of Operations to report battle casualties accurately to Washington within eight days after they occurred. The Adjutant General in turn was enabled to report to the next of kin two days after receiving the report of a casualty.

Civilian Employees

Over a million civilians were employed by the Army Service Forces at posts, camps, depots, arsenals, and other installations. Slightly over 6 percent of these were employed in Washington and in the nine Service Command Headquarters. About 30 percent were employed in various Service Command activities including the operation of posts, camps, and stations, maintenance shops, hospitals, and Reception Centers. About 21 percent were engaged in depot operations, and 10 percent in arsenals and other Government-controlled plants. Slightly more than 10 percent were employed in transportation activities at Ports of Embarkation and holding and reconsignment points. The remainder (about 23 percent) were engaged in a wide range of miscellaneous activities including procurement (6 percent), inspection, and civil engineering functions. Nearly one-half (about 47 percent) of all employees were "ungraded"—employees paid at hourly rates.

The Army Service Forces maintained careful control of wages in accordance with Government policy. The National War Labor Board delegated authority to the Army Service Forces permitting it to make limited wage increases, while maintaining the wage stabilization policy. The Army Service Forces in turn issued detailed instructions on wage administration to its field agencies. By 1943 all wages had been fixed in accordance with the Government's policy of paying the prevailing wage of the community.

Originally regional offices of the Civil Service Commission attempted to recruit civilian personnel for the War Department. It became clear in 1943, however, that direct recruiting was essential if sufficient personnel were to be obtained. Thereafter field installations were permitted to obtain employees directly or through the United States Employment Service. The scarcity of housing and transportation were major factors in recruiting and retaining a labor force. Frequently, Army installations were far removed from urban centers. This created a need for local civilian housing or improved transportation facilities.

High turn-over in the labor force and absenteeism plagued local commanders. Personnel losses requiring replacement rose as high as 70 percent per year. Part of this turn-over was caused by the tendency to employ persons without regard to specific abilities. Peacetime Government personnel procedures had devoted themselves almost exclusively to the process of hiring employees and placing them on the pay roll. The Army Service Forces, however, emphasized the importance of proper placement and training. A counseling program for employees was undertaken. Supervisor training, job methods training, and improved on-the-job training were extended to all field installations. These efforts did much to reduce turn-over and to assure an adequate operating force. Shortly after it was created, the Army Service Forces announced a civilian personnel policy to which it endeavored to adhere. Broad policies were established governing appointment, placement, opportunity for advancement, rates of pay, handling of grievances, safety and health, and employee organizations. In the months that followed the establishment of these policies, machinery was provided to assist the Technical Services, Service Commands, and all installations employing civilians in the administration of civilian personnel affairs.

Civilian employees were used as extensively as possible in operating jobs. Wartime working conditions often prevented the fullest utilization of civilian workers. For example, military personnel had to be used to supplement stevedores at Ports of Embarkation. However, throughout the war less than 40 percent of the operating personnel was military, and the Army Service Forces became the largest single employer in the history of the Nation.

Military Training

Two separate elements of training responsibility were assigned to the Army Service Forces: The training of service troops; and the training activities of the Army as a whole, examples of which are the Special Training Units, Women's Army Corps* training, the encouragement of preinduction technical training, and the Army Specialized Training Program.

Training programs for service units, and programs for the instruction of individuals were coordinated between the Army Ground and Service Forces. Within the Army Service Forces, the Office of the Director of Military Training was established as the responsible staff agency. It made plans for adequate staffs and equipment at training installations and devised and reviewed training programs. Correlation of the demand for and the supply of specialists was provided. Inspections of training activities were made in order to determine the extent to which they met required standards. The task of training individuals and units required men and facilities sufficient to care for

---

*Women's Army Auxiliary Corps from May 1942 to September 1943.

a peak training load of 700,000 individuals in September 1943. This total included 2,000 separate service troop units with a strength of 380,000 men. During the war units aggregating 1,290,000 men were trained for specific duties.

Early in 1942 most military training activities were conducted at Replacement Training Centers. The mission of such centers was basically to provide fillers for units and replacements for Theaters of Operations. Unit Training Centers were established late in 1942 that provided for the training of units as distinguished from individuals. The Service Schools for both enlisted men and officers were operated by the Technical and Administrative Services. There had been little coordination, training directives were inadequate, and training doctrine was not current. The Army Service Forces established standards for admission, instruction, and the teaching staff, and controlled the curricula and quotas for the output of trained personnel. In addition to the Service schools, civilian schools were used extensively for meeting specific training needs, such as the repair of railway rolling stock, radio repair, repair of diesel engines, assembly of motor vehicles, and petroleum refining. The use of civilian training facilities was confined to those institutions having specialized, technical, or other expensive equipment that it would have been uneconomical for the Army to duplicate. As needs declined during 1944, the number of civilian schools used was greatly reduced.

When the age limit for induction was lowered to 18 in November 1942, the Army established a Specialized Training Program, which utilized university facilities. This was initiated as a long-range program designed to meet the shortage of technically trained personnel, which necessarily followed the induction of college students. The Army was dependent upon colleges for the training of physicians and dentists. The colleges were the logical agencies for training engineers and linguists. The Army Specialized Training Program also served in some degree to assure the preservation of the existing educational structure of the Nation. By June 1943, 50,000 persons had been enrolled in this program, and at its peak in January 1944 over 145,000 individuals were in training at 227 different collegiate institutions. In January 1944 some 68,000 men were enrolled in the basic training course; 15,000 were taking engineering courses; 13,000, medical training; 13,000, area and language courses; and the remainder were enrolled in dental, veterinary, personnel, psychology, and other courses.

The shortage of manpower early in 1944 and the inability to supply ground force units for the invasion of France caused the War Department to reduce the strength of the Army Specialized Training Program from 145,000 to 30,000. Only the medical program, the engineering program, and some area and language studies were continued. At the same time, however, the Army Specialized Training Reserve Program for 17-year-olds was enlarged.

The abrupt cessation of hostilities prevented the Army from realizing the full benefits of the Army Specialized Training Program. However, the fact that over 1,600 of the men engaged in the manufacture of the atomic bomb were secured from the Army Specialized Training Program would indicate that the immediate contribution of the program to victory was not negligible. Many other extremely important technical tasks were performed by men who had been enrolled in the program. If the war had lasted much longer, the prewar supply of trained engineers and other technicians would have been exhausted, and the importance of the program as a source of replacements would have become increasingly evident.

Approximately 400,000 inductees who had received Grade 5 in the Army General Classification Test, or who were illiterate, or non-English speaking, were given instruction in Special Training Units. Rehabilitation Centers trained and restored over 39,000 AWOL's (individuals absent without leave) to duty. Approximately 139,000 members of the Women's Army Corps received basic training at specially established WAC Training Centers. Military personnel needed rather extensive retraining during the war. Men no longer required in their specialties received other types of training based upon their skills, military experience, and physical condition. Training programs for patients in convalescent hospitals facilitated their social and vocational readjustment to military or civilian life.

Good instructors were hard to find. When they were found, many were sent to oversea commands. One successful device employed in order to obtain instructors was the leadership training program. Individuals who had distinguished themselves during their basic training course were selected for further intensive training in the technique of instruction and the development of leadership. These, in turn, became instructors. A high degree of quality was obtained because the program was specifically designed for supplying personnel for training duties. Late in the war efforts were made to use individuals who had returned from oversea theaters as instructors. Many, however, were unsuitable for this purpose. In certain instances they considered themselves better adapted for operating assignments, and were not interested in undertaking a training job.

Service troop units were required in combat divisions, in corps, in armies, in Army Air Forces commands, and also in communications zones. The personnel for some of these service units was drawn from Replacement Training Centers, but in most instances inductees were sent directly from Reception Centers to Army Ground Force units without going through replacement training. Training was then conducted by the Army Ground Forces or the Army Air Forces, although a certain technical responsibility for doctrine remained with the Army Service Forces. On frequent occasions the Army Ground Forces and the Army Air Forces asked that individual officer or enlisted personnel or entire service units be given training by the Army Service Forces in particular specialties. The Ordnance School, for example, trained many mechanics, welders, instrument repairmen, and others for Army Air and Ground Forces units. Finally, the Army Service Forces was responsible for the unit training of certain designated service type units.

In 1942 the dividing line between Army Ground Forces and Army Air Forces unit training on the one hand, and Army Service Forces unit training on the other was not clearly drawn. Then the basic policy was adopted that all training of service units for assignment to tactical commands, up to and including armies and air forces, would be the respective responsibility of the Army Ground or Air Forces. The training of units for assignment to communications zones was an Army Service Forces responsibility. This dividing line was not always a satisfactory one. For example, there was little difference between the training required for the heavy maintenance company to be assigned to an army and that required for the heavy maintenance company to be assigned to a communications zone.

The Army Ground Forces and the Army Service Forces continuously reviewed the troop basis during 1943 and 1944 in order to eliminate any duplicating training responsibility. In addition, the mobilization training programs of these two major forces were brought into harmony with each other. Activation by the Army Service Forces of all service-type troop units, however, would have been a better solution. Initial unit training would then have come under one command. After initial unit training, tactical training as part of a combat command could have followed under the direction of the Army Ground or Air Forces. Under such a system the Army Service Forces would have transferred entire units to Ground or Air for incorporation in tactical commands, and better technical training could have been achieved.

In the early days of the war, the Army Service Forces trained and activated units as rapidly as possible in order to meet the requirements of War Department troop bases. This was done at the expense of individual replacement training. The pressure by 1944 was sufficiently relieved to permit the establishment of a more satisfactory system. The Army Service Forces then set up a preactivation training arrangement, by which inductees allotted to the Army Service Forces were assigned to an appropriate Training Center for their

CHART 14. TYPES OF MILITARY PERSONNEL PROCESSING CENTERS

INSTALLATION	FUNCTIONS
Induction Stations	To determine by examination whether registrants of the Selective Service System met physical, mental and moral standards of the Army and allocate personnel to Army and Navy.
Reception Centers	To process inductees, including the issue of certain items of clothing and equipment, classification, preparation of personnel records, immunization, applications for life insurance, initial assignment, and transfer to new installation, usually a training center or unit.
Special Training Units	To train newly inducted illiterate, non-English speaking and 5th grade personnel, to bring the individual to a 4th grade level.
Replacement Training Centers	To provide basic training.
Reassignment Centers	For the reassignment of personnel returned from overseas, battle casualties or surplus.
Redistribution Stations	To provide a period of readjustment for overseas veterans prior to reassignment.
Staging Areas	For the assembly of units at installations convenient to ports for shipment overseas.
Disposition Centers	Installations, usually at a staging area, to receive returnees for initial processing and transfer to a reception station.
Reception Stations	To process returnees from overseas either to a separation center for discharge or to a reassignment or redistribution center or training center for reassignment. Ordinarily temporary duty at home was given between reception station and subsequent assignment.
Separation Centers	To process personnel for release from the Service.
Separation Points	To discharge personnel locally in lieu of discharge at a separation center near a man's home.
Processing Centers	Installations, convenient to ports, to which were sent individuals absent without leave immediately prior to shipment overseas for subsequent shipment overseas.

individual basic military, technical, and team training. During the latter stages of their technical training, men were selected for filling specified units scheduled for activation. This system had several advantages. It gave full emphasis to individual training. It brought men together before the unit was actually established, thus reducing the personal adjustments required when the men were organized as units. It permitted better unit training designed for meeting field conditions. Substantial savings in training personnel and training equipment were also accomplished.

Shortages of manpower and the shifting requirements of oversea commanders throughout the war made it difficult to plan far enough in advance for the types of units that had to be activated and trained. Despite these difficulties, however, generally a high standard of individual and unit training was achieved. Arrangements permitted reasonable interchangeability among the technical agencies and major commands, and the demands of active Theaters were usually met satisfactorily.

Information and Education

The Information and Education Program was designed to inform the American soldier of the causes and background of the war, to keep him in touch with its progress, and to provide instruction in a wide variety of educational subjects by means of correspondence courses. Information and education officers were utilized at all echelons of command. Printed materials were supplied for discussion groups; "Newsmaps" were distributed; soldier publications such as "Stars and Stripes," "Yank," and camp newspapers were established; radio programs were broadcast to oversea troops. The Armed Forces Institute, an officially sponsored correspondence school, enabled military personnel to continue their education during off-duty hours and to prepare themselves for return to civilian life.

Originally, responsibility for the Information and Education Program was combined organizationally with that for managing post exchanges, the Army Motion Picture Service, and recreational and athletic activities. This proved to be unsatisfactory. Informational and educational activities were closely related to the whole scheme of military training, because their major objective was to inform the individual soldier of his stake in the defeat of the Axis. Moreover, the American soldier, like the American citizen, expected that he would be kept fully informed about developments in public policy and general events at home and around the world. Such a task required special personnel and a special approach to the problems involved. For the duration of the war, the Army Ground Forces, the

Army Air Forces, and oversea commanders established information and education officers in their headquarters and in subordinate commands. The Army Service Forces provided the materials and services necessary to the various programs. There was some question as to whether this type of central service was logically assigned. The Army Service Forces recommended on several occasions that the work be transferred to the War Department General Staff. After the conclusion of the war, the Information and Education Division was made a separate staff agency under the supervision of a Chief of Information reporting to the Deputy Chief of Staff.

Special Services

A part of the good morale of the soldier was attributed to the various special services provided by the Army, which included post exchanges, motion picture theaters, athletics, and other recreation. The Army Service Forces was charged with providing these services. Early in the war some quarters viewed these special services as frills, but their enthusiastic reception among the soldiers, and observation by commanders of their salutary effect on morale, brought general recognition of their importance.

Post exchanges were operated independently by posts, camps, and stations prior to the war. A special committee of 5 prominent merchandising executives in 1941 recommended the establishment of the Army Exchange Service in order to provide uniformity in standards and practices and centralized supervision. The Service established policies, provided financing, set up uniform methods of merchandising and control, and operated a central buying service. Some 960 price agreements were made with important suppliers of merchandise and equipment. The Defense Supplies Corporation lent 67 million dollars to supplement Army Exchange capital derived from fees and merchandising transactions. This money was loaned to post exchanges, at a low rate of interest, providing the latter with necessary capital. The Army Exchange Service had made available 78 million dollars by 30 September 1944 for establishing post exchanges in the United States and overseas. A new method of determining the amount of funds available in excess of the working capital needs of domestic exchanges was put into effect during 1944 and 1945. The surplus was sufficient to liquidate the debt owed the Defense Supplies Corporation. Subsequently, the Army Exchange Fund financed exchange operations, both domestic and oversea, without further borrowing.

The Quartermaster General procured and shipped to the Theaters the majority of the mass sales items, which in turn were resold to Theater exchanges. As merchandise became more difficult to procure, the Army Service Forces decided that it was unwise to permit domestic exchanges to use priorities in obtaining scarce items. The Quartermaster General accordingly procured certain scarce merchandise for resale through post exchanges in the Zone of the Interior. In order to prevent abuses, exchanges were restricted to the sale of articles of convenience and necessity to the soldiers.

The Army Motion Picture Service also operated with nonappropriated funds within the United States, and provided entertainment at the nominal charge of 15 cents. Motion pictures for oversea showing were supplied free of charge during the period of hostilities through the War Activities Committee of the Motion Picture Industry. The Army purchased and distributed projectors and other equipment; shortages were overcome with the assistance of the motion picture industry.

Within the United States each post operated recreational activities for the troops stationed there. The Quartermaster Corps purchased some 87 million dollars' worth of athletic equipment for use in oversea areas. The Army was successful for the first time in obtaining Federal funds for the welfare of enlisted men. Appropriated funds were accordingly employed in establishing library service at posts, promoting the distribution of books and magazines, establishing a handicraft and art program, and arranging various musical activities. Another important development was the establishment of special service companies, consisting of 109 enlisted men and five officers, which carried on recreational activities in Theaters of Operations. The Army Service Forces sent 40 such companies overseas during the war.

Chaplains

A most important service to troops was provided by the chaplains. There were 1,478 chaplains on duty on 7 December 1941, consisting of 140 Regular Army chaplains; 298 from the National Guard; and 1,040 from the Reserve. The peak reached during the war was over 8,000. In recruiting chaplains, a fair proportion among the various religious denominations was maintained. The Chief of Chaplains established a quota system based upon the religious census of the United States. To obtain sufficient chaplains, the maximum age for commissioning officers was advanced from 40 to 50, and to 55 for a brief period. Chaplains were provided in the ratio of 1 to 1,000 troops. The Chaplain School was established in February 1942 at Fort Benjamin Harrison, and was later moved to Fort Oglethorpe, Ga. It trained approximately 8,000 military chaplains during the war.

Some 1,500 standard Army chapels were constructed, and hundreds of simpler buildings were used. More than eight million Army Testaments were distributed. For oversea use, sets that consisted of a field desk, a field organ, and other appropriate items were provided. Recordings of religious services were made for use on transports and hospital ships.

Military personnel have testified to the vital service performed by chaplains and the value of their spiritual and moral counsel in maintaining morale under all types of conditions.

Medical Services

Medical service was furnished with exceptionally good results to a huge Army deployed over a vast geographic area. Had the Army deliberately selected the areas in which disease hazards would be the greatest and most varied, there would have been little deviation from the pattern cut out for us by the enemy. The Army was faced with the increased destructive power of modern weapons in addition to the hazards of disease. Despite the risks to which American troops were subjected, the death rates from disease were extremely low, and the record in saving the lives of the wounded was amazingly good. Deaths from disease were lower than in peacetime, lower than in the civilian male population of corresponding ages during the war period, and less than one twenty-fifth of the rate of World War I. The fatality rate for men wounded in combat fell to one-half of the rate obtaining in the last war, 4 percent as compared to 8 percent.

The Medical Department encountered difficulty in the procurement of an adequate number of doctors. It was estimated early in the war that 65,000 medical officers would be required. Medical officers were procured in 1942 through the activities of recruiting boards. Procurement through these boards, however, resulted in the withdrawal of too many physicians from certain communities. The boards were abolished at the request of the War Manpower Commission, which assumed responsibility for determining whether or not a particular physician could be spared from civilian practice for military service.

The War Manpower Commission and the Secretary of War in the winter of 1944–45 fixed a ceiling of 45,000 Medical Corps officers for the Army. This action was taken because the number of qualified physicians in the United States had declined so rapidly. Charges were made throughout the war that the Army was overstaffed with physicians. This was certainly not the case in the Zone of the Interior. A critical stage was reached and a shortage in trained medical personnel developed at fixed hospitals as a result of the oversea shipment of medical personnel. The economical and effective utilization of medical personnel, having extremely variable workloads, constituted a complex problem. The load placed on Medical Department personnel assigned

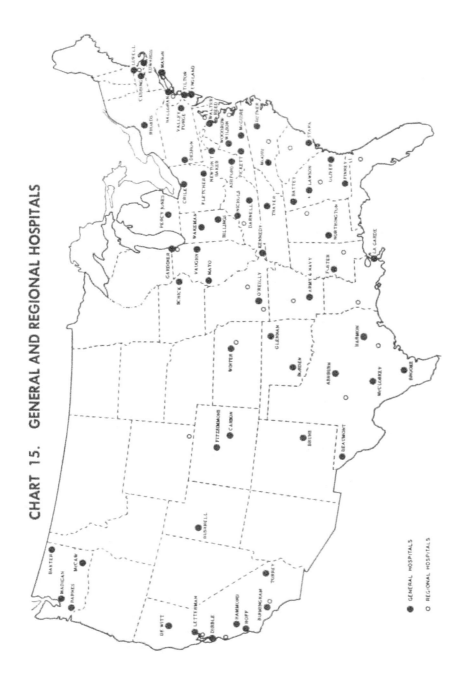

CHART 15. GENERAL AND REGIONAL HOSPITALS

to specific Theaters of Operations, and especially to units such as battalions, regiments, and divisions, varied with the weather, the climate, the season of the year, and most of all with military operations. The meeting of these variable loads with a minimum of personnel would have required the frequent and rapid transfer of medical personnel between units and major commands. Such a practice was impractical under the traditional method of giving each unit its own medical detachment, and was not attempted on a large scale during the war. Whether medical officers could have been better utilized by radically changing the organization of medical service within the Army is questionable.

Early in the war all nurses were recruited through the American Red Cross. However, many nurses were unwilling to enroll in that organization as a prerequisite to their appointment in the Army Nurse Corps. Arrangements were made for direct appointment, and the Surgeon General used the Red Cross solely as an administrative agency. As in the case of physicians and dentists, the uneven withdrawal of nurses from civilian communities precipitated control of their procurement by the War Manpower Commission. Critical shortages in the Army existed, however, and at one time the use of statutory authority was contemplated in order to obtain sufficient nurses. Although such authority was never obtained, adequate nursing service for the sick and wounded was supplied in the face of constant shortages, which required nurses to be on duty for abnormally long hours for extended periods. The use of Wacs and volunteer nursing aides materially eased this situation.

The hospital system in the Zone of the Interior was modified several times during the war. At the beginning there were two types of hospitals, general hospitals and station hospitals. The original concept was that station hospitals would provide emergency and general medical care to sick and injured military personnel at posts and camps throughout the United States. Patients needing prolonged or specialized medical care would be transferred to general hospitals. Two forces brought about changes in this traditional pattern of hospital organization. First, the rapid evacuation of sick and wounded from Theaters in 1944 began to fill the general hospitals. Second, the scarcity of highly specialized medical personnel necessitated readjustments in the methods of using hospital staffs. The Army Service Forces and the Army Air Forces designated certain hospitals as regional hospitals. Each such hospital received patients from all station hospitals, whether Ground, Air, or Service, within an area having a radius of approximately 75 miles. Regional hospitals were staffed with special personnel and operated in the same manner as general hospitals. The use of these hospitals for patients originating in the Zone of the Interior freed the general hospitals for patients returned from oversea theaters. The Army Service Forces at one time operated 32 and the Army Air Forces 30 regional hospitals.

No military patient was returned to a duty status until he was physically capable of fully performing all military duties. This policy required a physical reconditioning program that was begun during the convalescent period of the patient's hospitalization. Convalescent hospitals were established late in 1944. These facilities were less elaborate than general hospitals, usually being converted barracks or other troop accommodations. Convalescent hospitals were also economical in terms of the personnel and equipment required for their operation.

Conservation of hospital facilities was further effected by furloughing patients whose condition was such that continuous medical supervision was not required during convalescence. As a result of this policy, there were more patients normally assigned to hospitals than there were hospital beds during the early months of 1945. One further practice used to make the most effective utilization of specialized surgical and medical personnel was the concentration of this personnel in certain general hospitals. There were two general hospitals in 1945 specializing in the care of tuberculous patients, 19 specializing in neuro-surgery, seven in amputations, three in vascular surgery, two in the care of the blind, three in radium therapy, seven in plastic surgery, and three in tropical diseases.

Early in the war it was planned to provide station hospitals with beds numbering 4 percent of the troop strength of each post. This plan was based largely upon the experience of World War I. However, experience during World War II indicated that this number was excessive and the percentage was revised downward, first to 3½ percent and then to 3 percent, with corresponding reductions in the requirements for medical personnel. Originally a bed capacity of 100,000 was projected for general hospitals. This proved to be insufficient, however, and 50,000 additional beds were authorized late in 1944. There were 154,000 general hospital beds and 59,000 convalescent hospital beds in use in the United States at the end of hostilities. At the time of the surrender of Japan, there were in the United States 185,800 patients in general hospitals, of which 60,000 were on sick leave or furlough; 49,700 in convalescent hospitals, 14,000 on sick leave or furlough; 39,300 in regional hospitals, 2,100 on sick leave or furlough; and 33,800 in station hospitals, 500 on sick leave or furlough.

Hospital ships and other troop carrying vessels operated by the Transportation Corps were used in evacuating patients from overseas. Actually more patients were returned by modified troop ships than by hospital ships. About 10 percent of oversea casualties were evacuated by air, with the proportion running as high as 25 percent in the last months of hostilities. A Medical Regulating Office was established in order to govern the flow of patients from the ports to the general hospitals throughout the United States. When patients were returned from overseas, they were moved promptly from shipside to debarkation hospitals located near the ports.

The Medical Regulating Office issued instructions for the movement of patients to various general hospitals on the basis of reports from the debarkation hospitals. Although a part of the Surgeon General's Office, this office was physically located in the Office of the Chief of Transportation, with which it worked closely in directing the use of the Army's railway hospital equipment. Army equipment by 1945 consisted of 320 hospital ward cars, capable of moving 11,000 patients, and of 60 kitchen cars. The railroads provided additional equipment in order to meet peak loads. Whenever possible, patients were sent to the general hospitals nearest their homes. By the time hostilities ended, however, patients had to be sent to hospitals having available beds, regardless of the locality of patients' homes. Cases requiring specialized medical care were necessarily treated in hospitals equipped to provide the particular type of therapy needed.

In order to assure the highest level of technical competence and uniformity of treatment, small groups of expert consultants were assigned to the headquarters of each Service Command and oversea Theater. The consultants visited hospitals and advised their staffs, and inspected medical and surgical practice. This arrangement was useful in improving medical care. The monthly publication of the Army Medical Bulletin also kept medical personnel informed of best treatment practices.

The system for the medical care for battle casualties developed new characteristics in World War II. Originally it was intended that general hospitals, miles behind the combat lines, would provide definitive medical care for soldiers wounded in action. The system of battalion and regimental aid stations and division collecting and clearing stations was geared to a concept of static warfare. In World War II, evacuation hospitals, field hospitals, and mobile surgical hospitals worked very close to the combat front. This introduced a new concept of medical treatment. The wounded were moved promptly from the front lines to these hospitals. Here initial wound surgery was performed before a patient was sent to the rear areas. This surgery was intended only to remove the immediate danger to the patient's life. Reparative surgery was subsequently performed at general hospitals located in the Communications Zone. The third phase, reconstructive surgery and rehabilitation, was performed at general hospitals in the United States. This system of surgical treatment contributed materially to the fine World War II record of lives saved and also prevented many cases of permanent disability.

Great progress was made in both the prevention and treatment of diseases by employing new commercial equipment and drugs. Various sulfa drugs were remarkably effective against many diseases of military importance. Atabrine was developed as a substitute for quinine in the prevention and treatment of malaria. When properly used it was as effective as quinine, and in many respects it was preferable. Blood plasma and whole blood were of great importance in combating shock and hemorrhage. Sodium pentothal, a new anesthetic, was perfected. It was quick, reliable, and easily administered. The war immeasurably expedited the mass production of penicillin. This drug, at first made in almost negligible quantities, became available in steadily increasing amounts. Penicillin was successfully used in the treatment of infected wounds. Its use in the treatment of many diseases was also strikingly successful; for example, it reduced the treatment period for syphilis from 6 months to $7\frac{1}{2}$ days. The Army lost 1,280 man-days per thousand per annum in 1940 from venereal diseases; in 1945 it lost 244 man-days per thousand per annum.

The prevention and treatment of neuropsychiatric disorders assumed major importance in World War II. Efforts at the time of induction were made to screen and reject those persons who were mentally unfit for military service. The prevention of neuropsychiatric disorders, however, could not be solved by screening alone. Emphasis had to be placed upon good leadership, motivation, proper assignment, and incentive—all of which were potent factors in helping the individual to adapt himself to the stresses and strains of military environment. The establishment of neuropsychiatric clinics at training centers in order to render early treatment to individuals who had symptoms of maladjustment also prevented many potential neuropsychiatric casualties. The early treatment of combat neuroses within the divisional area produced excellent results, particularly in the Okinawa campaign. Other important neuropsychiatric advances were the development of group psychotherapy, the establishment of convalescent hospitals, and the adoption of the policy of treating neuropsychiatric cases rather than discharging the patient. Despite the progress made, much more work needs to be done in identifying and preventing the causes and in treating and rehabilitating neuropsychiatric casualties.

The consumption of medical supplies and equipment was not uniform overseas. The automatic supply of medical items proved to be most unsatisfactory. Some Theaters accumulated large surpluses, and others experienced temporary shortages. Each hospital required thousands of items that were essential to its proper functioning.

Supplies for a single hospital were frequently shipped in two or more vessels early in the war, with the results that supplies were frequently so scattered that it was impossible to consolidate them. This was finally overcome by the development of more efficient loading procedures at ports in the United States, although it continued to be troublesome throughout the war.

During the war specialized vehicles capable of providing direct medical support to forward troops, particularly to armored divisions, were constructed. A surgical operating truck was developed and standardized. It provided a mobile storeroom, a utility and sterilizer room, and, in emergencies, a field operating room. Other self-contained medical vehicles were developed for dental operating teams, optical repair teams, medical laboratories, and other specialized purposes.

Military Justice

Military justice was comprised of two separate functions: The enforcement of the Articles of War, and the control and training of military prisoners. The legal phases of these functions were the responsibility of The Judge Advocate General. Staff responsibility for disciplinary training was not clearly outlined until late in 1944 when the Correction Division was established in the Office of The Adjutant General.

Recognizing that speedy and effective punishment is one of the greatest deterrents to crime, The Judge Advocate General established procedures insuring the trial of offenders as promptly as might be consistent with justice. The average period that elapsed from the time of arrest and initial confinement until sentence was pronounced was reduced in the Army Service Forces from 28 days in 1943 to 13 days in 1944; in the Army Ground Forces from 28 to 23; and in the Army Air Forces from 27 to 24. "Military Justice Procedure," a Technical Manual prepared and distributed in 1945, provided an authoritative guide for the proper and fair handling of trials.

With general court-martial jurisdiction assigned to over 300 commanding officers, it was most difficult to assure equality in sentences. The Judge Advocate General reviewed general court-martial proceedings for legality and fairness during the trials, and uniformity and fairness in sentences. In the year ending 30 June 1945 over 19,000 records of trial by general courts-martial and 30,000 general court-martial orders were examined. Five branch offices with boards of review were established in order to relieve the Office of the the Judge Advocate General of the burden, and in order to facilitate the administration of military justice in the Theaters of Operations. These branch offices examined over 16,000 records during 1945. In June 1945 the Under Secretary of War established an Advisory Board on Clemency for reconsidering the cases of prisoners serving sentences, making recommendations for clemency, and adjusting and equalizing such sentences. Several Special Clemency Boards under the supervision of the Advisory Board were also established.

Early in the war military prisoners were generally confined in post stockades and in the Disciplinary Barracks at Fort Leavenworth. In 1943 the Army Service Forces, recognizing the extent of the loss of military manpower and the desirability of restoring men to duty when feasible, established Rehabilitation Centers. Over 34,000 prisoners were transferred to these Centers, and 13,900 men were restored to duty by June 1945. Of the number restored, only 11 percent again became general prisoners.

Every effort was made to discover and apply the best penal practices in Disciplinary Barracks. Adequate training programs were an important feature of the effort to restore men to duty. Military personnel were assigned to this work and regular training programs were established. The securing of suitable personnel was difficult, because those assigned as administrative officials or guards were likely to be those for whom other suitable military assignments could not be found. This interfered with the rehabilitation and proper treatment of prisoners. Abuses did occur. Fortunately, they were few, and immediate corrective action was taken as soon as they were uncovered. The utilization of psychiatrists and professional penal personnel did much to overcome these difficulties. Better types of guards were sought so far as possible, and standard practices were also introduced. By the end of the war there were eight Disciplinary Barracks and five Rehabilitation Centers in operation in the United States.

Military Police

The Provost Marshal General was responsible for the administration of police activities in the Army. As a result of the experience of World War I, a separate Corps of Military Police was established in September 1941. At its peak this Corps had a strength of over 210,000 men. The Provost Marshal General trained personnel in the Corps of Military Police. The duties of such personnel included the direction of motor traffic; occupational police duties; guard duty; the processing, transportation, and security of prisoners of war; the investigation of crimes involving military personnel; the apprehension of unauthorized absentees; and the maintenance of internal military security within the United States. Some 27 tables of organization and equipment were established for various types of Military Police units. In the Zone of the Interior 521 Military Police units of various types were activated of which 145 were prepared for oversea movement. Military police patrolled 60,000 of the 456,000 scheduled passenger trains each month in the United States. The Provost Marshal General trained 6,000 officers for Civil Affairs duties, 3,600 for the western Theaters, and 2,400 for the eastern Theaters. This program involved instruction both in military and a wide variety of economic, social, and political subjects. For training purposes the Army utilized the facilities of several universities, in addition to the Army's School for Military Government at Charlottesville, Va.

The detention of 425,000 enemy prisoners of war in the United States required the building of separate camps. The Army Service Forces encountered difficult problems of discipline. The most serious disciplinary problem involved certain German prisoners who administered their own "justice" by means of beatings, forced suicides, and kindred methods. This was dealt with by segregating Nazi and anti-Nazi prisoners into separate camps so far as possible, and through strict court-martial proceedings against offenders. Recalcitrant prisoners were punished by enforcing a "no work, no eat" policy.

The shortage of manpower that developed late in 1943 resulted in the use of prisoner of war labor. Prisoners who worked received 80 cents a day in canteen coupons or a credit to their prisoner of war trust account, in addition to the 10 cents a day allowed under the Geneva Convention. The 10-cent-a-day allowance was discontinued on 27 June 1945 for all enlisted prisoners of war who were physically able to work. Requests for prisoner labor were certified by the United States Employment Service, the War Food Administration, and the War Manpower Commission. As high as 95 percent of the prisoners, who could be employed under the terms of the Geneva Convention, were used by private contractors or at military installations. Money collected by the Government for the work of prisoners of war aggregated over 51 million dollars by August 1945. Use of prisoners for essential work on military installations resulted in an estimated saving to the Government of over 157 million dollars.

A program for the orientation and education of German prisoners of war in American ideals was initiated in September 1944. This was accomplished after working hours by making English language courses, films, and selected books and pamphlets available to the prisoners. After the surrender of Italy, approximately 70 percent of the Italian prisoners of war then in the United States were found to be sympathetic to the Allied cause and to the newly formed cobelligerent Italian Government. These men were formed into Italian Service Units under the command of American and Italian officers, and were paid $24 a month. They were employed as operating personnel at posts within the Zone of the Interior.

The Provost Marshal General was charged with the operation of the Prisoner of War Information Bureau (Enemy Section) for enemy prisoners of war and interned enemy civilians. He was also responsible for the operation of the American Prisoner of War Information Bureau, which provided a central exchange for information on American prisoners held by the enemy.

Internal security in the Zone of the Interior embraced both emergency and continuing protection, and the inspection of both War Department installations and privately operated facilities serving the War Department. Fire protection and safety programs were also included. Supervision of aliens and persons suspected of subversive activities, in facilities vital to the war effort, was under the jurisdiction of the Provost Marshal General. Control of enemy aliens working in war industry was also a responsibility of the Provost Marshal General. As a protection against sabotage and espionage, the Provost Marshal General supervised more than 3 million loyalty investigations of persons engaged in the war effort, and in addition assembled a file of the fingerprints of over 30 million persons.

Construction and Real Estate

The War Department had only 20 people experienced in real estate operations when war broke out in 1939. The huge requirements for land soon made it necessary to employ commercial firms in order to acquire the real estate needed for training grounds, depots, and other facilities. The mechanization of the Army, the extensive use of aircraft, and the destructive power of modern weapons required huge areas for training. Single sites of three million acres, or approximately 90 by 50 miles, were required for maneuver areas. At first the Quatermaster Corps entered into contracts with 10 different real estate brokers in order to acquire property. This step was a stopgap arrangement and was not satisfactory from the standpoint of fees and acquisition costs. The Quartermaster Corps subsequently employed real estate experts from the Lands Division of the Department of Justice, from other Government agencies, and from private business. The real estate function, in accordance with a statutory enactment of December 1941, was transferred from the Quartermaster General to the Chief of Engineers, who delegated the task of acquisition to the Division Engineers.

The final approval of major real estate transactions remained a function of the War Department because of the huge sums involved. Responsibility for establishing and supporting the need and for selecting the location of facilities was placed upon the using agency. Requests were made through the Chief of Engineers and the Commanding General, ASF, to the Under Secretary of War. After approval, the Chief of Engineers acquired all land needed by the Army Air, Ground, and Service Forces. This concentration of real estate operations in one agency made it easier to develop satisfactory policies and to supervise their execution.

Congress provided only $250,000 for land acquisition in January 1940. By the time the peak of the real estate program had been reached, 340 million dollars had been expended, and 3,500 installations were operating on 38 million acres of land, an area greater than the State of Michigan. These huge figures tell only part of the story. It was recognized, of course, that all this land would not be permanently needed. Maximum utilization was made of public lands by having them transferred to the Army from other departments of the Federal Government. Property was leased rather than purchased whenever this was economical. During the war 31,400 leases were consummated at an average annual rental of 88 million dollars. Housing, office and warehouse space, and space for special activities, such as garages and laundries, were generally acquired under lease. The most expensive installations, such as ordnance plants, camps, and airfields, were generally placed on land that was owned by the Government. Speedy mobilization required the leasing or purchase of many existing establishments and structures for training purposes. More than 550 large hotels and apartment houses were used. This action saved four to six months of construction time, reduced requirements for critical construction materials, and lightened the strain on a Nation that was rapidly approaching a manpower shortage.

The urgent need for speed was met only after certain legal and regulatory restrictions had been eliminated through statutory and other changes. The Chief of Engineers was authorized to acquire property by whatever means he deemed necessary. The exercise of the right of eminent domain was expanded. Restrictions on the ratio of rental to market value, designed as a peacetime economy measure, were lifted. Construction was authorized in advance of title clearance. A special statute provided the Secretary of War with authority to dispose of or lease real estate no longer required by the War Department, when such disposal was in the interest of National Defense. For example, because of advances in the technology of manufacturing, storing, and handling explosives, it was found that more than 250,000 acres of land previously acquired could be leased to civilian users for farming or other productive effort.

Careful analyses of the utilization of the facilities owned or leased by the War Department were made throughout the war. By the end of June 1945, utilization surveys resulted in the release of more than 2,000 rented properties, thereby effecting an annual reduction in rentals of approximately four million dollars. Certain installations declared excess by the using Service were converted to other uses. For example, all Army Personnel Centers and Separation Centers represented conversions of existing posts rather than new construction. The War Department provided facilities sufficient to separate more than 44,000 men per day at a cost of only about 12 million dollars.

On 16 December 1941 the Congress made the Corps of Engineers the construction agency of the War Department. Prior to that time the construction of airfields and oversea bases had been assigned to the Chief of Engineers, whereas the construction of cantonments, storage depots, and industrial facilities was the responsibility of the Quartermaster Corps. The centralization of all construction work in a single agency was an important administrative improvement. Construction costing more than 10.6 billion dollars was placed on Army real estate. Three thousand installations, providing facilities for the housing, training, transportation, and supply of 5.3 million troops in the United States at one time, were built. Peak activity in the United States was reached in July 1942, when 720 million dollars worth of construction contracts were placed. Thereafter, this activity declined steadily.

Because physical facilities had to be provided in advance for large-scale training, storage, and shipping operations, no delay could be permitted. Ordinary peacetime construction practices were inadequate for defense needs. Much of the planning and construction had to proceed concurrently. For this reason, the architect-engineer type of contract was developed for design and specifications. This brought architects and engineers and the construction contractor together on the job at the same time. The cost-plus-a-fixed-fee contract was the most widely used type of construction contract. This was indispensable, because accurate cost estimates upon which to base bids were not possible. Under the cost-plus-a-fixed-fee arrangement the Government reimbursed the contractor for the total cost of construction and paid him a fixed fee for his management services. The fee was based on an original estimate and did not vary with the actual costs of construction. There was some early confusion in Congress and among the public on this score, because it was thought that this type of contract might provide an incentive to increase costs. Careful supervision by resident engineers was relied upon to prevent unnecessary costs in construction work. In many instances the construction fees were reviewed and reduced during the progress of the work or after the completion of the contract. Although cost-plus-a-fixed-fee contracts were not generally favored in procurement operations, it is doubtful

CHART 16. ARMY CONSTRUCTION IN CONTINENTAL U. S.

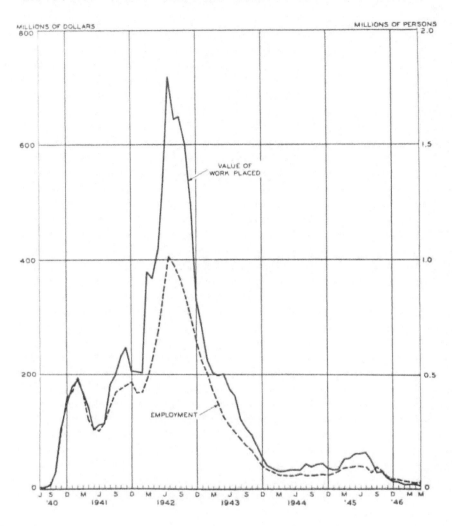

whether any other practices would have been useful in providing the facilities needed by the Army within the time available.

The building of a 60,000-man camp was a huge undertaking. Such large-scale construction could be handled by only a few contractors in the United States. For this reason projects were often divided and were built by several individual contractors. In other instances several contracting firms were encouraged to combine in order to undertake large projects. The Quartermaster General established an impartial board, later transferred to the Chief of Engineers, that recommended contractors for all contracts involving expenditures of over five million dollars. This was an important device for insuring the ability of individual contractors and for maintaining satisfactory relations with the construction industry.

The Army, Navy, and War Producton Board agreed upon minimum standards of wartime construction. The Army satisfied itself that no existing facilities could meet the need, before new construction was initiated. When construction was undertaken, only such stability and protection as would be required for war use was provided. The utilization of war materials was at all times keyed to the availability of resources. The Army rigidly adhered both to the letter and the intent of this policy of wartime construction. Frills were eliminated. Beautification and landscaping were sacrified. The Army made successive shifts from one material to another as the supply of each became critical—from steel to cast iron, to plywood, to lumber, to masonry. At every stage the objective was to obtain the most facilities in the shortest time with the materials most abundant at that moment. Thus, masonry construction was employed in certain instances, although it cost 15 percent more than lumber. Simultaneously, however, every effort was made to achieve economy. For example, the painting of buildings, both interior and exterior, was held to the minimum. During the war over 120 million dollars was saved by lowering painting standards. This saving was in addition to the saving in scarce pigments, fillers, and oils needed for other war uses.

Construction included the typical, temporary camp for housing and training troops, with barracks, warehouses, and administration buildings, and also such installations as airfields, depots, arsenals, proving grounds, hospitals, manufacturing plants, and some civilian war housing. In addition to purely military airfields, the Corps of Engineers built others financed with funds provided by and designed for ultimate use by the Civil Aeronautics Administration. Airfield construction involved constantly changing programs, plans, and specifications in order to meet changing military requirements. Fields constructed with runways, taxiways, and aprons designed for light fighter planes cannot accommodate heavy bombers. The B-17 and B-24 weighed approximately 70,000 pounds, and the B-29 weighed 135,000 pounds. These required heavier and longer runways. The The Corps of Engineers was designing runways capable of supporting 300,000 pound planes, such as the projected B-36, by the end of the war.

Hospital construction involved an expansion from an original capacity of 4,000 beds in general hospitals and 8,500 in station hospitals to 164,000 beds in general hospitals, 200,000 beds in regional and station hospitals, and 50,000 beds in convalescent hospitals. These facilities were in addition to the large number of dispensaries, auxiliary medical installations, and veterinary hospitals. Approximately 30 percent of the hospital program was accomplished by converting hotels or apartment houses into medical facilities.

Over one billion dollars was spent on the construction of War Department storage and shipping facilities during World War II. Storage facilities were expanded from a handful of depots in 1941 to 150 in 1945. Storage and loading facilities were enlarged at ports. Open storage space for vehicles and other equipment was constructed in addition to shed and warehouse facilities. Hard surfaces for such storage had to be increased in 1944, when it became evident that some equipment was deteriorating from standing in mud.

A huge program for the construction of industrial plants designed to produce the weapons of war was also necessary. Manufacturers were encouraged to finance privately the construction of new plants required for war production. The tax law of 1940 permitted the War Department to issue Certificates of Necessity that allowed the owner to amortize the cost of new plant over a 5-year period for income and excess profits tax purposes. From 1940 through December 1943, the War Department issued Certificates covering the cost of privately financed plants valued at 4.9 billion dollars. The plants financed in this manner were predominantly in the fields of transportation, petroleum, mining, fabrication, and aircraft manufacture. Less than 8 percent of the total provided facilities for the manufacture of such items as guns and ammunition. The War Department also sponsored certain facilities constructed by the Defense Plant Corporation. The Army Service Forces arranged Defense Plant Corporation financing amounting to 450 million dollars, of which 345 million dollars was for ordnance. In addition, Government-owned industrial facilities were constructed costing $3,250,000,000, exclusive of production equipment. In part this included $1,140,000,000 for powder and TNT plants, 690 million dollars for shell-loading facilities, and 300 million dollars for plants producing small arms and their ammunition.

Housing for civilian personnel was one of the most troublesome fields of construction. The peculiar needs of the Army dictated the construction of large installations, such as powder loading plants, in rural areas. Many of these required as many as 20,000 civilian workers. Adequate housing was necessary in order to recruit and retain these employees. Similar situations were encountered at large Army-owned plants. The President in February 1942 consolidated all Federal housing agencies in the National Housing Agency, giving it authority to construct civilian war housing, but no funds were immediately made available. Because early action was essential, arrangements were made for the Army to construct civilian war housing, with the understanding that the National Housing Agency would reimburse the War Department as soon as Congress made funds available. The National Housing Agency designated the War Department as its construction agent for a number of civilian housing projects, financing the construction from funds made available by the Lanham Act. The Corps of Engineers, using approximately 27 million dollars of National Defense Housing Funds, under this arrangement provided housing for approximately 35,000 individuals and 3,000 families.

During the war a compromise had to be made between complete decentralization of authority and the retention of adequate control over subordinate commanders responsible for construction activities. In 1942 new construction involving expenditures up to $10,000 could be approved by Division Engineers, and alterations, additions, and extensions up to the same amount by Service Commands. In April 1944 it was recognized that sufficient facilities had been constructed for the successful prosecution of the war, hence any new construction, alteration, or addition costing more than $1,000 required the approval of Headquarters, ASF.

The Chief of Engineers also directed several important, large construction projects outside the continental limits of the United States. These included air bases in the North Atlantic, the Caribbean, and South America. The Atlantic air bases served two purposes. They provided an air transport and ferry route to Europe and North Africa, and they provided bases for the air protection of allied shipping lanes in the Atlantic. These airfields were constructed on land leased from the British and from land made available by various American republics cooperating in hemispheric defense. The task of the Corps of Engineers was to construct bases after diplomatic arrangements had been made and specific fields designated for American development. The operation of the fields was under the jurisdiction of the Army Air Forces, the Caribbean Defense Command, and United States Army Forces in South America.

The construction of a highway from the United States to Alaska had been proposed a number of years prior to World War II. A Presidential Commission, for example, reported favorably on such a project in 1930. In the prewar years, however, the War Department did not believe that such a construction project was justified purely from the point of view of national defense. The United States and Canadian Governments in August 1940 established the Permanent Joint Board on Defense. This Board in November of the same year recommended the construction of an airway to Alaska through Canada. The route selected was one previously determined by survey to be the most practicable flight route. The Alaskan International

Highway Commission in May 1941 issued a report recommending immediate construction of a highway through Canada to Alaska. During the summer the War Department General Staff concluded that an overland highway route was desirable in light of the unfavorable trend of international events and the danger of interrupted sea communication to Alaska. The highway would also service the airway, operation of which was being delayed because of the isolation of the airfields.

Alaska was exposed to enemy attack after Pearl Harbor with its terrible naval losses. Alaska was on the shortest route from Japan to the United States. For three or four weeks following Pearl Harbor, many merchant ships leaving west coast ports were attacked by enemy submarines. Enemy submarines and surface vessels were detected off the west coast and in Alaskan waters on 41 separate occasions during January 1942. The War Department in February 1942 directed the Corps of Engineers to construct a highway that would service the string of airfields and provide uninterrupted land communication with Alaska. In March 1942 an agreement was made with Canada respecting its construction. The Alcan Highway was begun at the town of Dawson Creek in British Columbia and was extended to the northwest for 1,428 miles across Yukon Territory to Big Delta, Alaska. The pioneer roadway was completed on 20 November 1942 in a little more than 7 months. This roadway was used during the winter of 1942. By August 1943, when the Japanese were driven from the Aleutians, improvements on the Alcan Highway were approximately 70 percent complete. The highway continued to serve as a supply route for the airfields during the remainder of the war. There was some controversy over the route selected and the preference given to road instead of railroad construction. The decision on both points was made in the light of military considerations. The route was selected because of the location of the airfields, and a highway was built in preference to a railroad because it was the most satisfactory and quickest means of establishing a supply route between the airfields.

The Canol project, approved by the War Department and the Joint Chiefs of Staff, was another aspect of the precautions taken for the defense of Alaska. It involved the drilling of wells and the extraction of oil from fields located on the MacKenzie River in the Yukon Territory; the transportation of crude oil by pipe line from Norman Wells to Whitehorse, a distance of 577 miles; and the building of a refinery at Whitehorse and a gasoline pipe-line distribution system along the Alcan Highway and to Skagway on the sea route to the United States. The Chief of Engineers started the construction of the project in the spring of 1942. The pipe-line distribution system was completed in November 1943. The Whitehorse refinery began operations on 30

April 1944. The project cost 133 million dollars, of which some 31 million dollars was for the distribution pipe lines.

Considerable criticism was leveled at the Canol project, particularly the crude oil extraction at Norman Wells and the refinery operations at Whitehorse. The project was undertaken in light of our extremely precarious situation in the Pacific in 1942 and 1943, and although its practicality was questioned, it was continued as insurance against subsequent unfavorable developments in the war against Japan. The decisions on the project were made from the military standpoint and followed what appeared at the time to be the safest course. The Canol project was one of the preparedness measures which fortunately proved to be nonvital.

The Inter-American or Pan-American Highway has been planned for many years to connect South American countries with the United States and Canada. Parts of the 3,250-mile route were completed prior to the war. In 1942 Congress approved a project to complete more than 900 miles, to close gaps and to improve inferior existing roads in order to provide a land route between the United States and the Panama Canal. This work was undertaken by the War Department and executed under the supervision of the Chief of Engineers. During the first 6 months of the war, ships were lost within sight of the Atlantic coast, in the Gulf of Mexico, and in the Caribbean Sea. The successful countermeasures that eliminated the submarine menace from American waters insured uninterrupted sea communication and thus made the Pan-American Highway militarily unnecessary. The War Department canceled its project in October 1943 and the work was stopped.

The operation of utilities and the maintenance of the Army's physical plant required more attention as the war progressed. The electric lines employed by the Army in the United States totaled 23,000 miles. The roadways were sufficient to span the United States 25 times. Other utilities included over 9,000 miles of sewer lines, over 3,000 miles of railroads, 10,000 miles of water mains, and 2,500 miles of gas lines. A system of cost accounting was set up in order to measure repair and utility performance at posts, camps, and stations. Experience indicated that this system was a helpful tool in reducing costs. A fuel conservation program that included cutting off heat after 10 o'clock at night and during the day in barracks reduced fuel consumption from 25 to 40 percent. Temperatures of 68° to 70° were maintained in hospitals and offices during the day. It became evident in 1945 that maintenance standards were too low for many structures, and deferred maintenance work on permanent buildings was resumed. The Army Service Forces gave increasing attention to the maintenance of all structures that the Army expected to use in the postwar period.

Communications

At the start of the war the communications system was designed to meet the needs of an Army of 1.6 million, operating largely within the continental limits of the United States. The Army in 1940 had fairly simple telephone systems at posts, camps, and stations and a manually operated radio circuit. These facilities were grossly inadequate for handling war traffic. To serve the larger wartime Army, communications facilities had to be expanded in the United States and established throughout the world. The first step involved the acquisition of domestic radio circuits so as to make their frequencies available for oversea communication activities. The Army transferred 44 telephone systems to commercial companies for operation and maintenance early in 1942 in order to relieve itself of these responsibilities.

What eventually became the Army Command and Administrative Network was started in June 1942, when a radio net was established between Australia, Hawaii, San Francisco, and Washington. The network was further extended by establishing a high-power station at Karachi, India. Installations were made by 14 task force radio detachments that were activated at Fort Monmouth and sent overseas with the matériel required for erecting the necessary facilities. A teletypewriter network later replaced the radio net within the continental United States. The Chief Signal Officer controlled this network, eliminated unnecessary circuits, leased new facilities, and consolidated independent networks.

Research during the war resulted in major improvements in communications engineering. Teletypewriter transmission was coordinated between land lines and radio. Transmission speed was increased from 60 words a minute to 100 words a minute. Two-way direct conference teletypewriter service was developed. New equipment made it possible to establish a "belt line" route that permitted the sending of a message from Washington completely around the world in three and one-half minutes, relayed automatically at Asmara, New Delhi, Brisbane, and San Francisco. The communications system was expanded until it handled traffic that reached a peak of more than 50 million words a day, or as many as are found in 500 novels. Because of the need for speed, mechanization supplanted manual operation wherever possible. Automatic devices were developed to decipher messages. The use of security scramblers was also an important development.

The Army Airways Communications System included both radio communication and navigational aids. Signal networks were needed wherever air transport routes were established. In 1942 signal troops were organized and assigned to four sector headquarters of the Army Airways Communications System. Teams from these sector headquarters were sent to any part of the world where airways signal construction work was needed.

Important communications services were provided at the conferences of Allied leaders at Quebec, Cairo, Teheran, Malta, Yalta, and Potsdam. At each conference direct teletypewriter channels to the War, Navy, and State Departments and to the White House were installed. For example, the signal facilities for the Yalta conference required 250 tons of equipment, 20 tons of it being transported by air from the United States. This equipment was placed in operation within nine days. The system worked so efficiently that a message sent from Yalta to Washington required less than one hour for filing, cryptographing, transmission, decoding, and delivery.

In wartime the security of communications transcends other problems of military security. This was the responsibility of the Signal Security Agency. Fast, secret communication was provided by changing from manual to machine systems. There were many significant secret developments in this field during the war.

The volume of messages transmitted by wire and radio became greater and greater as the war continued. Because the volume threatened to overload existing facilities, special efforts were made to reduce the load. Upon the recommendation of the Army Service Forces, the War Department issued instructions designed to eliminate verbiage from messages and to prevent the use of radio communications when airmail would serve equally well. Signal personnel scrutinized messages carefully and, where appropriate, questioned the need for radio transmission. These measures reduced the volume of traffic.

Transportation

The Army Service Forces transportation mission, which did not include air transport, was to assure sufficient land transportation, locate adequate water shipping for Army needs, and operate Ports of Embarkation.

The Army Service Forces established a Transportation Corps in 1942 in order to handle the major task of moving men and supplies promptly within the United States and to oversea Theaters. Transportation played a decisive role throughout the war, affecting virtually every phase of the Army's activities in the Zone of the Interior and in oversea areas. The successful accomplishment of the mission may be largely attributed to the consolidation of transportation functions within a single Service.

CHART 18. MERCHANT SHIP TONNAGE AVAILABLE FOR UNITED NATIONS SHIPPING

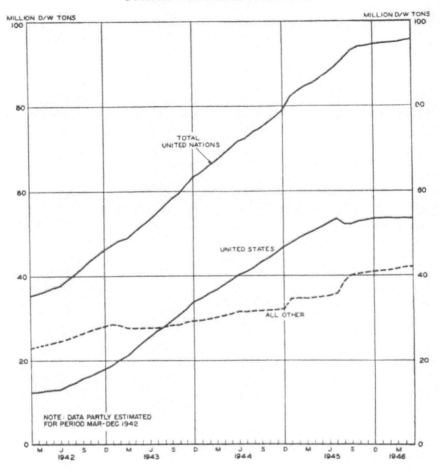

The construction of troop transport and cargo vessels was a responsibility of the Maritime Commission; landing craft were supplied by the Navy. Vessels were allocated by the War Shipping Administration. The efficient employment of the allocated shipping was the responsibility of the Army Service Forces.

The United States and Great Britain in January 1942 established a Combined Shipping Adjustment Board in order to pool merchant shipping and to make the best possible use of all ships under the control of the two nations. As of December 1941 the combined cargo and tanker shipping resources amounted to 41.6 million deadweight tons, of which 11.4 million was American. By the end of the war

CHART 19. PORTS OF EMBARKATION AND THEATERS SUPPLIED

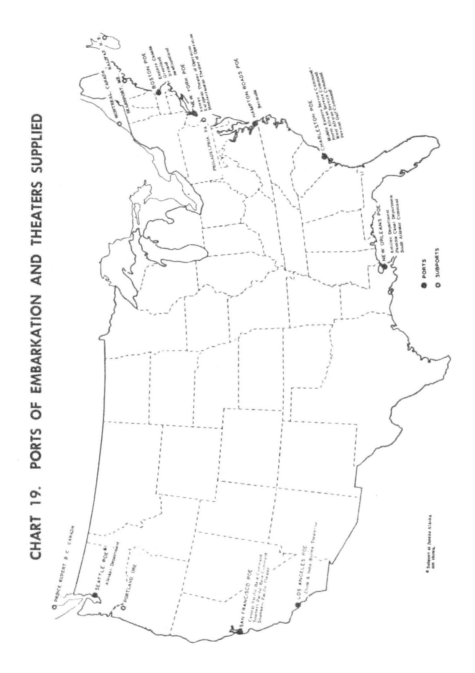

142

the combined shipping resources totaled 90.8 million deadweight tons, of which 54.1 million belonged to the United States. In practice the Combined Shipping Adjustment Board functioned only when the British or the American forces required the assistance of the other. The United States provided the British with considerable cargo shipping, and they in turn aided the United States in transporting troops. In the calendar year 1944, for example, the United States made 6,350,000 deadweight tons of cargo shipping available to the British, or about 20 percent of the total. The British in turn transported about one-fourth of the American troops sent overseas in that year. Military shipping needs were controlled within the United States by the Joint Army-Navy Military Transportation Committee, on which the Chief of Transportation represented the Army Service Forces.

At the beginning of the war it was necessary to estimate the Army's shipping requirements by various types of vessels: cargo ships, tankers, transports, and combat loaders, and of assuring that the needs for various types of ships were included in the construction program of the Maritime Commission. In 1943 an imbalance developed in the program, cargo carrying capacity exceeding troop transport capacity. In order to meet this situation the British made available passenger vessels, particularly the Queen Mary and the Queen Elizabeth, for the transport of American troops. In addition, the Maritime Commission instituted a program to convert troop transports into cargo vessels. Other conversions were similarly made later in the war. Examples of these were the additional hospital ships required in 1944, and the troop transports needed in 1945 for redeployment and the return of troops to the United States for discharge.

Securing the fullest possible utilization of the ships made available to the Army was extremely important. Careful planning of cargo loading assured proper use of hold space, and the deck loading of cargo ships and tankers also increased the capacity of vessels. By August 1944, Army ships carried loads averaging 90 percent of the bale cubic capacity. The shipment of fully assembled aircraft was largely accomplished by constructing special superstructures on tankers. By the end of the war, 535 tankers had been equipped for deck loading, and 19,000 airplanes had been delivered overseas by this means alone. Aircraft were also transported on converted aircraft carriers and on Liberty ships.

At various times delays in the unloading of cargo vessels at oversea ports severely handicapped the dispatch of supplies. In February 1943 there were 88 vessels waiting to be unloaded at Noumea, New Caledonia, and Espiritu Santo in the South Pacific. Similar congestion occurred in both the Atlantic and Pacific in the latter half of 1944. During the time operations in the European Theater depended upon the Port of Cherbourg and the beaches of Normandy, and awaited the opening of the Port of Antwerp, the unloading of supplies could not keep pace with shipments. Cargo vessels were held as floating warehouses for considerable periods. In October 1944, 290 ships were waiting to be unloaded in the European Theater. In the Pacific the absence of unloading facilities on Leyte and the destruction of port facilities at Manila caused a shipping jam that was broken only by a reduction in shipping schedules.

At the peak of its operations the Transportation Corps used eight major ports of embarkation, five subports, and three cargo ports. The commanders of all these were held responsible for meeting oversea supply requisitions, including the assembling of supplies and the loading of them on outgoing vessels. In providing an orderly flow of supplies into ports, the Army Service Forces established a system of cargo planning that fixed definite periods within which supply action was to be taken by depots and Technical Services. Procedures were developed whereby the movement of carloads from depots to ports was closely supervised, and each shipment was carefully controlled until the actual loading was completed. In order to assure constant contact and up-to-date information on shipments, the New York Port conducted daily two-way teletype conferences with the European and Mediterranean Theaters, and the San Francisco Port communicated similarly with the Southwest Pacific and the Pacific Ocean Areas.

Extraordinary safeguards were necessary during the loading and oversea shipment of ammunition. Special ammunition piers were constructed in isolated places, and special controls were exercised so as to avoid the accumulation of large concentrations of ammunition or explosives near the loading piers. These precautions were so effective that the largest tonnage of explosives in Army history was moved without serious mishap.

A first major transportation objective within the United States was to prevent the congestion at ports that had so seriously impeded oversea transport in World War I. With the cooperation of the Association of American Railroads, the Transportation Corps early in the war instituted a careful system of traffic control that limited cargo shipments to ports. This proved to be so effective that the number of freight cars on hand at any port rarely exceeded more than 10 days' loading capacity. This was very different from World War I, when freight cars waiting to be unloaded in New York were backed up all the way to Pittsburgh.

Efficient utilization of existing railroad freight equipment was of the utmost importance. A continuous program was conducted for the purpose of achieving maximum loading and the quick release of cars. A reduction of back hauling and cross hauling was accomplished. One

CHART 20. ARMY CARGO SHIPPED OVERSEAS

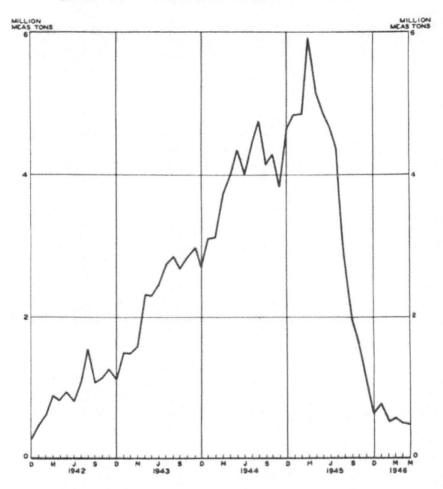

of the most prominent features of this program was the rapid release of cars. This was stimulated by encouraging competition among the Army's largest freight handling points.

Delays and difficulties experienced early in the war in connection with the large numbers of movements of less-than-carload lots of military freight were overcome by establishing consolidating stations, where such freight could be assembled and shipped in full carload lots. This operation assured the Army of control of the main course of movement and greatly decreased transit time. Important byproducts of the undertaking were reduced freight charges and fuller utilization of available freight cars. It was so successful that Navy,

Marine Corps, and Coast Guard shipments were later included. By the end of the war more than 2 million tons of freight had been handled in this manner at an estimated saving of more than 13 million dollars.

Army freight rates were kept as low as possible. One of the most ambitious projects undertaken in this field, that of translating hundreds of thousands of items of Army freight, many of them new to commerce, into the classification ratings contained in rail carriers' guides, was responsible for vast savings in freight charges. Negotiations with the Association of American Railroads yielded other large savings in the form of rate adjustments.

The Office of the Chief of Transportation routed all Army passenger movements of groups of 40 or more persons. Requests for such movements were conveyed to the Association of American Railroads, which assembled the necessary rolling stock and established time schedules. The Defense Plant Corporation financed the construction of additional special troop sleepers and improved kitchen cars designed by the Transportation Corps. Rail transport was handled so efficiently that it was only when large numbers of troops returned from Europe after VE-day that American railroads encountered serious difficulty in meeting military personnel transportation requirements. Even this difficult problem was solved by means of joint cooperation among the Office of Defense Transportation, the railroads, and the Army Service Forces. The Army agreed to take coaches within 48 hours when Pullmans were not available for movements. At the same time the Office of Defense Transportation eliminated Pullmans for general traffic on runs of less than 450 miles.

The best possible utilization of rail equipment required some leeway in carrying out troop movement orders. As issued by the War Department or troop commanders, these orders specified only an approximate date of movement and left the precise day and time to be fixed by the Transportation Corps. This practice permitted transportation authorities to schedule movements in and out of military reservations in a way that assured almost continuous use of the same equipment. The shunting of empty equipment for great distances was thereby avoided.

Troop movements into and through Ports of Embarkation were highly specialized operations. Troops were first routed to staging areas in proximity to the ports. There they came under the jurisdiction of the Port Commander for processing and loading. Final physical examinations were given, shortages or defects in equipment were corrected, and pay accounts and personal affairs were settled, within a very short period. The ports designated transports for the movement, and assigned units to individual vessels, while troops were being processed. Every unit and every man was assigned definite space. When the time came for embarkation, trains carried men from the staging areas to ferries or directly to the dock in loading order. Soldiers went aboard and to their designated places without delay. Fifteen thousand men were frequently embarked on the Queen Mary or the Queen Elizabeth in less than three hours. From December 1943 until the end of the war in Europe, the number of troops and other passengers embarking for oversea destinations exceeded 200,000 a month. The peak month was January 1945, when some 295,000 troops were sent overseas. Usually about 66 percent of the passengers were dispatched to Atlantic destinations, and the other one-third to the Pacific. Two-thirds of all embarkations on the East Coast were made at the New York Port. Boston handled approximately 18 percent and Hampton Roads 15 percent. On the West Coast 68 percent of all embarkations were handled at San Francisco. Seattle handled 24 percent, and Los Angeles approximately 8 percent.

Combat loading introduced special complications in transportation operations. The Western Task Force for the invasion of North Africa proceeded from the United States to the western coast of Africa for the assault near Casablanca. Considerable confusion attended this operation, largely because it was a first operation and because of the inexperience of personnel engaged in the undertaking. The task force commander was given the responsibility for the combat loading. The Army Service Forces assembled the ships and assisted in the loading at Hampton Roads. Supplies and equipment were loaded for ready discharge upon arrival overseas and in the order in which they would be needed on shore. When the convoy finally departed, it consisted of 28 ships carrying 38,000 men, 728 tracked vehicles, over 5,000 wheeled vehicles, and some 90,000 measurement tons of cargo.

In May 1943 the reinforced 45th Division was loaded at Hampton Roads for the assault upon Sicily. This operation proceeded much more smoothly. The Army Service Forces prepared the movement orders; the port commander was given greater responsibility for the loading operation; the division was collected at the new staging area which had been constructed in the vicinity of the port; and cargo was more carefully identified. The task force consisted of 23,000 men and 45,000 measurement tons of cargo loaded on 26 ships.

Combat loading required transports that were armed for defense and equipped to unload their own heavy cargo. This type of loading was wasteful of cargo space, because the needs of combat rather than full utilization of space was the governing factor. Actually only 50 to 65 percent of the cargo space was utilized. Moreover, men and supplies were loaded on the same vessels. It was necessary for the Transportation Corps to supervise combat loading, because of the lack of training and experience of troop commanders in such a highly

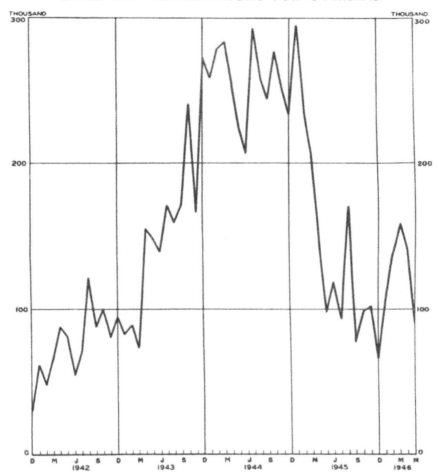

specialized operation. Because of the shortage of shipping, the Army Services Forces opposed combat loading, except when it was indispensable. Reinforcements for Normandy after D-day were not combat loaded, although the European Theater originally requested such loading.

The Transportation Corps, established after the creation of the Army Service Forces, had no procurement organization at the outset. There had been little need before the war for purchasing transportation equipment for military use. By the time the necessity arose, the Navy and the Maritime Commission had pre-empted practically all available facilities for producing marine equipment. The Army had to utilize small manufacturers and the remnants of the industry in order to obtain barges, harbor craft, and other necessary equipment. Commercial designs were used extensively, although efforts were made to adapt specifications to various climates, beaches, and specialized uses. Special maintenance and repair vessels, refrigerator-mounted barges, rescue boats, and special tugs were developed. Many craft from other sources were pressed into service. The impossibility of standardizing marine equipment made maintenance and the procurement of spare parts difficult. Nearly 8,000 self-propelled vessels and over 6,000 nonpropelled vessels were purchased during the war. Little difficulty was encountered in the procurement of railroad equipment, although the rolling stock had to be adapted to various gage widths and to special terrain features. Some 7,000 locomotives and over 97,000 railway cars were procured.

There were few officers in the Regular Army who had transportation training or experience. Railroad companies, steamship companies, and industrial shippers made personnel available to the Army to the fullest possible extent. Many of these men were commissioned in the Army, and others served in a civilian capacity. Most of them had little or no military experience, and time was required to acquaint them with Army practices and procedures. Other personnel were obtained through Officer Candidate Schools and Service schools that trained them for specific transportation jobs. By the end of the war a highly trained corps had been developed.

Finance

The War Department had no central organization for managing its fiscal affairs before 9 March 1942. Budget estimates had been prepared independently by each agency. A War Department budget committee screened these estimates prior to their submission to the Bureau of the Budget; this was the full extent of centralized staff supervision of fiscal matters.

The separate Arms and Services were not accountable to a central agency for allotted funds other than those included in the summaries of expenditures made by the Chief of Finance. No adequate central records of commitments or obligations were kept. Although the Chief of Finance controlled the issue of allotments as a safeguard against the allotting of funds in excess of appropriations, the Chiefs of Services limited their controls to a report of the status of an allotment after all funds thereon had been obligated. No monthly status report of funds was required. The absence of a coordinated system subjected the War Department to the danger of overexpending its appropriations without detecting the fact until afterwards.

The lack of a coordinated system of allotting, accounting, auditing, and disbursing appropriated funds, plus the shortage of trained personnel, gave rise to problems that could be solved only by placing responsibility for the supervision of these important functions in one office. This was accomplished by appointing a Fiscal Director in the Army Service Forces.

The magnitude of War Department appropriations and the expansion in number and size of installations made it necessary to establish a system for accumulating accurate accounting information in summary form. Commanders at each echelon could then appraise the current progress of the military program. All operating agencies were required to have a fiscal officer. The responsibilities of such officers were clearly defined; they were an important part of the Army Service Forces managerial organization. The Fiscal Director established uniform standards, concepts, and technical procedures. Reports on the status of funds were submitted through the same channels as those used for allotments. The Fiscal Director consolidated these data in summaries that were made available for War Department use.

The 14-fold increase in expenditures during the Fscal Years 1941–1945 and the expansion and deployment of the Army throughout the world required an extensive disbursing system. Prompt payment of all War Department obligations was essential: salaries of military and civilian personnel, invoices on construction and supply contracts, and transportation bills had to be met promptly, and amounts due the Government had to be collected. In order to accomplish these tasks, personnel were trained and procedures were simplified. Certifications of essential facts replaced the voluminous documents required in peacetime in justification of disbursement vouchers. This change was achieved by legislation to which the General Accounting Office interposed no objection. Payments to carriers were greatly expedited by using microfilm records and by making it unnecessary to associate copies of bills of lading with specific vouchers.

The great volume of disbursing records made it impracticable to centralize such primary records in Washington. The Army Service Forces established four regional accounting offices in the United States where disbursing officers' accounts were sent. Headquarters, ASF, also established similar centralized fiscal offices in each of the major Theaters of Operations. All disbursing officers' accounts were processed through these offices. The General Accounting Office, for the first time in its history, established its own accounting offices adjacent to these regional offices. Army examiners first reviewed disbursing officers' accounts and supporting data. These were then turned over to the General Accounting Office for final settlement. The General Accounting Office examination and settlement never lagged more than three or four months behind current payment, in contrast with the several years required to settle accounts after World

War I. When suspensions in Army disbursing officers' accounts were interposed by the General Accounting Office, it was not difficult to reconstruct the circumstances of the payment and to provide the additional information requested by the General Accounting Office. A greater time lag would have made prompt and satisfactory reply almost impossible. By the end of the war suspensions on vouchers, other than those involving cost-plus-a-fixed-fee contracts, were less than two one-thousandths of 1 percent of total payments.

In order to control cost-plus-a-fixed-fee contracts, the contractor and Army officials audited all costs before payments were made. In addition, a complete duplicate set of documents had to be sent to the General Accounting Office in Washington for auditing and settlement. Each review included a detailed check of every transaction. The Army Service Forces simplified this procedure by taking over certain of the contractors' audit personnel, by introducing a uniform selective auditing procedure in examining contractors' claims, and by persuading the General Accounting Office to establish its own auditors at the site of large projects where cost-plus-a-fixed-fee contracts were used. These practices greatly improved the efficiency of the accounting activities required for this type of contract.

Fiscal activities included more than the preparation of budget estimates, the control of obligations, and central control of disbursing activities for the entire Army. There were many additional tasks that had to be undertaken. One of the most important was the payment of family allowances and allotments. By 30 June 1945 there were 4.4 million active family allowance and 3.8 million voluntary allotment accounts. Despite this great volume, the Office of Dependency Benefits was able to mail eight million checks for the June payment by 1 July. In addition, the Fiscal Director deducted 55 million dollars a month for the payment of 10 million Government life insurance allotments.

The sale of war bonds was actively promoted among all military and civilian personnel throughout the War Department and the Army. Arrangements for handling bond deductions were unsatisfactory until the activity was greatly decentralized. It was desirable to persuade soldiers overseas to refrain from spending their pay because of the adverse effects of such spending upon the local economy. The establishment of soldier deposit accounts and free service in transmitting funds from overseas to the United States did much to accomplish the desired objective. By June 1945, military personnel were spending only 15 percent of their pay overseas; the remainder was retained in or was returned to the United States.

Banking facilities were provided at military installations in the Zone of the Interior. Contractors were assisted throughout the war in obtaining financing through guaranteed loans from private banks and advance payments on war contracts. Insurance costs chargeable to the Government by contractors were controlled in order to avoid unnecessary coverage and to minimize the cost of essential insurance. This resulted in the saving of hundreds of millions of dollars. Various types of military and special invasion currencies were obtained for use in overseas areas through the Treasury Department. Exchange rates for such currencies in terms of American dollars were established by the Treasury Department in consultation with the State Department.

Fiscal management in World War II represented an outstanding achievement. The largest appropriations in Government history were handled efficiently, and payments were made promptly to military and civilian personnel, to contractors, and to common carriers.

Printing

Printing and publishing activities in the War Department during the war were big business. There was no central office for the control of this work at the time of the reorganization of the Army in 1942. Each Arm and Service was responsible for its own publications. The Procurement and Accounting Division in the Office of the Secretary of War merely maintained accounts of the charges made by the Government Printing Office against the War Department appropriation for printing and binding. The Army Service Forces established a Publication Division in The Adjutant General's Office in the latter part of 1942, with general responsibility for the initial printing and distribution of all Army Service Forces publications. The Publication Division became the central publishing agency of the Army Service Forces, and in addition served the entire Army in many phases of printing.

The publications of the various Technical Services in 1942 were distributed by Technical Service depots. In order to reduce the number of publications and improve procedures, an Adjutant General Depot was established in each of the nine Service Commands, and a distribution system was set up. Publications and stocks of printed forms were sent from the printer to these depots, and from there they were distributed to posts, camps, and stations located within the respective Service Commands. This service was provided to all units of the Army Ground Forces, and was available to all units of the Army Air Forces. War Department publications were made available to Air Technical Service Command depots for redistribution to Army Air Forces stations. The latter distribution system duplicated the service that Adjutant General Depots were prepared to render to all posts.

An analysis of publishing in 1943 disclosed that the distribution system functioned badly, and that the printing was frequently of poor quality. Excessive quantities of some publications were produced. Some important publications were poorly printed and were without adequate illustration. A review mechanism was established and The Adjutant General given responsibility at the highest echelon. All initiating agencies in turn were held responsible for screening manuscripts in order to determine the need for them. Controls were subsequently provided for the distribution of publications and stocks of printed forms in order to curtail procurement. A stock control system was established. Finally in 1944 additional controls were introduced governing the production of publications and blank forms, whether printed at the Government Printing Office, printed under contract, accomplished in field printing plants, or produced as manuals to accompany equipment manufactured by industrial contractors. Between April 1943 and September 1945, The Adjutant General's Office reviewed 34,900 manuscripts of proposed publications and disapproved 2,400 as nonessential. Furthermore, the number of Army field printing plants was reduced from 70 to 35; at the same time production increased 20 percent, and the average annual cost of operation per plant dropped 17 percent. A reduction of $2,750,000, or 20 percent, for contract field printing was accomplished in the Fiscal Year 1945.

Photography

Photography, a responsibility of the Chief Signal Officer, was used as an important tool during the war. Motion pictures and film strips were major adjuncts to the programs for training, orientation, and education. The Army Pictorial Service served both the Army Service Forces and the Army Ground Forces. This Service produced training films of all types and entered into contracts with the motion picture industry in order to supplement its own production. More than 2,500 motion picture films were produced. Over 300,000 prints of these films were placed in film libraries, which in turn supplied the prints needed for military training purposes. Military personnel both in the United States and in oversea Theaters were kept informed of tactical and technical problems and developments through the exhibition of combat films.

Because of the large number of requests for training films, a special board representing the War Department, the Army Ground Forces, and the Army Service Forces was created in order to establish film production priorities and to insure that only essential training films were produced. In addition, the production of films was placed on a scheduled basis, thereby reducing production time as much as one half.

From among hundreds of thousands of still pictures taken by Signal Corps cameramen, 423,000 prints were assembled in the War Department Film Library for training, intelligence, informational, and historical purposes. At the end of the war, communications and photographic facilities permitted the transmission of color photographs of the Potsdam conference by radio for the first time.

Maps

The Army Map Service in the Corps of Engineers was established to collect, evaluate, and disseminate terrain intelligence. Without maps an army cannot travel or fight. The task of mapping various areas was divided among the United States and its Allies. International conferences established mapping policies, insured uniformity of map design, and coordinated map production and distribution. Advance programming was essential, because it took about 8 months to convert an aerial photograph of an operational area into a usable map for delivery into the hands of troops. Maps were produced and distributed in a shorter period than this, but at the expense of quality and detail. A war of movement required an astronomical number of maps. The Army Map Service throughout the war supplied 488 million copies of over 65,000 different maps for operations overseas.

Post Management and Housekeeping

The military post or camp where troops were trained in the United States was the focal point of service to the combat forces in the Zone of the Interior. The Army Service Forces managed the military posts utilized by the Army Ground Forces throughout the war. The task was comparable to that of operating a hundred or more large cities. The men had to be housed, and the sick and injured given medical care. Installations, such as laundries, service clubs, bakeries, and libraries, were required. Each post had a complete utility system that included water supply, electricity, sewage disposal, telephone service, and transportation facilities. Other services included fire protection, the paving and maintenance of roads, the maintenance of grounds, insect and rodent control. Boilers and furnaces were kept in repair, and garbage was removed. Vehicles and equipment were repaired, and outworn equipment was sold as scrap. Military and civilian personnel were paid, religious services were provided, mail was delivered. Supplies were stored in warehouses and issued as needed, motion picture theaters operated, and men and supplies were moved in and out of these installations by motor and rail. All of these facilities and services had to be provided coincident with the training of troop units. For this reason, post management was a logical responsibility of the Army Service Forces. The Army Ground Forces was able to devote itself entirely to the training of troops. The Army Service Forces appointed the post commanders who maintained the permanent facilities of a post for the ground troops in training. In reality, the post commander was the business manager of the installation. Some services of the types enumerated above were rendered to the Army Air Forces, although to a lesser extent.

The management task was a large one. It involved the providing of all the services in the most economical and efficient manner possible. It required the assembling of many different professional and technical specialists in order to provide the needed services. It was the post commander's job to insure that common facilities were utilized to the fullest extent, that common labor was shifted from one activity to another to meet peak loads, and that each service was adequate. Such responsibilities called for administrative talents of a very high order.

Posts were grouped under the nine Service Commands for supervisory purposes. The Service Commander and his staff insured that operations at each post were performed satisfactorily. The Service Command Staff included many professional and technical specialists who assisted in coordinating all phases of post management.

The system of post management introduced no new principle of military organization, but it did represent a departure from previous practice. Corps Area Commanders and post commanders in the 1920's and 1930's theoretically possessed the authority and responsibility for the economical management of military installations. In practice, however, the trend during these years was to give greater freedom of action to technical and professional specialists. Corps Area Commanders, and even post commanders, received separate allotments of funds from the Chiefs of Services in Washington. Each Chief of Service communicated directly with his counterpart in the field and, in effect, governed his activities directly. Corps Area Commanders by 1942 had, to all practicable purposes, become figureheads. This was changed after the organization of the Army Service Forces. Single allotments of funds and bulk personnel authorizations were made directly by the Commanding General, ASF, to the Commanding Generals of the Service Commands. They in turn made allotments as they saw fit to post commanders. All official instructions were issued in the name of the Commanding General, ASF, to Service Commanders. Informal consultation between technical specialists at all echelons was encouraged, but the chain of command was carefully preserved. This was essential in order to insure the most economical and efficient performance of many different services. It created a single, well-understood organization for operating and supervising services in the Zone of the Interior. The Service Commander was the recognized agent of the Army Service Forces for carrying out activities other than procurement, depot storage, construction, and trans-

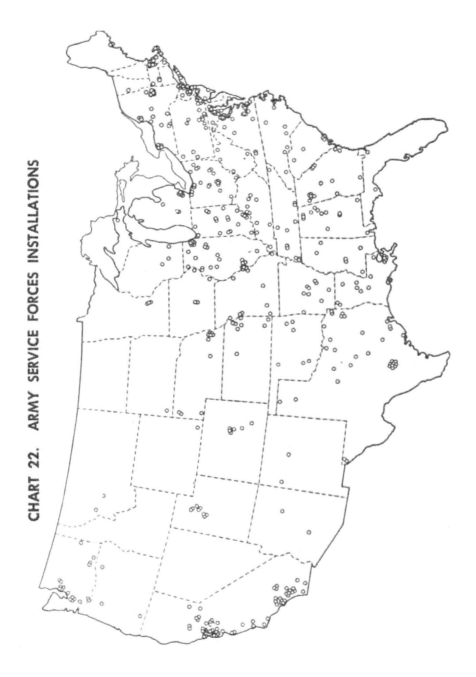

CHART 22. ARMY SERVICE FORCES INSTALLATIONS

portation within his area. A well-organized and efficient hierarchy of supervision was thus established. Each Service Commander and post commander, within the limits of general policies established by Headquarters, ASF, was expected to adjust programs and activities to meet local situations. As much discretion as possible was vested in these officers. This did much to prevent excessive centralization of authority and activity in Washington.

There were two complications in the system of post management. There were certain installations over which the Chiefs of Technical Services had exercised complete authority prior to 1942. These included such installations as depots, proving grounds, schools, general hospitals, and certain training centers. The fault in this arrangement was that the Surgeon General, for example, was thus responsible for more than just medical service at general hospitals. He was also responsible for supply activities, personnel activities, repairs and utilities, and other operations needed in maintaining such large military installations. The Chief of Engineers was similarly concerned with more than purely engineering activities. Nominally, at least, he was expected to supervise medical service, fiscal service, and other non-engineer activities at stations under his command. In order to avoid this anomalous and duplicating situation, these posts were designated as Class IV installations. The commander of such an installation was responsible to the Service Commander for all common services, and to the Chief of each Technical Service in matters involving that particular Service. This arrangement had the advantage of recognizing a single, common, supervisory organization for the broad range of service duties at any large military post, and of preventing the duplication of these services in the Office of each Chief of a Technical Service.

The second complication involved relations with the Army Air Forces. The Army Air Forces directly operated all services at airfields and other posts under its jurisdiction. The Air Surgeon supervised medical service at airfields; the Surgeon General supervised medical activities at all other military posts. The Air Provost Marshal supervised internal security and police matters; the Provost Marshal General supervised these activities for other installations. The Air Quartermaster supervised quartermaster supply activities at airfields; the Quartermaster General was the top supervisory authority for all other installations. Thus the supervisory hierarchy within the Army in the Zone of the Interior was duplicated.

Decentralization of authority and responsibility, a single well-recognized supervisory hierarchy for post services, the efficient and economical management of all common services—these were the essential elements and objectives of the system governing the administration of military posts by the Army Service Forces.

Chapter 7

LOGISTICS IN THEATERS OF OPERATIONS

The procurement and production job in the United States was organized and well under way by the end of critical year, 1942. The organization of an adequate system of supply and service in support of oversea operations still had to be developed. It was reasonably sure that munitions could be produced and shipped on schedule, but there was less reason, then, to be confident concerning the performance of the supply mission in support of forces in combat.

The Army Service Forces' operational responsibility ended when supplies were delivered at an oversea port. Plans prepared by the War Department had provided that Theater Commanders would be designated in those areas where combat operations would take place. These commanders would have complete control over all Army activity in their areas. This principle had been accepted in World War I, and there seemed to be no reason to question its validity for World War II. Accordingly, the commanders of Theaters of Operations and other oversea forces were made responsible for supplying and servicing troops within the areas under their command.

The complexity of the oversea supply mission was not well understood when the war began. There were oversea ports to be operated, where troops and supplies could be unloaded. There were storage depots and large cantonments to be constructed and operated. There were pipe lines for gasoline distribution, repair and maintenance shops for damaged and worn equipment, laundries, bakeries, radio stations, telephone systems, truck lines, railroads, disciplinary barracks, rest camps, hospitals, publishing facilities—all these and a hundred other facilities and activities were necessary to the support of combat forces in their operations against the enemy. The rapid forward movement of armies made in infinitely difficult to provide them with balanced supply and services. The combat commander had to be relieved of the preoccupation of supplying and servicing his forces; at the same time he had to be confident that supply and services would be adequate.

Plans for the logistic task in Theaters of Operations were only sketchily drawn during the years before Pearl Harbor. The experience of the Services of Supply of the American Expeditionary Force in World War I had established a rough precedent. Even this was an inadequate guide for World War II, because our forces had depended largely upon British and French supplies after their arrival overseas in 1917–18. World War I was not a war of movement as was World War II. Army doctrine in 1942 called for the creation of Communications Zones in major Theaters of Operations. The responsibilities of these Communications Zones resembled those of the Army Service Forces in the Zone of the Interior. The absence of procurement on a large scale was the major difference. Army doctrine gave little indication of the size of the job, its essential characteristics, its tremendous complexities, or of the organization and procedures that would be required. For the most part, Army schools and the War Department General Staff in peacetime planned, trained for, and studied combat operations. To a great extent the Army neglected the logistic problems of operations. This was a deficiency that proved to be costly.

Insufficient provision was made in War Department plans for service troops. The Commanding General, ASF, pointed out this deficiency immediately after the creation of his command, but he was unable to convince the War Department General Staff until after the North African compaign. Operations in North Africa in 1942 were initially impeded by the shortage of service troops and by a failure to prepare adequately for the operation of a Communications Zone. Drastic and urgent action corrected these deficiencies. The lessons learned were applied in Sicily and Italy. When Normandy was invaded, personnel for a Base Section for supply operations accompanied the assault troops as they landed. Gradually the supply and service forces were expanded into a large Communications Zone whose Advance Section moved forward with our combat forces as they crossed France and the Low Countries and penetrated Germany.

The gigantic logistic achievements in oversea Theaters during World War II owed less to foresight or advance planning than to the ingenuity and selfless devotion of thousands of officers and men in the service organizations.

The invasion of France and the defeat of Germany absorbed the greater part of our logistic effort from the closing months of 1943 until VE-day. Into that series of operations were crowded most of the logistic problems encountered in other Theaters, and also a number of problems that were peculiar to it.

The invasion of Normandy was necessarily preceded by a long period of preparation in the United Kingdom. The Theater's share of the task was to disembark the troops sent from the United States and to house, train, and equip them fully. The second part of the job was to unload, store, and issue the supplies necessary for their support and to prepare for the actual invasion. This effort required vast military construction. The mounting of the operation against North Africa in the summer and fall of 1942 virtually denuded the United Kingdom of American service troops. This postponed the construction of depots and housing facilities. The construction, however, of the airfields necessary for strategic bombing was expanded steadily during this period. The general construction program was again under way on a large scale by the spring of 1943. The Army Service Forces rushed engineering troops overseas in order to hasten the building of warehouses and cantonments. Depot companies were sent to store and issue the mounting piles of supplies, and port companies were dispatched to unload the ships and clear the docks.

American preparations in the United Kingdom by D-day had changed the Isles into a vast fortress. The Theater's Services of Supply had built housing for 1.2 million men, hospitals for 94,000 men, and tented accommodations for another 30,000; 20 million square feet of covered and 44 million square feet of open storage space had been provided; 270 miles of railroads had been constructed. There were 163 different airfields, supported by three base depots, and seven combat crew and replacement centers, with accommodations for 454,000 men and 8.5 million square feet of storage and shop space. About 60 percent of the accommodations for the Army Air Forces represented new construction built by British and American engineers. Some 77 percent of the hospital program had been constructed by the British; American engineer troops had built the remainder.

The planning and preparations for the actual invasion proceeded in the meantime. Special types of equipment were devised by modifying existing equipment or were obtained by making emergency requisition upon the United States. The equipping of each assault unit was painstakingly planned. The transportation of succeeding waves of troops was carefully phased. The loading of supplies in British ports and the unloading of them in France were arranged in great detail. Supply personnel dispatched definite quantities of supplies to specific ports in southern England, and even specified the vessels for their shipment to France. British and American logisticians planned and constructed two large artificial ports to be floated to the coast of France. Over 1.5 million tons of materials went into the construction of the American port called "Mulberry A." One hundred fifty-eight sea-going tugs towed the prefabricated parts from England to the Normandy coast. Mulberry A covered two square miles, with moorings for seven Liberty ships and 15 smaller craft. Unfortunately, a terrific storm between 19 and 22 June demolished this artificial port, which considerably delayed supply operations.

Another delay occurred because the port of Cherbourg was not captured until 27 June, two weeks behind the original schedule. The harbor had been so thoroughly demolished that another three weeks were required to repair the damage and open the port for service. The supply organization in the Theater had to continue the use of two open beaches, Omaha and Utah, in supplying the combat forces as a result of this combination of circumstances. During June and July over 800,000 long tons were delivered over Omaha and Utah, and over 900,000 men and 315,000 vehicles were landed. Virtually the entire resources of the American Army at the time of the Saint Lo breakthrough on 25 July 1944 had reached France over the two beaches.

Substantial tonnages continued to move into France over the beaches until November, when bad weather stopped these operations. Cherbourg had been opened as a supply port late in July. It received over 400,000 long tons in November, exclusive of bulk petroleum products and vehicles. Cherbourg was then the only port of any importance in the hands of the American Army.

After the break-through at Avranches, the lightning-like advance of the Third Army and the swift progress of the other Allied armies expanded the area of operation and overextended our supply lines. Storage dumps in Normandy could not be moved forward rapidly enough. Even at the end of October, 73 percent of all supplies on the continent were still stored in the Normandy area. Supply personnel attempted to postpone as long as possible the day when the forward advance must stop for lack of adequate support. The wreckage of the French railway system temporarily placed the entire transportation burden upon truck transport. Dependence upon truck transport resulted in a heavy expenditure of vehicles, tires, and spare parts. The "Red Ball Express" route opened on 25 August, and expanded until it extended over a circuit of more than 700 miles. Finally, late in October, the reconstruction of bridges and roadbeds, the overhauling of rolling stock, and the arrival of new equipment enabled the railroads to take over most of the transport of supplies. Engineer troops had rebuilt or repaired 750 miles of track by the end of August. The Red Ball Express ceased operations on 16 November. On its peak day it hauled over 12,000 tons; it delivered more than 400,000 tons to the front lines during its period of operation.

The distribution of petroleum products was accomplished in part by laying a pipe line under the English Channel. Operation PLUTO, as it was called, was completed soon after D-day and reached a daily capacity of a million gallons. Only a few miles of pipeline had been laid on the continent before the Saint Lo break-through. In the confused period that followed, motor transport, rail, and barge lines hauled gasoline and oil to the forward areas. The pipe lines followed as rapidly as possible. The Transportation Corps of the Communications Zone was operating 198 Quartermaster Truck Companies with a total of 9,500 vehicles by December 1944. Fourteen of these companies operated motor tankers.

The rapid advance of the troops across France left large supply depots far behind in Normandy, and almost no facilities existed between these and the front line troops. The job of supply personnel now was to build a supply system for the front lines. At the same time the Supreme Allied Command was determined to press the attack forward as fast as possible. Supply personnel tried to deliver commodities directly from Normandy to the armies on the German border. The system was not effective, and Cherbourg and other smaller ports were jammed. Front line troops obtained the needed food, ammunition, and petroleum products, but lacked many spare parts, quantities of medical supplies, and other items. Armies sent trucks all the way to Cherbourg to get supplies for themselves. Early in September Allied troops captured Antwerp with its port installations intact. German troops were not driven from the approaches to Antwerp, however, until the middle of November, and the port was not opened until December. In that one month service troops unloaded 420,000 long tons at Antwerp. It took only one-fourth as much effort to supply one division from Antwerp as from Cherbourg. Capacity at Cherbourg was sufficient to supply a maximum of only 13 divisions. Antwerp could supply 50. The use of the port of Antwerp was divided between the British and the Americans. In December supply depots were moved forward. Liege became the principal forward depot area, and other depots were established at Charleroi, Mons, Namur, Lille, and Verdun.

The Germans launched a counteroffensive on 16 December 1944. The forward flow of supplies was halted and many supplies were evacuated to the rear. The enemy did not capture a single gasoline dump. The drive was stopped, and the Allied Forces were again on the offensive in January, when the normal forward flow of supplies was resumed. For a time in January and February the Germans succeeded in seriously interfering with port operations at Antwerp by using the V-2 bomb. Antwerp unloaded only 74,000 tons of supplies in the third week of January. By the middle of February, however, the disruption had lessened and the weekly tonnage was up to 134,000.

Over 4.6 million long tons of American supplies poured onto the Continent during December, January, and February. The rail yards at Liege handled 35,000 tons every day during the month of February. Supply operations in March mounted sharply when American railroad battalions extended their efforts in getting supplies forward. Twenty-four hours before the crossing of the Rhine on 23 March, 460 cars of engineer bridging equipment, 765 cars of quartermaster and ordnance supplies, 80 cars of jerricans, 80 cars of oil and lubricants, 16 cars of mail, and eight troop trains were moved to the front. In the month between 11 February and 11 March, the highways of France handled a million troops and 2.8 million tons of supplies.

As the northern armies swept across France, American and French Forces invaded southern France on 15 August 1944. The first great supply need was to obtain a port. Toulon fell on 25 August and Marseilles on the 27th. Marseilles had been systematically wrecked, but within one month the port was restored, and by mid-October it was handling 100,000 tons a week. The Sixth Army Group in the south received 1,556,279 tons of supplies through Marseilles by the end of December. Supply activities in the north and south were brought together in February 1945 under a unified command.

From March 1945 until VE-day, supply personnel were once again confronted with the difficult task of keeping rapidly advancing armies supplied. There were more munitions and facilities for the task than in the preceding autumn. Pipeline companies advanced almost as rapidly as the combat troops. Air transport was used to drop and land supplies. Stocks stored along the French frontier were moved across the Rhine by truck in great quantities. Engineer troops constructed a railroad bridge across the Rhine in 10 days, and railroads were operating into the heart of Germany by the first week in April. Fighter strips and larger air fields were constructed behind the front lines.

Throughout the invasion and the operations that followed, service troops never failed to deliver the mail. Radio programs, picture shows, and post exchange supplies were also provided, and daily newspapers were printed and distributed. Medical troops and hospitals followed the combat forces as fast as they moved forward. Air evacuation to hospitals in England began on D plus 3. Field hospitals and evacuation hospitals were set up immediately behind divisions. Communications Zone hospitals were only a short distance behind the armies. The wounded and injured were promptly moved back through a series of hospitals until they could be evacuated to the United States for final medical care.

Signal troops provided communications for United States operations on the Continent. Signal troops were among the first to land on D-day. A mobile radio station, in operation by noon of the second day, provided a channel between the beachhead and Plymouth, England. Wire and radio stations were moved along with the troops. The communications center in Paris handled 25,000 telephone calls a day. The long distance switchboard handled another 5,000 calls every 24 hours. There were 250,000 miles of wire strung on the Continent as a part of the American communications system by the end of 1944. The radio center handled a traffic volume second only to that of the War Department in Washington. More than 50,000 messages a week were sent and received. Within 25 days after the equipment reached Paris, a radio transmitter was sending and receiving trans-Atlantic radio messages. A radio and wire teleprinter system connected more than 107 principal headquarters, dumps, depots, and rail heads with the center in Paris.

Accomplishments in the European Theater of Operations were paralleled by equally magnificent efforts in other Theaters. In North Africa supplies were hauled all the way from Casablanca to Tunisia in support of the final drive upon the Germans there. The Mediterranean ports shipped supplies for the invasion of Sicily. The reconstruction of the port of Naples and the rehabilitation of the Italian railroad system were major achievements. Almost no one had visualized the immense distances and the virtually complete lack of facilities that American troops had to overcome in the Pacific. By the time the Germans were defeated in Europe, the Philippine Islands had been rewon, and American troops were driving the enemy from Okinawa, which was within fighter-plane range of the Japanese home islands. Air fields and storage dumps were hacked out of the jungle. A road from Ledo, linking with the old Burma Road, was constructed across 271 miles of mountains, virgin jungle, rice fields, and torrential streams. Pipe lines had been laid in India, roads constructed in New Guinea, harbor facilities installed where none had ever existed before. There were deficiencies, in spite of all the efforts expended in support of our combat troops. That none of these proved to be disastrous was fortunate. An appreciation of these deficiencies should pave the way for the development of improved logistic doctrine in the future.

There was no common pattern of organization to be used in performing logistic functions in oversea Theaters. There was a Services of Supply in North Africa and later in Italy. It was superseded in September 1944 by a Communications Zone, which in many respects resembled the Communications Zone in Northern Europe. There was a Services of Supply in the European Theater until D-day, when it was supplanted by the Communications Zone. There was also a Services of Supply in the Southwest Pacific until the completion of the Philippine Campaign. It then was superseded by entirely new commands of broadened scope.

In not a single instance was the organization the same, nor was the assignment of responsibilities comparable. Each Theater Commander had a different conception of the role to be played by his supply command. The Army Service Forces at one time suggested to the War Department that a standard supply organization for Theaters be established. The recommendation was rejected. The organizational dissimilarities may be illustrated by a comparison of the European Theater of Operations after D-day with the Southwest Pacific Theater.

The Supreme Headquarters, Allied Expeditionary Forces, in Europe had a joint staff of American and British officers. The Chief of Staff to the Supreme Allied Commander was also Chief of Staff for the European Theater of Operations. As Commander of the American Forces in Europe, the Supreme Commander had under him the United States Naval Forces in France, the Sixth Army Group, the Twelfth Army Group, the United States Strategic Air Forces, the First Airborne Army, and the Communications Zone. The Communications Zone was the supply organization for American combat forces. The same General Staff and Special Staff served both the European Theater of Operations and the Communications Zone. For a time the Commanding General of the Communications Zone was also Deputy Commanding General of the Theater. This was an effort to recognize the Communications Zone as the supply and service agency for the entire Theater. The arrangement was never clear-cut. The lines of authority and responsibility between the staff sections of Supreme Headquarters and the Communications Zone were confused. The Air Forces to a great degree had their own independent service organization. There was little integration of Army and Navy service activities. The Communications Zone was organized into a number of geographic sections which expanded as the armies moved across France. There were many different organizational units making up the Communications Zone in addition to the Base, Intermediate, and Advance Section Headquarters. The extent of the authority of Communications Zone Section commanders and of the Special Staff units was not clearly delineated.

The Supreme Allied Commander in the Southwest Pacific Theater during September 1943 was also Commanding General of the United States Army Forces in the Far East. The General Headquarters Staff was composed largely of Americans. A separate American staff, apart from the Commanding General and Chief of Staff, served the United States Army Forces in the Far East. At this time there were three operational components in the United States Army Forces in the Far East: the Sixth Army, the Fifth Air Force, and the Services of Supply. The Services of Supply had six Base Sections in Australia and an Advance Section in New Guinea. Here again there was some confusion between the functions of the Services of Supply and those of the staff of the United States Army Forces. In general, Services of Supply officers had much less authority of a Theater-wide nature, and supply activities were confined more to the operating of facilities

in Australia and in bases at a considerable distance from the combat fronts. This difference in part can be attributed to the peculiar combat condition in the Southwest Pacific.

No Theater worked out a satisfactory solution to the problem of the organizational location and responsibilities of its Technical Service officers. In the Zone of the Interior, the Surgeon General was also Surgeon General of the Army; the Chief of Ordnance was Chief of Ordnance for the whole Army. In this capacity they had responsibilities that were Army-wide in scope. On the other hand, Theater Commanders were apparently reluctant to recognize the soundness and practicability of such an arrangement. The Special Staff of the Communications Zone was also the Special Staff of the American Army in Europe in February 1945. After VE-day, however, this was changed and separate Special Staffs appeared for the Theater and for the Theater service force. In the North African and Mediterranean Theaters there were separate Technical Service staffs in the Services of Supply and in Theater Headquarters. When the Services of Supply was eliminated in 1944, a single Special Staff served the Theater as a whole. In the Southwest Pacific there were Special Staffs for the American Command and for the Services of Supply. As was to be expected, such duplications of Special Staffs resulted in uncertainty respecting authority and responsibility, and in large headquarters having overlapping functions.

The lack of uniformity in the functions assigned to service forces in the Theaters was evident in several instances. In the Southwest Pacific the control of shipping and the determination of priorities was vested in General Headquarters. All control of cargo shipping in the European Theater was the responsibility of the Chief of Transportation of the Communications Zone. Signal communications throughout the Southwest Pacific were handled by the Chief Signal Officer of General Headquarters, but in the European Theater the operating of the communications network was a responsibility of the Signal Officer of the Communications Zone. In the Mediterranean Theater, military rail service was under the direct supervision of the Theater Commander, but in the European Theater it was a Communications Zone activity. In North Africa the Services of Supply operated the replacement system. In France it did not. Army commanders in the Pacific operated extensive supply services of their own, with the Services of Supply far separated geographically from the Army areas. In southern France the Communications Zone operated all installations within a few miles of the combat forces. The combat commander in the latter case depended upon the Communications Zone for the closest possible support of his forces.

These differences in organization and function were evidence of a lack of standard doctrine governing logistic activities in Theaters of Operations. They created many complications in Theater relationships with the Army Service Forces. They made the training of supply officers for oversea duty a difficult task. No one could predict what functions these officers might be called upon to perform. A standard concept of the role of service forces and their organization in relation to the Theater and to the combat forces was greatly needed.

Adequate oversea port facilities were indispensable to military operations. Because of the lack of such facilities, Commanders in both the European Theater and the Southwest Pacific relied upon cargo vessels from the United States as floating depots. A lack of storage facilities and congested unloading facilities made such practices inevitable. They necessarily interfered with the orderly shipment of supplies from the United States and with the best utilization of our limited shipping resources. In Europe, as the armies hastened across France in the summer and autumn of 1944, intermediate depots, where supplies could be sorted and subsequently shipped forward as required by the combat troops, were badly needed. This deficiency had to be rectified before orderly supply became possible. In the Pacific, supplies were scattered from island to island. Supplies and facilities were not moved forward as rapidly as combat troops advanced into new areas. This resulted in the wasteful use of supplies, facilities, and service troops.

In the latter days of the New Guinea Campaign, loaded ships moved directly from the west coast to the invasion forces. Cargo vessels were on the way to Hollandia before American troops landed there. In the meantime, supplies were left at bases far to the rear. The same problem had occurred in North Africa after the fighting front shifted to Italy. A vigorous "roll-up" of bases no longer close to the fighting front should have been standing logistic procedure.

Perhaps the greatest single deficiency in oversea supply systems was the lack of adequate stock control. Orderly supply operations depended upon detailed knowledge of the quantities of supplies on hand and their exact location. The Army Service Forces endeavored to maintain stated inventories in the Theaters equal to 50 to 120 days supply. Such stock levels were almost meaningless without accurate consumption and inventory records. There was no uniformity between Theaters, or even between Technical Services within a Theater, in maintaining records of supply levels, or of using these records in the preparation of the requisitions. The supply information transmitted to the United States often contained many important errors. The critical cigarette shortage in the United States in late 1944 largely resulted from requisitioning that had failed to include consideration of quantities en route or held in ships. There were occasions when duplicate requisitions were sent to the United States for supplies that, according to Army Service Forces records, had been delivered to a Theater some time previously. Shortly after D-day, the European Theater found that it could get supplies more quickly from New York than from the British Isles. This was because confusion existed regarding the locations of stocks in Britain. Even at the end of the war there was not a single Theater that had a completely adequate stock control system in operation.

The great complexity of oversea supply and service operations had its effect upon service troop requirements. Seldom did Theaters find that they had an adequate number of service troops. For example, General Headquarters, Southwest Pacific, gave priority in 1942 and early 1943 to the shipment of combat forces from the United States. Then suddenly in September 1943 the Southewest Pacific asked for an additional 29,000 service troops by June 1944. These could be supplied only at the expense of Army Service Forces training in the Zone of the Interior. Part of the service job in the Theaters was performed by native civilians. In North Africa, Sicily, and Italy they were employed extensively under trained supervisors provided by the Army. The acquisition of large numbers of German prisoners of war helped meet the manpower situation in France. In Australia only a limited number of civilian workers were available. In New Guinea natives were employed as extensively as possible. Every Theater was constantly confronted with shortages of manpower in performing its supply and service functions.

The Army Air Forces operated its own supply and administrative services in the several Theaters during World War II. Air Service Commands in each Theater duplicated the work performed by the Communications Zones to a considerable extent. There were sound reasons for Army Air Forces' performance of those special supply and service functions that were directly related to its combat mission. On the other hand, there was less reason for the duplication of base depots, construction troops, and transportation facilities. This was wasteful of both supplies and manpower.

Inadequate advance planning, shortages of supply and service troops, and organizational confusion further compounded the already intricate and complex logistic task in Theaters of Operations. Overall performance of the oversea logistic mission was magnificent, despite the absence of adequate precedent. Lessons have been learned that are of great significance. To ignore these lessons would be perilous.

Chapter 8

MANAGEMENT

The Army Service Forces, originally named the Services of Supply, comprised a vast military, industrial, and transportation organization that encompassed the United States. Its management problem was unprecedented in size and complexity. At its peak, the Army Service Forces directly employed more than a million persons and drew on the efforts of several million more who were in the employ of War Department contractors. It operated more than 3,500 facilities and installations and engaged in practically every type of human activity. It was formed by consolidating 21 separate agencies, and had to obtain positive results speedily, without benefit of proved organization or tested methods of operation. It had simultaneously to plan and to build its operating structure. The application of techniques of good management was essential for success. Little could be accomplished without highly qualified personnel in key positions. The tasks to be performed and the schedules to be followed had to be determined. This called for continuous planning in specific terms. Sound policies, simple systems, standard procedures, and efficient methods were required. Assurance that the job was being done could only be obtained by continuously checking performance against pre-established objectives and standards.

Organization

The number and variety of different agencies inherited by the Army Services Forces gave rise to numerous organizational problems. The first involved the integration of such major units as the large supervisory staff that had been directed by the Under Secretary of War, the major portion of the Supply Division, War Department General Staff, and others. Another was to determine the place of the Administrative Services, such as The Adjutant General, the Provost Marshal General, the Chief of Chaplains, the Chief of Special Services, and the Chief of Finance, in the organization. Still other problems involved the role of the Corps Areas (later renamed Service Commands) and adjustments to be made among the Supply Services (later known as Technical Services).

The organizational pattern which was developed recognized three types of agencies: Staff Divisions, Technical Services, and Service Commands. The Staff, organized along functional lines, also included the former Administrative Services. In order to reduce the number of individuals reporting directly to the Commanding General, ASF, Staff Directorates were established whenever several Staff Divisions in a related field could be more efficiently controlled by this means. The Transportation Corps was created, thereby combining certain work previously done by the Quartermaster General and the Supply Division, War Department General Staff. All automotive procurement was concentrated under the direction of the Chief of Ordnance. Statutory authority was secured for one important adjustment in the responsibilities of the Technical Services: construction, repairs and utilities, and real estate functions were transferred from the Quartermaster Corps to the Corps of Engineers. Otherwise, the Technical Services functioned largely as they had before the reorganization. The Commanding General, ASF, was able through his staff to exercise close supervision over Technical service activities, to plan and promulgate uniform policies and procedures, and to act as a single responsible commander charged with all supply and service functions.

By the time the Corps Areas were placed under the command of the Army Service Forces, they had lost virtually all the tactical functions assigned to them by the amended National Defense Act of 1920. They were soon reorganized and renamed Service Commands, becoming the major field agencies for the performance of logistic responsibilities other than procurement, storage, construction, and transportation. The basic aim was to place as many field activities as possible in the Service Commands. The Technical Services were regarded in part as staff agencies. This policy was never carried to its logical conclusion. The Commanding General, ASF, in the fall of 1943 presented to the Secretary of War a plan that would have implemented the policy. It is believed that implementation of this plan would have greatly simplified organization and operations. The plan was disapproved by the Secretary of War. Consequently, a group of installations and field activities remained under the direct command of the Technical Services throughout the war. The most important were ports and their auxiliary facilities, procurement offices, depots, and construction divisions and districts. The Service Commands, however, were made responsible for common types of service activities at all Army Service Forces installations within their geographic areas, regardless of the lines of command. The supervision of military training was assigned to the Service Commands, whereas the control of training doctrine and schedules remained with the Technical Services.

Organizational adjustments within the major elements of the Command were made by the Staff Division, the Chief of Technical Service, or the Service Commander concerned. In order to assist key executives and supervisors throughout the Army Service Forces in the solution of their own internal organizational problems, a manual was published that carefully described the basic principles of good organization. Standard organizational patterns were prepared for the common types of subordinate elements, such as Technical Services, Service Commands, posts, hospitals, and Personnel Centers. The principles of staff and line organization were set forth in graphic and narrative form. A detailed manual on Army Service Forces organization was also published, kept up-to-date, and distributed to 35,000 supervisors, providing them with a clear statement of the divisions of responsibility and authority.

The respective roles of the Technical Services and the Service Commands in such matters as the maintenance of equipment, military training, and the supply of labor were never clearly delineated. This was impossible without making substantial changes in the responsibilities of the Technical Services. The Staff Divisions required to coordinate the common actions of the Technical Services, and the Technical Services themselves, constituted a Headquarters that was large and frequently ponderous. In order to avoid waste and duplication in such common actions as the maintenance of real property, some installation commanders were under the command of both a Technical Service and a Service Command. Such anomalies could only have been eliminated by the complete adoption of the staff-line principle, under which all field activities would have been conducted by the Service Commands.

Supervisory Personnel

The Army Service Forces constantly sought to place the most able individuals obtainable in key jobs. Shortly after its formation, it initiated surveys of job requirements and analyzed the applicant's or incumbent's qualifications for all important supervisory positions. The surveys revealed a need for higher personnel standards, more careful assignment, and the recruiting of personnel with specialized technical and industrial experience. For example, one survey showed that 25 percent of the personnel were misassigned and that 31 percent of the jobs were overrated. Immediate corrective action was undertaken, and the surveys were extended to cover all officers and key civilians in the command. Progress reports on the status of individual assignments were instituted. Assignments were reviewed on the job by trained review teams. A personnel clearing house was established in Headquarters, ASF, where requisitions were filled by carefully matching job requirements with the background and experience of the person considered to fill a position. Ninety-five percent of the misassignments made during the war were corrected. Personnel placement experts from the business world directed the program. Outstanding civilians in their field were commissioned and assigned. Only two percent of all the officers in the Army Service Forces were Regular Army officers. The work of appraisal, recruitment, and the selective replacement of key personnel continued throughout the war.

Policies

One of the first concerns of the Army Service Forces was whether the necessary policies had been established, and, next, whether the policies had been implemented by clear-cut instructions that were fully understood. Correspondence was continuously checked for indications of failure to provide policy guidance. The coverage of policies was tested in important fields by systematic surveys. A typical example was the review of the administrative machinery for the disposition of excess and surplus property. Many policy gaps were plugged as a result of the survey. Most of these gaps were traceable to a failure by higher authority to make determinations respecting Lend Lease, reciprocal aid, excess fixed installations, surplus property, and captured and surrendered enemy equipment.

The Army Service Forces reviewed policies not only for coverage, but also for soundness and consistency. A survey of the administration of nonappropriated funds provides an example in this field. It was discovered in 1943 that numerous abuses and weaknesses existed. There was no central supervisory agency in the War Department, no uniformity in accounting, no clear designation of activities properly financed with nonappropriated, as opposed to appropriated, funds. New policies and a new system providing control over the accumulation, use, and final disposition of both nonappropriated funds and property acquired with these funds were established.

The Army Service Forces was criticized in the early days of the war for the quantity and quality of its written instructions. Beginning in 1942, directives and instructions were screened carefully, standardized, and consolidated into a daily circular. This provided better control, as well as greater convenience for those who had to carry out the orders. Thereafter, a noticeable decrease in the volume of instructions emanating from Headquarters, ASF, was evident. Sixty Army Service Forces publications affecting the assignment of enlisted men were consolidated into a single circular having less than 10 percent of the original volume. Sixty-six War Department and Army Service Forces instructions dealing with property disposition were replaced by the publication of a single Army Service Forces Manual and one War Department Technical Manual.

Planning

Planning in the Army Service Forces was one of the most important aspects of management. Proper planning divided over-all objectives into their constituent parts, and scheduled these in detailed, quantitative terms. Such schedules were furnished to all elements of the command concerned with the accomplishment of a mission. Classic examples of failures in this direction were the several construction projects that, prior to Pearl Harbor, were so secret that months passed before officers responsible for planning the work were informed of requirements. One of the first tasks of the Army Service Forces was to spell out objectives. A Director of Plans was appointed in order to insure that the necessary detailed plans were prepared and coordinated. The watchword here was "how much and when?" The Army Supply Program was developed, which established detailed supply requirements, which in turn governed procurement activities. Current and long-range troop lists were prepared from War Department General Staff data on troop activation, training, and supply. An Operational Project System was instituted for securing and providing for the exceptional supply needs of the Theaters of Operations. Shipping and movement schedules were prepared, and evacuation and hospitalization were planned in detail. Advance operational data provided by the Combined and Joint Chiefs of Staff were promptly disseminated to those engaged in preparing detailed logistic plans.

Procedures

An intensive program for the standardization and simplification of general procedures was an important part of the effort to improve management techniques. Simple, uniform, well-understood procedures, systems, and methods of doing business were essential in the large and complex undertakings of the Army Service Forces. Detailed, standardized techniques, described in a procedural manual, were utilized for the analysis of existing procedures and the presentation of new ones. The principal technique was the development of the flow chart.

Page Intentionally Left Blank

Page Intentionally Left Blank

Page Intentionally Left Blank

CHART 28. EXAMPLES OF ANNUAL SAVINGS FROM PROCEDURAL SIMPLIFICATIONS

PROCEDURE	RESULT
Daily Sick Report............	601,000 man days saved in form preparation
Enlisted Personnel Pay and Allowances	360,000 copies of documents eliminated
	600,000 man days saved in preparation of forms
Enlisted Personnel Retirements	1,800 hospital beds made available
Furlough	417,000 man days saved in document preparation
Individual Clothing and Equipment Record	11,200,000 copies of documents eliminated
Physical Reclassification of Officers	1,000 hospital beds made available
	365,000 man days saved for personnel being processed
Reception Center Operations.	500,000 man days saved for personnel being processed
	935,000 copies of documents eliminated
Retirement of Officers.......	7,200 hospital beds made available
	2,645,000 man days saved for officers being retired
Separation Center Operations.	24,800,000 man days saved for personnel being separated from Army
	500,000,000 copies of documents eliminated
Procurement Office Purchasing.	18,000,000 copies of documents eliminated

Bill of Lading Procedure	24,000,000	copies of documents eliminated
	6,000,000	separate document preparations eliminated
Vendor's Shipping Document	33,500,000	copies of documents eliminated
	5,050,000	separate document preparations eliminated
Reduction in Shipping Schedules for West Coast Ports	$460,000,000	matériel eliminated from pipeline
Station Supply Procedures	30,000,000	copies of documents eliminated
Quartermaster Fixed Laundry Procedures	69,700,000	clerical operations eliminated
	416,000	copies of documents eliminated

An early, important procedural improvement was the development of the War Department Shipping Document. Previously, there were almost as many forms and methods for recording the shipment of supplies and equipment as there were shippers. None was fully adequate. A basic form was developed that reduced the work of preparing the form to one-eighth of that previously required. Ninety-five million pieces of paper, and the work required to prepare them, were eliminated annually. Checking operations at depots, stations, and ports were reduced 25 percent. The same papers followed a shipment from the depot, through the port, to the oversea Theater. They were a major factor in accomplishing proper notification of shipment to oversea consignees.

More than one-half million soldiers received medical discharges during the first nine months of 1943. At that time, 49 separate forms and an average of 20 days were required to effect discharge, and the soldier occupied a hospital bed badly needed for a war casualty during this period. The Army Service Forces developed and published a complete, new procedure. The new procedure effected discharge in only three days, eliminating 32 of the 49 forms previously required. This acceleration resulted in an estimated annual saving of 6.2 million hospital bed days, or more than ten 1,000-bed hospitals; 230,000 man-days annually in hospital operating personnel; and 43.8 million dollars per year in pay, allowances, and the cost of retaining such personnel in hospitals. Other improvements in the procedure provided the soldier, the Veterans' Administration, and all other agencies concerned with vital information that aided the soldier in making his transition from military to civilian life.

Procedures were published in manuals that generally utilized graphic methods of presentation. In addition to improving operations, these manuals served for instructional purposes. Over 75 War Department Technical and Army Service Forces Manuals containing improved procedures were issued during the war. Many existing forms were eliminated and consolidated in the course of the standardization and simplification of procedures. A Forms Control and Standardization Program was established in order to control the number and character of printed forms used by the command. The results were notable. Over 200,000 forms were inventoried, reviewed, and their use regulated; 6,100 were simplified and 125,000 were eliminated.

Work Simplification

The Army Service Forces comprised a wide variety of small groups engaged in an enormous number of activities at 3,500 installations throughout the United States. The simplification of the work of these units posed an unprecedented management problem, which was attacked on two fronts. One was the streamling of the common procedures applicable to many installations; the other was an extensive program of work simplification.

Established professional techniques for the analysis and simplification of work were made available by industry. The vastness and urgency of the problems made them unique. The orthodox industrial approach, involving careful and laborious studies of individual units by trained engineers, was out of the question. Neither the time nor the personnel was available. A solution was evolved through a series of tests in the latter part of 1942. It consisted of the Work Simplification Program, the major features of which were the reduction of recognized industrial engineering techniques to their basic and fundamental aspects; the dissemination of clear, simple, instructional material based upon the simplified techniques; the training of hundreds of people at all levels of the organization in the application of these techniques; the establishment of a program of surveys throughout the organization; the maintenance of a progress performance record on the number of surveys that were conducted; and continued emphasis by high command on the importance and value of the program.

The basic techniques of the Work Simplification Program were: The "process chart" for systematic analysis of administrative operations, the "gang process chart" to fulfill the same purpose for materials handling operations, the "lay-out chart" for physical lay-out, and the "operation chart" for eliminating unnecessary individual work-motions. Probably no program for applying management techniques has ever before been undertaken on so extensive a scale and at such a tempo. More than 10,000 persons were instructed in the standard methods developed. Thirty thousand persons participated in the actual surveys. More than 73,000 separate projects were undertaken and completed. The activities reviewed involved the employment of approximately 800,000 persons. The savings in manpower averaged 18 percent of the personnel surveyed, or the equivalent of 144,000 persons.

Work Measurement

The Army Service Forces developed its Work Measurement Program in order to provide an accurate measure of the efficiency of operations. Its techniques included the use of standard work units for various common activities, the recording of man-hours expended per work unit, and the comparison of the required man-hours with established standards. Standard man-hours divided by man-hours expended indicated effectiveness. A comparison of similar activities showed where improvements might be made and where personnel was not being properly utilized. It provided a measure of the effectiveness of personnel employed on current work load. The use of such an "effectiveness ratio" made it possible to compare the efficiency of personnel utilization of dissimilar activities and operations, and also permitted the consolidation of the effectiveness indices for installations and larger commands. This important characteristic was exploited by establishing a monthly analysis of work measurement throughout the command as a part of the Monthly Progress Report.*

The Work Measurement Program was designed primarily to provide post commanders with a management tool and to assist them in keeping the strength of organizational units at the proper level. It made it possible for them to transfer personnel promptly between various activities as the work loads fluctuated; to evaluate the effect of improvements in organization, procedures, methods, equipment, and training; to estimate future personnel requirements; to compare the performance of similar activities and installations, and to detect those having the most or least economical operations. The program was put into effect in over 600 installations and covered over 80 percent of all the operating personnel of the Army Service Forces.

---
*See p. 190.

CHART 30. WORK SIMPLIFICATION—GANG PROCESS CHARTS

LOADING REPAIRABLE TIRES TO TRUCK

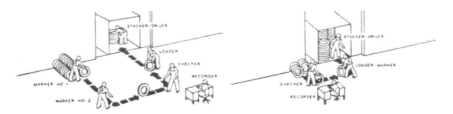

BEFORE   **AFTER**

IMPROVEMENTS

1. SPEED OF OPERATION INCREASED BY:
   - A. COMBINING OPERATIONS OF MARKER NO. 2 AND LOADER.
   - B. HAVING INSPECTORS CHALK SERIAL NUMBERS WHEN INSPECTING TIRES.
   - C. CHANGING THE SEQUENCE OF STEPS IN THE OPERATION.
   - D. LOCATING THE RECORDER NEARER THE CHECKER, MAKING IT EASIER FOR HER TO HEAR AND ELIMINATING USELESS REPETITION.
   - E. REDUCING THE DISTANCE TIRES TRAVEL FROM STORAGE TO VAN – AVERAGE 71 TO 41 FEET.
2. WAITING TIME ELIMINATED BY:
   - A. BALANCING THE GROUP.

RESULTS

1. 55% REDUCTION IN STEPS REQUIRED TO HANDLE EACH TIRE – 18 TO 8 STEPS
2. 33% REDUCTION IN SIZE OF GANG – 6 TO 4 PERSONS

CHART 31. OPERATION AND LAYOUT STUDY, WRAPPING PROCESSED AUGERS IN KRAFT PAPER

Service Control

As a service organization, the Command strove to render the best service possible. Work measurement was a quantitative measure of the utilization of personnel, but did not provide a measure of the quality of their performance. To fill this need the Army Service Forces initiated the Service Control Program. Two hundred important activities were selected, and each was analyzed in terms of two objectives: a Minimum Service Objective that represented an "average" or "norm," which, if not attained, represented unsatisfactory performance; and a Target Objective that represented better-than-average performance based upon the attainments of the most efficient activities or installations. Spot checks at frequent intervals determined how well the objectives were being met and where corrective action was needed.

Management Ideas From Within the Organization

The Army Service Forces sought ideas for the improvement of management from all its employees and military personnel. It maintained an active employee suggestion system. Under this program

CHART 32. WORK MEASUREMENT

SECOND SERVICE COMMAND

DATA FOR MONTH OF AUGUST 1945

INSTALLATION, ACTIVITY, OR OPERATION	EFFEC- TIVE- NESS	MAN-HOURS EXPENDED - TOTAL NUMBER	MAN-HOURS EXPENDED - MEASURED HOURS	MAN-HOURS EXPENDED - % MEAS.	MAN-MONTH EQUIVALENT OF TOTAL MAN-HOURS	PERSONNEL ASSIGNED END OF MONTH - TOTAL	OFFICER	ENLISTED	CIVILIAN	OTHER
TOTAL ALL INSTALLATIONS	88	11,045,354	5,262,483	48	52,249	56,241	4,252	22,588	19,698	9,703
TOTAL ALL POSTS	89	6,608,820	3,303,066	50	31,083	34,150	1,776	16,019	9,911	6,444
Camp Upton, N. Y.	97	425,588	115,001	27	1,970	2,488	253	1,226	699	310
Fort Dix, N. J.	98	2,895,064	1,124,378	39	13,403	14,635	662	9,474	2,281	2,218
Fort DuPont, Del.	64	267,934	209,304	78	1,340	1,568	89	533	262	684
Fort Hancock, N. J.	107	83,602	46,111	55	387	420	19	103	298	0
Fort Jay, N. Y.	99	330,093	207,016	63	1,650	1,617	113	491	754	259
Fort Miles, Del.	115	78,880	38,305	48	394	451	30	83	303	35
Fort Monmouth, N.J.	75	343,158	210,153	61	1,589	1,744	191	424	915	214
Fort Niagara, N. Y.	85	261,743	214,663	82	1,212	1,031	73	557	152	249
Fort Slocum, N. Y.	84	380,519	108,072	28	1,762	2,216	87	832	199	1,098
Fort Tilden, N. Y.	88	36,717	22,124	60	184	209	16	48	139	6
Fort Totten, N. Y.	75	191,974	83,268	43	889	988	54	531	394	9
Fort Wadsworth, N. Y.	92	58,345	34,722	60	292	361	22	70	269	0
Pine Camp, N. Y.	86	538,700	358,399	67	2,694	2,733	91	997	1,071	574
Post Eng Atl. City, N. J.	70	17,348	15,476	89	80	69	4	0	65	0
Post Eng Clifton, N.J.	99	16,677	14,319	86	77	93	2	0	75	16
POW Camp, Mitchel Fld, NY	125	10,390	10,390	100	48	49	3	46	0	0
POW Camp, Popolopen, N.Y.	84	18,497	17,692	96	86	89	3	49	0	37
QM Laundry, N. Y.	50	96,199	96,199	100	443	554	2	0	513	39
Serv Comd Ord Shop, N. Y.	82	288,913	152,564	53	1,338	1,431	19	0	1,412	0
U.S.D.B. Greenhaven, N. Y.	92	268,479	224,910	84	1,243	1,404	63	535	110	696
ADJUTANT GENERAL DEPOT										
New York, N. Y.	104	88,767	75,534	85	511	483	14	16	453	0

CHART 33. EXAMPLES OF SERVICE IMPROVEMENTS IN ASF

Activity	Most deficient performance	Month of occurrence	Situation as of August 45
Percentage of replies to overseas radio communications delayed beyond 2 days.	52.5%	Jan 45	12.1%
Age of oldest unpaid transportation bill.....	42 days	Dec 41	14 days
Commercial bills unpaid over 60 days in procuring offices	12,800	Nov 44	4,270
Commercial bills unpaid over 60 days in disbursing offices	4,170	Nov 44	311
General Accounting Office uncleared suspensions on hand	24,400	Feb 44	8,360
Terminations in process 4 months or more:			
War Department total.................	1,480	Jun 44	311
Fixed price contracts.................	1,360	Jun 44	255
Cost-plus-fixed-fee contracts...........	132	Aug 44	56
Time to settle terminations with claims:			
All claims........................	5.4 months	Feb 44	2.2 months
Claims over $10,000.................	7.3 months	Apr 44	2.6 months
Demurrage charges accrued................	$136,000	Oct 44	$82,000
Loading time ships in U. S. Ports............	8.2 days	Apr 44	6.5 days
Depot tons handled per 8-hour man days by receiving and shipping employees	2.9 short tons	Oct 43	5.89 short tons
Warehouse refusals.......................	5.7%	Jul 44	1.2%
Unavailability of stock in individuals depots...	17.3%	Nov 44	13.4%
Average time from confinement to sentence for General Courts Martial cases	51.3 days	Nov 42	8.7 days
Average time for General Courts Martial cases from confinement to final action by reviewing authority	79.2 days	Jan 43	13.2 days
Civilian accident frequency rate.............	13.2 per 1,000 strength	Feb 43	5.7 per 1,000 strength

244,000 suggestions were received. Of these, 36,800 resulted in concrete action providing savings in time and money. In 1943 a project was undertaken that utilized the suggestion system technique on an organized, intensive, and high-level basis, covering basic policy, organizational, and procedural matters, upon which 4,200 major recommendations were received. Over 60 percent were found to have merit in simplifying and improving operations.

Statistical Reporting

The chief purpose of statistical reporting in the Army Service Forces was to measure current progress against objectives in terms of both quantity and time. It was one of the follow-up mechanisms. The statistical service inherited by the Army Service Forces did not meet this requirement. A mass of statistical information was available from centralized mechanical compilations, but the time lag was so great that the data were of little or no used for managerial purposes. The coverage was inadequate and concerned mainly with procurement, leaving other major fields of activity such as distribution, transportation, personnel, and training virtually untouched. The existing reports were fragmentary and often did not include the same information periodically; therefore they could not be used to compare or measure progress. In order to correct this situation and to furnish reports for operational purposes, a Monthly Progress Reporting System, covering all major activities of the command, was installed. The main characteristic of this system was quantitative comparison of objectives and accomplishments. If a report did not serve as a basis for action, it was eliminated. In its final form the Monthly Progress Report measured more than forty fields of activity, devoting a separate publication or "Section" to each.

An example of the data collected was the comparison of deliveries with forecasts of deliveries. Monthly deliveries and forecasts were shown as percentages of the Army Supply Program, which itself was the production goal. In the field of distribution the total storage space available provided an objective standard against which space utilization was measured. Automatic supply requirements for oversea bases were compared with the supplies on hand at those bases, afloat, and at Ports of Embarkation for shipment. In the transportation field, ships sunk, ships constructed, capacity of ships in Army service, loaded freight cars on hand at ports, volume of inland freight, and troop movements were closely watched in order to anticipate bottlenecks and to provide remedial action.

Monthly summaries of significant data from all fields of activity were presented in the Analysis Section of the Monthly Progress Report. This became the most vital part, since it drew attention to the most important current developments and pointed up the situations needing corrective action. The Monthly Progress Report constituted a valuable guide to managerial action, and was reviewed by the Commanding General and his Staff at periodic conferences. It also served Staff Directors, Chiefs of Technical Services, and Service Commanders as a guide to corrective action within their own organizations.

Reports Control

At the beginning of the war a large number of reports were prepared that filled no real need, and a great many man-hours were wasted on their preparation. A Reports Control System was established in order to insure that only necessary reports were made, and that these included only essential data. Periodic surveys eliminated reports of limited use. Reports were consolidated wherever practicable. A continuous control over new reports was accomplished through the assignment of control approval symbols. No report could be prepared in the field without such a symbol. The effectiveness of this program is indicated by the fact that almost 1,000 of the 1,500 reports originally approved were eliminated as the need for them diminished. In June 1945 the War Department General Staff established a Reports Control System, for the entire Army, based upon the system developed by the Army Service Forces.

Personnel Control

It became evident early in 1943 that there would be a critical manpower shortage. It was incumbent upon the Command to do its job with the minimum number of both military and civilian personnel. This required a system that controlled the number of personnel employed. The key to personnel control was the Personnel Allotment System. At first the method for allotting personnel to elements and agencies of the organization covered only the military. Allotments were centrally controlled and were made, upon application, for individual activities and installations. This system was too cumbersome for a vast and expanding organization. It was also impractical in that a central Washington office could not render sound judgment respecting the myriad requests from the field for additional personnel. Accordingly, an improved method for controlling the number of personnel in the organization was installed. The new system was basically one of making quarterly authorizations for the total number of military and civilian personnel that could be employed by each major subordinate element. These elements then sent personnel authorizations

CHART 34. ASF ACTIVITY AND PERSONNEL INDEXES

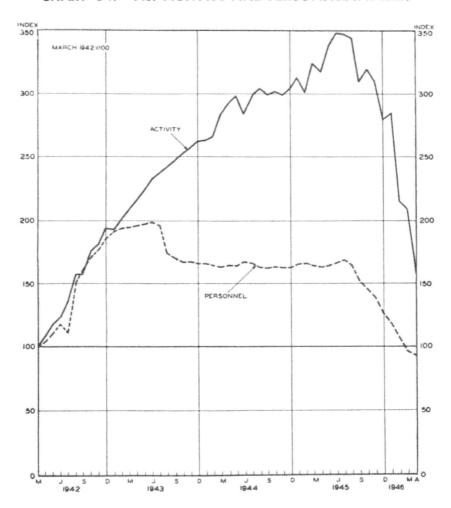

to their subordinate units, and they in turn made subsidiary authorizations. Monthly reports on a standard form were submitted through channels to Headquarters, ASF, on the numbers actually employed. The system provided strict accounting for and control of all personnel employed, and gave each echelon of command the greatest possible flexibility in handling personnel authorizations. The Technical Services and Service Commands established Personnel Control Units to make military and civilian personnel authorizations and to insure maximum personnel utilization. The work of the units was closely correlated with the Work Simplification and Work Measurement Programs.

In the 2-year period from June 1943 to June 1945, the operating personnel of the Army Service Forces was reduced 225,000, or 16 percent, in the face of an increased work load of 30 percent. This reduction was not solely the result of the operation of the personnel control system. The reduction resulted from all the combined efforts to improve management and increase efficiency during the period.

Control Units

Management was so important to the Army Service Forces that a Control Division devoted solely to its improvement was established. This Division had no exclusive right to its assigned function; rather it provided the stimulation and the leadership required to develop various managerial programs. Some 400 similar units were established in the Technical Services, the Service Commands, and at posts, camps, and stations. Much of the managerial improvement described in this chapter originated in these units. The control idea spread to the Service Forces in the Communications Zone of the European Theater and to the Service Commands of the Pacific. Never before in history has such a broad attempt at critical self-analysis and improvement been made. The concept of control was recognized in professional circles as an important management development of the war.

Chapter 9

ARMY SERVICE FORCES RELATIONSHIPS

The reorganization of the War Department in March 1942 had two fundamental aims. One was dictated by the enormous expansion of the organization from its peacetime structure. That structure had been designed for sudden expansion, to be sure, but during the relative inactivity of the interwar years the War Department General Staff had been able to perform many purely administrative and even operational functions. Under the avalanche of administrative work brought on by the war, the General Staff was obliged to decentralize the work of running War Department machinery in the United States. For this purpose there were established three major commands—Air, Ground, and Service—thus freeing the General Staff for supervisory activities and for strategic and operational planning.

The first purpose of the reorganization was subsidiary to the second. The operating functions of the War Department in the Zone of the Interior were considered as falling into two groups: one, primarily tactical, the preparation of troops for combat; the other, primarily administrative, the provision of supplies and services for the troops. The former mission was divided between the Army Ground Forces and the Army Air Forces, and the second was assigned to a single agency, the Army Service Forces. The whole arrangement was designed to conserve effort through specialization and the consolidation of functions: the General Staff was free to perform its proper mission, planning and over-all direction; the Ground and Air Forces were free to perform their proper missions, the training and organization of combat forces.

This organization was generally effective throughout the war and fully justified its underlying theory. That it failed to achieve all that was hoped from it was because of certain inherent contradictions between the theory and its implementation. In part, the failure was the result of uncertainty and disagreement regarding the extent to which the organizational structure should be consistently shaped to the two basic aims described above. From this uncertainty flowed most of the difficulties in the relations of the Army Service Forces with other War Department elements. Throughout the discussion of these relationships that follows, two main groups of problems stand out: Those derived from divergent views concerning the functions that the Army Service Forces should perform for the Army Air Forces, and those resulting from the lack of clarity in defining the role of the Army Service Forces in the logistic planning activities of the War Department.

Within the War Department

On the whole, the relations of the Army Service Forces with the War Department General Staff during the war were harmonious and productive. For the most part, the devolution to the Army Service Forces of detailed logistic planning responsibilities in support of the plans and policies of the General Staff worked out effectively in practice. The Command successfully assumed the enormous administrative tasks assigned to it, and throughout the war there was no serious criticism by the General Staff of the manner in which the Army Service Forces fulfilled its responsibilities.

A tendency soon developed in the General Staff, however, to go beyond the conception of a small staff concerned only with general policy-making and planning. The General Staff began to expand and to enter other fields. New Special Staff divisions were created from time to time. In some cases these simply took over functions assigned to the Army Service Forces; sometimes they encroached upon these functions, duplicating them in part, and raising many problems of coordination.

The Personnel and Supply Divisions of the War Department General Staff duplicated in many particulars the activities of the Directors of Personnel, Supply, and Matériel of the Army Service Forces. The Logistics and Theater Branches of the Operations Division, War Department General Staff, not only relied heavily upon the Director of Plans and Operations, ASF, for logistic data and support, but tended in some measure to duplicate his activities.

During the early part of the war, the Intelligence Division, War Department General Staff, operated directly within the structure of the Army Service Forces until the Intelligence Division, ASF, was firmly established. Despite some duplication of effort, the two agencies worked together effectively. As the war progressed, many important intelligence activities were transferred by G-2 to the Intelligence Division, ASF, such as military and civilian censorship and the Counter Intelligence Corps. On the other hand, contrary to this trend, G-2 took over direct control of certain important intelligence operations of the Signal Corps.

All financial matters in 1943 were finally consolidated under the Fiscal Director, ASF. Almost immediately, however, certain fiscal functions were transferred to a new Budget Division of the Special Staff. The War Department Manpower Board, created to establish and control personnel ceilings in the major commands, had representatives in the Service Commands and largely duplicated the personnel utilization programs of the Army Service Forces, particularly the Work Measurement Program. New Divisions were created for Civil Affairs and Research and Development, and each attempted to perform duties that had also been assigned to the Army Service Forces. In all, six organizational units were either transferred from the Command to the War Department General Staff level during the war, or were established at that level to handle functions already assigned to the Army Service Forces.

This tendency to shift logistic matters to the General Staff level betrayed an unwillingness to recognize the Army Service Forces as the supply and service agency for the entire Army and to establish the Commanding General, ASF, as the staff advisor to the Chief of Staff within this field. The development reached its culmination during the closing months of the war when a War Department order authorized the Surgeon General to formulate policies by dealing directly with the General Staff and independently of any control by the Commanding General, ASF. Somewhat later, against the protest of the Commanding General, the Chiefs of the Technical Services were accorded similar authority. The end of the war and the immediate focusing of attention on the larger question of post-war military organization engulfed this issue, just as it was becoming crucial. How it might have affected the logistic conduct of the war, had the war continued, can only be conjectured. Despite this clear drift of policy, the underlying operations of the Army Service Forces were little affected, and the Command maintained in actual practice almost exclusive control over the logistic functions assigned to it by the March 1942 reorganization.

The relations between the Army Service Forces and the Army Air Forces gave rise to an even sharper jurisdictional issue. The directives for the reorganization of March 1942 were vague on two crucial points: The services that the Army Service Forces was to provide for the Army Air Forces and the precise nature of items "peculiar to the Army Air Forces," for which the latter was to have exclusive procurement responsibility. The Army Air Forces established a duplicating medical and hospital service in the United States. Fortunately, this duplication did not extend to oversea Theaters. The Army Air Forces also had duplicating facilities for the storage and distribution of common supplies. It undertook the production and distribution of training films. It established independent publication depots. It prescribed its own procedures for the supply of air stations and for officers' clubs and messes. It demanded and obtained the right to independent action in such common service fields as repairs and utilities, mortuary procedures, the sale of coal, the operation of telephone and telegraph systems, the sale of scrap, and the administration and auditing of non-appropriated funds. It dealt independently with such civilian agencies as the War Production Board, thus tending to place in the latter's hands purely military decisions affecting allocations within the Army.

The Army Air Forces justified duplication in all these matters on the ground that the services and activities in question were essential to and integral parts of the air mission and that they could not be performed by another agency without jeopardizing the success of that mission. This conviction was undoubtedly sincere. In contrast to the divergency in policy between the Army Air and Service Forces Headquarters, however, was the strikingly successful practice among some of the field agencies of the two Commands of freely rendering whatever mutual assistance might best utilize available personnel and facilities.

The most acute and significant issue between the two Commands concerned the transfer to the Army Air Forces in the fall of 1944 of many service functions at air installations hitherto performed by ASF Service Commands. This transfer resulted from a decision by the Chief of Staff that funds for many of the common supply and service activities performed by the Service Commands at Army Air Forces installations should be under Army Air Forces control. The decision applied also to allotments of personnel. Thereafter, two independent and duplicating administrative systems existed, one for the Air Forces and another for the Ground and Service Forces.

The Army Air Forces procured aircraft and related items under the March 1942 reorganization; thus, similar procurement functions, with their separate personnel, facilities, and the systems, were performed by both the Army Service Forces and the Army Air Forces. These included purchasing, contract termination and renegotiation, disposal of surplus property, labor supply, and distribution. In contrast to this, the Under Secretary of War, the responsible War Department official in such matters, designated the appropriate Army Service Forces Staff Division as the supervising agency in each common activity. Throughout the war the Under Secretary utilized the Staff of the Army Service Forces instead of setting up a large duplicating organization within his own office.

The fundamental soundness of a single supply and service agency in the War Department was demonstrated by the harmonious and satisfactory relationships developed between the Army Service Forces and the Army Ground Forces. The latter from the beginning depended upon the Army Service Forces to handle its supply and administration, thereby leaving it free to fulfill its primary mission of activating and training troops for combat. The Army Service Forces provided and managed all supplies and services at posts where troops were trained by the Army Ground Forces. Any problems that arose were generally settled locally because of the clear-cut delineation of duties and responsibilities. Joint action by these two major Commands was standing operating procedure. For example, the Army Pictorial Service produced and distributed training films for both Forces. The printing and distribution of publications and blank forms was handled by the Army Service Forces for both Commands. Joint mess funds were established. In short, many of the activities that the Army Air Forces regarded as an integral part of the air mission were performed by the Army Service Forces for the Army Ground Forces on a basis that was both satisfactory and economical.

With the Navy

The War Department and the Navy Department had little in common at the beginning of the war, either in the form of policies or of traditions. Real cooperation had not been established, particularly with respect to logistics. Each Department had its own agencies for the procurement of equipment and supplies, although the Army had begun to procure small arms and ammunition for both Services. There was little similarity in the purchasing and pricing policies of the two

Departments. The Army and Navy each had its own storage depots, repair facilities, and Ports of Embarkation. Each had its own medical services and hospitals. Each dealt independently with the railroads, and each had its own ocean shipping service. Each had a construction organization and its own communications service. The Army and Navy each recruited its own manpower; policies and regulations governing personnel also differed materially.

Efforts had been made periodically, prior to the war, to integrate the two Services. The Joint Army-Navy Board, formed for the purpose of establishing uniform operational policies, had no appreciable success in its efforts to coordinate supply and service activities. Except in the Army and Navy Munitions Board, created to prepare plans for industrial mobilization (and engaged primarily in issuing preference ratings during the war), the two Services had made no concerted effort to coordinate their logistic activities or to eliminate the waste resulting from the duplication of their common supply and administrative functions.

After Pearl Harbor the tremendous pressure of war and the urgent need for supplies and equipment forced a greater measure of cooperation upon the two Services. Almost three years passed, however, before action resulted in real coordination of logistic activities.

Many joint committees established during the war worked together harmoniously and effectively, some under the Joint Chiefs of Staff and others independently. The Army and Navy Munitions Board, the Joint Army-Navy Petroleum Board, the Army and Navy Selective Service Committee, and many others did excellent work. Cooperation extended into certain phases of logistics. The Army Service Forces procured an increasing number of items, including subsistence and motor vehicles, for the Navy. The Navy purchased fuel oil, landing craft, and other items for the Army. The Army Service Forces operated combined induction stations for both Services. Purchasing policies and contract forms were standardized to some extent, and standard pricing for some items was established. Uniform regulations for contract terminations were also developed. Some of the duplications in communications and transportation services were eliminated, and a small degree of standardization in specifications was achieved.

Two major efforts were made during the war to achieve closer relationships. The first was a series of joint Army-Navy procurement studies prepared by a committee under the direction of the Under Secretary of War and the Secretary of the Navy late in 1944. The resulting report recommended the establishment of Joint Matériel Chiefs, under whom a Joint Director of Matériel would direct procurement activities for both Services. Other recommendations were made for the encouragement of joint purchasing in specific fields. The War Department urged the establishment of the Joint Matériel Chiefs, but the proposal was dropped. The same fate befell many of the other recommendations, although a few resulted in closer cooperation. The latter included the joint procurement of certain medical supplies and equipment, and closer coordination in the purchase of standard stock items such as textiles, clothing, shoes, and athletic equipment.

In spite of all efforts, the two Services were still far apart in the handling of logistics when the war ended. Many gains were achieved only after months of negotiation. Many pressing needs for joint action were never met.

With the Combined and Joint Chiefs of Staff

The Combined Chiefs of Staff (British and American) and the Joint Chiefs of Staff (Army, Air Forces, and Navy) were primarily concerned with the strategy and the planning of combat operations. Logistic planning, however, was inseparable from strategy at every stage. The most tentative strategic decisions could not be made without careful consideration of basic logistic limitations. Relations among the Combined Chiefs of Staff, the Joint Chiefs of Staff, and the Army Service Forces were accordingly close and constant. They were maintained principally through representatives of the Army Service Forces on various committees of the Combined and Joint Staffs that dealt with matters of logistics, and by the presence of the Commanding General, ASF, at various conferences between the President and the British Prime Minister.

It was the duty of the Army Service Forces, first, to advise the Staffs respecting the logistic aspects of proposed operational plans and, second, to provide support for the plans selected for implementation. Long negotiations often preceded important decisions because of the conflicting interests involved. Many decisions ultimately were made at the highest international level by the President and the British Prime Minister. Decisions were often made too late for adequate logistic preparations. Changes in plans were constantly made. The Army Service Forces had to anticipate decisions and to base its actions upon careful conjectures. Fortunately, it was able to forecast probable operational plans with some accuracy because of its close working relationships with the Operations Division of the War Department General Staff. Such forecasts were dangerous, because of the possibility of making serious errors that would result in the waste of time, men, and materials.

The need for unanimous approval in committee action and the complexity of the problems encountered all contributed to delays and changes that seriously hampered supply programs. The provision of the lead time required for procuring supplies and equipment was always of the utmost importance to the Army Service Forces. Frequently the margin was so small that adequate preparations were nearly impossible. A problem, gradually corrected as the war progressed, was the lack of recognized procedural channels for the coordination of matters being considered by various committees. The Joint Chiefs of Staff in the early days of the war reached many decisions that had important logistic implications, but on which the Army Service Forces had not been consulted. A Review Unit was established in Headquarters, ASF, that was advised of all pending actions and through which the views of the Army Service Forces could be presented directly to those working on joint and combined matters. This unit did much to solve the problem of coordination. Lack of adequate representation on various committees also added to the difficulties encountered by the Army Service Forces. This was particularly true of the Joint Logistics Committee; its subsidiary, the Joint Logistics Plans Committee; and the important Joint Military Transportation Committee. Considering the great responsibility of the Army Service Forces for the support of logistic operations and the fact that these committees dealt exclusively with such matters, a representation of one member out of six (which was the situation on the Joint Logistics Committee) scarcely gave the Command an effective voice in the deliberations of the committees.

The International Division, ASF, was charged with the operations of the Munitions Assignment Committee (Ground), a subsidiary of the Munitions Assignment Board. This committee, composed of British and American representatives, assigned military ground items to claimant nations in accordance with policies established by the Combined Chiefs of Staff and the Munitions Assignment Board. This system worked well, except for some difficulty in obtaining policy guidance from higher echelons. The Army Service Forces was the point of contact for the several military staffs and missions of the United Nations whenever they became eligible to receive military items under the provisions of the Lend-lease Act. Except for the

British and Russians, the International Division acted as spokesman for all the United Nations when they requested the assignment of munitions.

The committee system of the Combined Chiefs of Staff and Joint Chiefs of Staff did all that could be expected of it during the war. Although not the best system, it was probably the best that could be devised under the existing circumstances.

With Civilian War Agencies

The War Department in its relations with the civilian war agencies recognized from the outset the general principle that the civilian agencies were responsible for the over-all mobilization and utilization of national resources. These agencies were expected to allocate materials and services between military and other users. The War Department procured its supplies and services, maintaining that procurement, production, storage, and distribution were inseparable parts of a single process that was essential to the effective direction and supply of the Nation's military forces. Most of the difficulties encountered by the Army Service Forces in dealing with civilian agencies arose from the absence of clear definition of the responsibilities and authority of the civilian agencies, from the absence of effective systems for the conduct of their business, and from the delays in resolving jurisdictional disputes. In general the civilian agencies provided the Army with the materials and services it required, but the war had come to an end before workable operating relationships were fully developed. That working relationships were achieved can be attributed primarily to the devoted efforts of individuals working for the common good and not to any preplanned and carefully thought-out organizational system.

A multiplicity of new autonomous agencies was created in order to meet specific problems as they arose. These agencies reported directly to the President in most cases. The jurisdictional limits of each agency were often ill-defined. Not until the Office of War Mobilization and Reconversion was created in May 1943 could interagency disputes be settled promptly. By then most of the important jurisdictional controversies had been laboriously settled after months of negotiation.

Since practically every civilian activity had a counterpart in the Armed Forces, the Army Service Forces dealt constantly with every

Government war agency. The most significant relationships were in the fields of procurement, manpower, and transportation. Many different agencies handled the civilian phases of these activities.

CHART 35. COMMITTEES OF THE COMBINED AND JOINT CHIEFS OF STAFF WITH ASF REPRESENTATION

Combined Committees	Joint Committees	Purpose
Combined Administrative Committee (1 ASF member out of 6 U. S. members)	Joint Logistics Committee (1 ASF member out of 6)	To provide logistics guidance and advice to the Chiefs of Staff on joint and combined matters, as well as matters where supply interests of the Army and Navy conflict
None	Joint Logistics Plans Committee (1 ASF member out of 6)	A subordinate of the Joint Logistics Committee designed to prepare joint logistics plans for operations.
Combined Military Transportation Committee (2 ASF members out of 6 U. S. members)	Joint Military Transportation Committee (2 ASF members out of 6)	To determine requirements and availability of cargo and passenger shipping, make recommendations as to allocations and to handle all joint and combined problems regarding shipping
Munitions Assignment Board (Washington) (1 ASF member out of 6 U. S. members)	Joint Munitions Assignment Committee (1 ASF member out of 5)	To allocate finished munitions for the proper logistics support of operations
Combined Communications Board (1 ASF member out of 4 U. S. members)	Joint Communications Board (1 ASF member out of 4)	To provide communications, guidance and advice to the Chiefs of Staff on joint and combined matters as well as matters where conflicts exist between the War and Navy Departments
Combined Civil Affairs Committee (No ASF representation)	Joint Civil Affairs Committee (1 ASF member out of 6)	To handle civil affairs problems within the limits of military responsibility
None	Army-Navy Petroleum Board (1 ASF member out of 4)	To coordinate the procurement, allocation, overseas shipment and storage of petroleum and petroleum products for the Army and Navy

CHART 36. PRINCIPAL CIVILIAN AGENCIES WITH WHICH THE ASF HAD DEALINGS

Civilian Agency	ASF Element	Subject of Relationships
INTERNATIONAL		
Combined Raw Materials Board	Director of Matériel	Critical raw materials
Combined Production and Resources Board	Director of Matériel	Critical end items
Combined Shipping Adjustment Board	Chief of Transportation	Shipping allocations
Combined Food Board	Quartermaster General	Combined food problems
United Nations Relief and Rehabilitation Administration	International Division	Supplies for relief and Rehabilitation
Joint War Production Committee, United States and Canada	Production Division	Industrial production
Material Coordinating Committee, United States and Canada	Production Division	Production of raw materials
British-American Joint Patent Interchange Committee	Director of Matériel Judge Advocate General	Patent interchange
Foreign Economy Administration	International Division	Lend-lease and civilian supply
PROCUREMENT		
War Production Board	Director of Matériel Technical Services	Allocations of raw materials; industrial facilities, production scheduling
Petroleum Administration for War	Quartermaster General	Allocations, procurement and distribution of petroleum products
Solid Fuels Administration for War	Quartermaster General	Allocation and procurement of solid fuels
War Food Administration	Quartermaster General	Allocation, procurement and distribution of food
Rubber Bureau, War Production Board	Production Division Chief of Ordnance	Allocation of rubber and production of synthetic rubber
Office of Scientific Research and Development	Research and Development Division Technical Services	Scientific research for military purposes
Office of Price Administration	Purchase Division Technical Services	Price limitations on military items and rationing

Civilian Agency	ASF Element	Subject of Relationships
Office of War Mobilization and Reconversion	Director of Matériel	Solution of issues between agencies
Smaller War Plants Corporation	Purchases Division Industrial Personnel Division Provost Marshal General	Placement of contracts with smaller plants and internal security
Defense Plant Corporation	Director of Matériel	Industrial construction
Defense Supplies Corporation	Director of Matériel	Industrial facilities
Rubber Reserve Company	Production Division	Stockpiling of rubber
Metals Reserve Company	Production Division	Stockpiling of critical metals
Procurement Division	Director of Matériel Technical Services	Procurement of common items
War Contracts Price Adjustment Board	Purchases Division	Contract renegotiation
Surplus Property Board	Readjustment Division	Surplus property
Department of Commerce	Readjustment Division	Disposal of civilian type items
Reconstruction Finance Corporation	Readjustment Division Storage Division	Disposition of surplus and storage therefor
Office of Contract Settlements	Readjustment Division	Settlement of contracts
COMMUNICATIONS		
Board of Communications	Chief Signal Officer	Utilization of radio, telephone, and telegraph facilities
MEDICAL		
Veterans Administration	Surgeon General Fiscal Director Adjutant General	Medical treatment, pensions, National Service Life Insurance
American Red Cross	Surgeon General	Recruitment of nurses; blood donors, prisoners of war
American Medical Association	Surgeon General	Recruitment of doctors
American Dental Association	Surgeon General	Recruitment of dentists
United States Public Health Service	Surgeon General	Health matters
TRANSPORTATION		
Maritime Commission	Chief of Transportation	Shipbuilding program
Shipbuilding Stabilization Committee, War Production Board	Chief of Transportation	Shipbuilding program
War Shipping Administration	Chief of Transportation	Allocation and operation of commercial vessels
Interdepartmental Shipping Priorities Advisory Committee, War Production Board	Chief of Transportation	Shipping priorities

Civilian Agency	ASF Element	Subject of Relationships
Office of Defense Transportation	Chief of Transportation	Rail and motor transport within Zone of Interior
Transportation Control Committee	Chief of Transportation	Traffic moving to ports
Interstate Commerce Commission	Chief of Transportation	Rail and motor transport within Zone of Interior
Association of American Railroads	Chief of Transportation	Rail transportation
Federal Emergency Warehouse Association	Storage Division Chief of Transportation	Warehousing facilities
Public Roads Administration	Chief of Transportation	Highway projects
MANPOWER		
Selective Service System	Military Personnel Division	Quotas for military manpower and induction
War Manpower Commission	Industrial Personnel Division	Mobilization of industrial manpower
National War Labor Board	Industrial Personnel Division	Labor disputes affecting war production
National Labor Relations Board	Industrial Personnel Division	Management-Union relations
Department of Labor	Industrial Personnel Division	Labor relations
National Housing Agency	Industrial Personnel Division	Housing for industrial personnel
Committee for Congested Production Areas	Director of Matériel Industrial Personnel Division	Facilities and relief in congested areas
Office of Defense Health and Welfare Services	Industrial Personnel Division	Housing and facilities for industrial personnel
Civil Service Commission	Industrial Personnel Division	Civilian personnel employment
United States Employment Service	Industrial Personnel Division	Labor supply
Committee on Fair Employment Practice	Industrial Personnel Division	Race Discrimination problems
Office of Economic Stabilization	Industrial Personnel Division	Wage stabilization and plant take-overs
FISCAL AND ADMINISTRATIVE		
Bureau of the Budget	Fiscal Director	Appropriations
General Accounting Office	Fiscal Director	Settlement of Accounts
Government Printing Office	Adjutant General	Printing War Department publications

Civilian Agency	ASF Element	Subject of Relationships
Post Office Department	Adjutant General	Army mail
Treasury Department	Fiscal Director	Foreign exchange
Office of War Information	Bureau of Public Relations, ASF Section	Public relations
Department of Justice	Judge Advocate General Chief of Engineers	Claims for and against War Department and military personnel land acquisitions War Frauds
	SECURITY	
Office of Civilian Defense	Provost Marshal General Chief, Chemical Warfare Service Chief of Engineers	Plant security, Preparations against bombing and gas attack
Federal Bureau of Investigation	Intelligence Division	Personnel investigations and counter espionage
War Relocation Authority	Provost Marshal General	Removal of Japanese from Pacific coast
Office of Censorship	Intelligence Division	Censorship intercepts

The War Production Board was established shortly after Pearl Harbor. The Army, largely through the Office of the Under Secretary of War, had been dealing since early in 1941 with its predecessors: the Office of Production Management, the Priorities Board, and the Supply Priorities and Allocations Board. Steps had been taken to set up a priorities system in order to control requirements for materials, and the Army and Navy Munitions Board had been assigned the task of issuing preference ratings for munitions. Controls over contract clearance and placement had already been established. The Executive Order establishing the War Production Board vested complete authority over war production in the Chairman. Because this might be interpreted as divesting the Army of essential control over its own procurement, a subsidiary definition of this authority was essential. An agreement in March 1942 between the Under Secretary of War and the Chairman of the War Production Board reaffirmed the responsibilities of the War Department for its own procurement and supply and recognized the responsibility of the War Production Board for the allocation of raw materials, components, and facilities. Although frequently attacked, this agreement remained the cornerstone of the working relationships between the two agencies.

The first major issue that arose under this agreement was the allocation of critical war materials. The Army Service Forces maintained that the War Production Board gave insufficient consideration to strategic needs. The War Production Board was urged to establish firmer controls over all echelons and to devise an organization capable of speedier action. (The Army Service Forces at the same time developed better methods of computing its own requirements and developed the *Army Supply Program.) The dispute engendered was widely characterized as an attempt by the Army Service Forces to take over the functions of the War Production Board. In reality it was merely the insistence of the Army Service Forces that a system be established capable of meeting the critical needs of the military establishment. There was never an attempt to usurp the War Production Board's power to make allocations nor to limit its control over production. Actually both the War Department and the War Production Board made adjustments as a result of the controversy. The limited resources dictated the lowering of Army requirements; the Army Service Forces made further improvements in their computations; and the War Production Board tightened its control over raw materials. The actions taken in the last field finally culminated in the establishment of the Controlled Materials Plan. This scheme had been originally sponsored by the Army Service Forces after the War Production Board had tried unsuccessfully to operate the Priorities Requirements Plan. The Controlled Materials Plan provided allocations of specific quantities of critical raw materials to the Army and other claimant agencies, which they in turn allotted to their contractors. The Controlled Materials Plan was outstandingly successful.

Production scheduling was the second element of controversy between the War Department and the War Production Board. When deliveries fell behind schedule the War Production Board charged the Army with bad planning. The War Production Board questioned and attempted to lower the goals of Army schedules when they were not met. The Army Service Forces asserted that only the Army knew its own needs, and that failures were attributable to inefficiency in the control of raw materials and manpower. Actually the Army Service Forces had initiated close production scheduling early in 1942, and continued to do its own scheduling within the limits of the Army Supply Program, subject to review by the War Production Board.

These two major issues were examples of the controversies and the constant interplay of forces that characterized relationships between the War Production Board and the Army Service Forces. The underlying urgency was to obtain a high degree of mobilization quickly and to balance requirements against resources. Many of the difficulties

---

*See page 57.

resulted from inadequate systems and procedures and the inability to obtain prompt decisions on jurisdictional matters.

Problems of the same type were encountered in other fields. The Department of Agriculture finally assumed centralized control of the whole agricultural program for the war. The Army Service Forces, however, made most of the food procurements for all Government agencies. Rubber remained critical throughout the war. The Army, through the Office of the Under Secretary of War, assisted in the development of the synthetic rubber program. An effective allocations system was devised under the Office of the Rubber Director, War Production Board, and the Army Service Forces obtained most of its requirements. Because of the over-all authority of the Petroleum Administrator for War, the work of the Joint Army-Navy Petroleum Board, and the integrated nature of the petroleum industry, few major difficulties were encountered in this phase of war production. The Army Service Forces worked closely with the Office of Price Administration. Specific exemptions for broad categories of military articles were worked out, although the Armed Forces were unable to obtain blanket price exemptions for military supplies. In the vital field of research and development, the cooperation and assistance of the Office of Scientific Research and Development was invaluable. The latter constantly informed the Army Service Forces respecting progress of the fundamental research conducted by civilian institutions, and consequently was able to direct work into fields that were of importance to the Army.

The Army Service Forces dealt with the Combined Raw Materials Board and Combined Production and Resources Board almost entirely through the War Production Board. The Combined Raw Materials Board divided raw materials among competing interests, and its actions, therefore, had a direct bearing upon the allocation of these materials to the Army. The Combined Production and Resources Board performed the same function with respect to critical manufactured items. The Army Service Forces was able to present its requirements indirectly to the Board by means of its participation on a subcommittee. However, the existence of other allocating authorities increased the complexity of activities in this field.

Except for its close and continuous contacts with the Selective Service System, the most important relationships of the Army Service Forces in the manpower field were with the War Manpower Commission and the National War Labor Board. Adequate industrial manpower was vital to the Army Service Forces because, in the production of military equipment and supplies, shortages of manpower were as serious as the shortage of raw materials or facilities. The need to deal with many agencies with overlapping functions, and the reluctance of the War Manpower Commission to take strong or definitive action in the allocation and control of industrial manpower were of serious and continuous concern to the Command.

The Army Service Forces maintained close and constant liaison with the War Manpower Commission, both in Washington and in the field, in order to promote effective control over the recruiting and referral of industrial workers. This led to the participation of the Command in the establishment of policies and procedures for that purpose. Although the Army Service Forces constantly pressed for more efficient operation, the War Manpower Commission employed few effective controls. The Army Service Forces also attacked the problem of labor shortages by other means, including voluntary manpower rationing, ceilings, priority referral, and special recruiting campaigns. It assisted management in dealing with a bewilderingly large number of agencies, which included the Office of Defense Health and Welfare Services and the Committee for Congested Production Areas, in attempts to ease housing shortages and other conditions that contributed to labor shortages. In spite of the fact that shortages of industrial labor were the greatest single impediment to war production in the winter of 1944–45, the problems stemming from inadequate organization and controls were never satisfactorily solved.

Strikes and work stoppages in war plants were closely related to labor shortages. In this field the Army Service Forces worked harmoniously with the National Labor Relations Board. The Board formulated Government policies in labor matters and resolved labor disputes. Close working relationships were maintained and careful consideration was given by the Board to the effect of a particular strike upon war production. The Army Service Forces and the National Labor Relations Board worked together in the handling of strikes that interfered with war production, plant seizures, and wages. Although some friction developed, particularly in the case of Government-owned, privately-operated plants, this was an outgrowth of divergent views and no serious disagreement arose.

The Army Service Forces from time to time was directed to take over and operate vital facilities when work was stopped by labor disputes. Such cases were not confined to plants working directly for the War Department. In each case, the President issued an Executive Order directing the Secretary of War to assume control of a particular facility, and the Secretary of War in turn directed the Commanding General, ASF, to operate the plant. The most spectacular instance was that of the railroads. The Government assumed control of the Nation's railroads on 27 December 1943 in anticipation of a strike called for 30 December. The War Department had previously prepared a detailed plan for this contingency, which was placed in effect immediately. The president of a large railroad company was designated as advisor to the Chief of Transportation, who directed the operations of the railroads. Other consultants included railroad labor and management officials. The Association of American Railroads and the American Short Line Railroad Association made their staffs available to the War Department. Seven regional directors were appointed from among leading rail executives. Some 600 commissioned officers were assigned to work with individual carriers. Because the Government was in control, the strike-call was revoked, employees remained at work, and it was not necessary for military personnel to operate the roads. When the danger of interrupted service had passed, the railroads were returned to the owners on 18 January 1944. By the end of January, 680 out of a total of 780 railroads had signed releases that precluded the prosecution of any claim against the United States for loss during Army operation.

The Army Service Forces in the year ending 30 June 1944 took over the operation of industrial facilities on seven different occasions. These included 13 leather manufacturing companies in Massachusetts, 10 textile manufacturing plants, the utility system of the city of Los Angeles, a radio tube and lamp company, and an automobile parts manufacturing company. In each instance production was restored to normal within a short period of time. The plants were returned to private operation as soon as the basic disagreement between management and labor was settled. In the year ending 30 June 1945, the Army Service Forces took over a total of 21 industrial plants. These included cotton mills, a steel plant, a machine tool plant, a foundry, a meat-packing company, a rail car manufacturing company and a chemical company. Seven of these facilities had been returned to private management by the summer of 1945. Thirteen plants were returned to private management in the next few months. Control of the last plant was relinquished 18 October 1945.

The most controversial of all cases was that involving Montgomery Ward & Co. This firm was not engaged in any business of direct concern to the War Department. Since other Government agencies were not prepared to operate the company, the President directed the Army to take over its management, after deciding that its continued operation was indispensable to the war effort. The top officials of the firm opposed Government operation, contesting its legality in the courts, so the Army Service Forces had to assume an active part in the management of the company. The firm was still under Government control on VJ-day.

The effects of military demands upon the civilian economy were felt most directly in the field of transportation. The enormous commercial shipbuilding program absorbed extensive raw materials, men, and facilities. The movement of troops and military supplies sharply curtailed civilian railroad passenger and freight traffic. As in the case of procurement, the War Department maintained its right to exercise control over the use of the transportation facilities made available to it, but recognized the right of civilian agencies to make allocations and determine policies. In order to assure the inclusion in the shipbuilding program of its needs for cargo vessels and transports, the Army Service Forces submitted its requirements to the Maritime Commission after they had been adjusted and approved by the Joint Chiefs of Staff. Other agencies did likewise, and the program was frequently adjusted by balancing the respective needs against available resources.

The War Shipping Administration made allocations of available cargo vessels, transports, and tankers among the claimants. It had been created to control the operation, purchase, charter, requisition, and use of all noncombatant vessels under the control of the United States. An Executive Order had lodged full authority in the War Shipping Administration for the allocation of American Shipping. Since this broad authority required definition, the Army Service Forces and the War Shipping Administration in June 1942, with some difficulty, reached an agreement that governed all their future relationships. Under it the Army Service Forces operated all Army-owned vessels and troop transports assigned to it. It also had complete control over the loading of cargo vessels assigned to the Army, as well as over the operation of all necessary commercial piers and terminals. Cargo vessels were assigned to the Army on a voyage basis, so that the War Shipping Administration could control the character and routing of return cargoes.

The Office of Defense Transportation set policies on the use of rail transportation within the Zone of the Interior. The Army Service Forces had a vital interest in the railroads and cooperated in establishing these policies. It dealt directly with the Association of American Railroads in contracting for specific hauls. The Office of Defense Transportation exercised only general supervision, and largely left problems of rail utilization to be worked out between the Army Service Forces and the railroads. Prior to issuing policy directives, the Office of Defense Transportation gave the Army Service Forces an opportunity to comment upon them and make recommendations. This same cooperative practice was not followed by the Interstate Commerce Commission, however, and its orders occasionally had an adverse effect on Army movements. The Office of Defense Transportation, after considerable negotiation, worked out a block release system with the Army and other shipping agencies in order to avoid port congestion. Each agency was allocated specific amounts of cargo which they were permitted to move into designated ports each month. The claimant agencies selected their own cargoes within the established limits and issued unit permits.

The Army Service Forces was in constant touch with many other civilian war agencies. It worked closely with the Lend-lease Administration and with the Foreign Economic Administration on matters of international aid and civilian supply. It assisted the Office of Civilian Defense in the preparation of programs and in the training of civilians for meeting bombing and gas attacks. It also developed a working arrangement with that agency for protecting industrial plants against sabotage. It maintained close liaison with the Federal Bureau of Investigation on personnel security matters, assisted the Office of Censorship, and worked with the American Red Cross and the American Medical Association. Many of these relationships were hampered by inadequate planning, vague definition of functions and policies, and by the multiplicity of the agencies.

Chapter 10

THE TRANSITION TO PEACE

The postwar activities of the Army Service Forces were of extremely varied tempo and purpose. In contrast to the steady acceleration of activity and the single-minded emphasis upon greater and greater quantitative objectives that were characteristic of wartime activities, the end of the war introduced a period of diminishing activity in certain fields and of intensification in others. Nor did the contrast end there. The very process of deceleration in many cases resulted in an actual intensification of effort and in an increase in the number of new problems. For example, fiscal and budgetary activities multiplied because declining appropriations and expenditures stimulated efforts to liquidate outstanding obligations and to recover unliquidated balances. For many other activities, such as transportation, the end of hostilities brought an abrupt change in direction which, for a time at least, demanded equal if not greater efforts than before. Throughout the Army Service Forces the reduction of personnel ceilings usually outdistanced the decline in the work load and placed heavier burdens upon dwindling staffs. Demobilization, like mobilization, called for new procedures, new organization, and new facilities. At the same time, it was necessary to combat a decreasing sense of urgency and the natural tendency to freeze existing organizations and cling to established positions.

A facile distinction cannot be made between the activities of demobilization which were marked by a quickened tempo, and the activities which merely continued from war into peace at a diminishing tempo. The postwar period must be considered as a whole, at the risk of obscuring the continuity which in many fields marked the transition from war to peace.

Demobilization Planning

The Army Service Forces started planning for demobilization in April 1943. By that time the Allies had gained a foothold in North

Africa, but had not yet landed in Sicily. Victory in Europe was still an objective, and victory in the Pacific only a hope. A special Planning Division, established in Headquarters, ASF, initiated a series of demobilization studies. By July 1943 the War Department decided that, since demobilization planning affected all major commands, this Special Planning Division should be transferred to the General Staff level. Within the Army Service Forces the job of demobilization planning was continued by the Planning Division.

Decentralization was an important feature of Army Service Forces demobilization planning and action. The Planning Division operated under policies established by the Joint Chiefs of Staff and the Special Planning Division, and supervised the planning activities of the various Staff Divisions of the Army Service Forces. Plans prepared by the Divisions were, in turn, worked out in detail and executed by the operating elements of the Technical Services and the Service Commands. Over-all demobilization plans were translated into a series of "actions" that were assigned to the Staff Divisions and Technical Services. A Section of the Monthly Progress Report measured the progress of demobilization planning after May 1944.

Demobilization plans were geared to the broad strategy of the war. There were three phases: "Period I," extending from the defeat of Germany to the defeat of Japan; "Period II," extending from the defeat of Japan until all our Armed Forces, except occupation troops, had been returned; and "Period III," covering the postwar period. Although the chief objective in Period I planning was redeployment against Japan, it was recognized from the beginning that a partial demobilization was necessary between the defeat of Germany and final victory in the Pacific. Period I activities were estimated to be about one-quarter demobilization and three-quarters redeployment. Demobilization swung into full operation only upon the defeat of Japan.

The Army Service Forces encountered difficulties in adjusting its planning to policies established by higher authority. In certain instances, the absence of policy decisions by higher authority delayed demobilization. Frequently the Army Service Forces had to make its own assumptions. Many of these were later adopted as War Department policy. Sometimes its decisions were reversed, thereby causing embarrassment and confusion. In some cases, too, decisions essential to demobilization could not be obtained from civilian agencies having jurisdiction over broad Government policies.

The original War Department plan was that troops would be redeployed directly from Europe to the Pacific during Period I. Later the War Department General Staff reversed this, deciding that all combat and many service troops were to be redeployed through the

United States so the men could visit their families and receive redeployment training.

The War Department General Staff originally planned to give precedence to troops from Europe destined for redeployment to Pacific Theaters over troops being shipped home for separation. Shortly before VE-day this decision was reversed. An interim basis for the separation of high score personnel was establishsd, and personnel to be separated were moved with personnel to be redeployed. This arrangement placed additional burdens, not contemplated by existing plans, upon transportation and separation facilities.

Demobilization could not be based purely upon military considerations. A good example was the separation of personnel with high Adjusted Service Rating scores during the redeployment of troops to the Pacific. Again, in recognition of civilian demands, the Army in 1944 established surplus disposal procedures that distinguished between civilian-type property and property having only military utility.

In order to overcome the natural inertia and reluctance of organizations to reduce or terminate their activities, the day after the surrender of Japan the Army Service Forces proposed, and the Chief of Staff accepted, a restatement of the mission of the Army. This mission was limited to demobilization, to the support of occupation forces, and to the provision of reasonable requirements for the postwar period. The Chief of Staff directed that expenditures of men, money, and matériel not immediately related to these purposes be eliminated. The need for the rapid discharge of military personnel was emphasized, and all officials were directed to resist any tendency to continue activities, to demand services, or to retain personnel, supplies, equipment, or facilities that were not clearly necessary to the announced mission. In the Army Service Forces this was reduced to a terse slogan: "When in doubt, cut it out."

Demobilization of Personnel

The demobilization of personnel required compromises involving the desires of the men and their families, the economic needs of the Nation, and the imperatives of the military situation. Priority for the release of military personnel was based upon a survey of the opinions of a cross-section of the soldiers themselves. The plan devised by the G-1 Division of the War Department General Staff for the demobilization of personnel was announced on 30 August 1944. On that date Readjustment Regulation 1-1 established a discharge procedure based upon length of service, service overseas, service in combat, and parenthood. These factors determined the Adjusted Service Rating for each individual. This calculation was made twice: First, on 8 May

1945, VE-day, and later, on 2 September 1945, the date of the Japanese surrender.

The limiting factor in the demobilization of personnel was originally thought to be the availability of transportation. Careful logistic studies were made of shipping, rail capacity within the United States, and air transport. By VJ-day there was sufficient transport capacity to execute the plans of the War Department General Staff. As of VE-day, plans based upon the distribution of military personnel by residence and upon the capacity of the rail network in the United States, contemplated 18 Separation Centers. By September 1945, 22 Separation Centers were actually in operation, and by 1 November, 27 had been activated. The capacity of these centers was augmented in September by Separation Points located at posts, camps, and stations. Broadly speaking, the bottleneck in releasing personnel was neither transportation nor separation capacity. Congestion resulted from the rapid, progressive lowering of the point score for discharge, and the application of the theory that a man in the United States, regardless of the need for his services, should not be discharged until men in oversea areas with higher scores were available for discharge. This situation was corrected in October by permitting the release of surplus personnel in the United States.

Personnel demobilization required the establishment of detailed separation procedures, and the provision of housing and operating personnel, medical examinations, and assistance in readjustment to civilian life. Recognizing these needs, the Army Service Forces established a pilot separation center at Fort Dix, N. J., early in 1944. As a result of on-the-job experience, procedures were developed that greatly reduced the processing time, and reduced and simplified the paper work required in releasing men from the Army. The number of basic forms prepared for each person separated from the Army was reduced from 32 to 6, and the processing time was cut from 5 to 2 days.

The Army Service Forces prepared careful and detailed plans for troop movements in anticipation of both VE-day and VJ-day. On VE-day, movement orders for units being sent to the European Theater were rescinded. On VJ-day, orders were issued diverting to American ports all ships carrying troops from Europe to the Pacific through the Panama Canal. These orders changed the routing of some 48,000 men aboard 18 ships. Similarly on VJ-day, out-bound movement orders from the United States for 478 units comprising a personnel of 83,000 were canceled. Fourteen hundred units scheduled for direct redeployment from Europe were ordered returned to the United States.

One can best appreciate the snow-balling problems of personnel

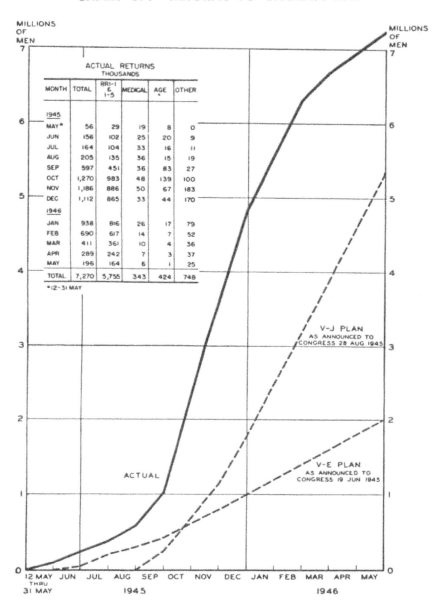
CHART 37. RETURNS TO CIVILIAN LIFE

separation by examining the quantitative record of achievement. During the period from 1 September 1945 through 31 May 1946, separations of military personnel totaled 6,689,000, including separations at hospitals, War Department Separation Centers, Army Service Forces Separation Points, and Army Air Forces Bases. The Army Service Forces accomplished 90 percent of this over-all achievement. The peak monthly rate of separation was reached in October 1945, when 1,270,000 were released. This was more than 3 times the peak rate of induction into the Army and more than twice the total number of separations (581,000) during the 4 months between VE-day and VJ-day.

Matériel Demobilization

Matériel demobilization required advance planning, the decentralization of responsibility, and the integration of programs. Supply movements involving enormous tonnages had to be abruptly reversed on both VE-day and VJ-day. As early as October 1944 all matériel destined for oversea shipment carried distinctive markings which indicated whether shipment was to continue or be held up in the event of victory. This arrangement was known as the "stop and ship" system. On VE-day and again on VJ-day supplies en route, except certain categories such as subsistence, exchange items, and medical supplies, were stopped. Similarly, prior to those two dates provision had been made for the cancellation of outstanding requisitions from each of the Theaters.

Upon the surrender of Japan, all shipments from European depots to the Pacific were halted. Forty ships en route to India and the Pacific were ordered to return to the United States. Loading operations were discontinued on 69 ships in United States ports; 25 of these were ordered to discharge their loads, and 44 sailed after making cargo adjustments. Rail cars awaiting unloading were returned to depots, and cars en route from plants or depots to the ports were stopped. Three hundred twenty-three out of a total of 354 operational projects were canceled. Cancellations involved oversea construction or special issues of equipment required for combat operations. Matériel demobilization had actually started as soon as the Supply Control System [1] was introduced in 1944. Supply Control made it possible to dispose of stocks when a 12-month supply of civilian-type items, or a 24-month supply of military-type items, was exceeded.

In 1943 and again in 1944 a special Army Supply Program [2] based

---
[1] See page 58.
[2] See page 57.

upon the assumption of victory in Europe was computed. After VE-day a third Army Supply Program was prepared in anticipation of victory over Japan. These programs naturally envisaged drastic reductions in procurement. Prior to VE-day, procurement schedules were reduced in anticipation of victory in Europe. During Period I, further cutbacks were planned which assumed the defeat of Japan. These cutbacks in procurement were effected through the termination of entire contracts, by partial terminations that reduced the quantity to be delivered, and by withholding contracts for quantities of matériel originally programmed.

Peak procurement plans for the two-front war were embodied in the program of 28 February 1945. On that date the figure for the current year was slightly above 27 billion dollars; for the calendar year 1946 it was 23.1 billion dollars. During March and April, the cessation of hostilities with Germany was anticipated by program reductions of almost 5.8 billion dollars for the calendar year 1945, and about 7 billion for 1946. The end of the war with Germany on 8 May 1945 gave further impetus to cut-backs. During May and the following 2 months the program was further reduced to 20.1 billion dollars for 1945 and 14.8 billion for the one-front war with Japan during the 1946 calendar year. Finally, upon the collapse of Japanese resistence on 14 August, the 1945 figure was reduced to 15 billion dollars or about 55 percent, and the 1946 schedule to 1.7 billion, or less than 8 percent of the 28 February 1945 program.

Two other important actions, taken immediately after the conclusion of hostilities, had immediate effect on the War Department's procurement program. On 21 August, a week after Japan's collapse, the President directed that steps be taken to bring Lend-lease operations to a close. Early in October, hearings were begun before the House Appropriations Committee contemplating the rescission of $1,729,561,000 previously appropriated for Lend-lease purposes.

The War Department endeavored, following VJ-day, to employ competitive bidding for all procurement. Advertising for bids in all fields of procurement was instituted, but in most cases bids were not offered. Manufacturers were unwilling to sell to the Army, preferring to utilize their facilities for the manufacture of products for civilian markets. It became necessary, in the absence of bids, to negotiate most procurement contracts during the first 6 months of 1946. In many cases these negotiations were forced by using Civilian Production Administration priority orders that prevented manufacturers from obtaining raw materials unless they provided the Army with its requirements.

Contract termination procedures suitable for the great activity anticipated after victory had long been under discussion. New stand-

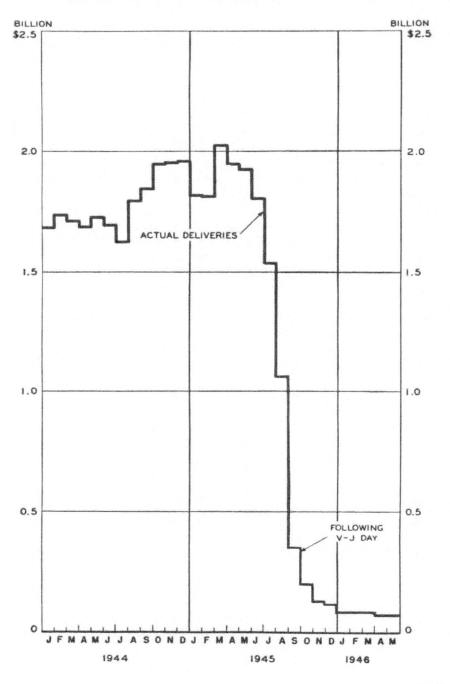
CHART 38. ASF PROCUREMENT DELIVERIES

ard termination regulations applicable to both the Army and the Navy were published during 1944. Officer personnel with civilian or military experience in the terminating and settling of contracts and the disposing of contractors' inventories were selected during 1944 and trained in a number of contract termination schools. The end of hostilities found the Army Service Forces prepared with an adequate staff of specially trained personnel.

The surrender of Japan was announced at seven o'clock, Eastern War Time, the evening of 14 August. At five minutes past seven the Technical Services released previously prepared telegrams directing procurement districts to terminate contracts. Within two days 60,000 contracts, with a value of 7.3 billion dollars, were canceled. It would be inaccurate, however, to think of contract terminations as a postwar activity. The administration of contract terminations was a continuous function throughout the war as well as during the period of demobilization. While the greatest concentration of terminations came on VJ-day, the aggregate value of terminations initiated during the period of hostilities (29.1 billion dollars) substantially exceeded the terminations initiated between VJ-day and 31 May 1946 (16.9 billion dollars). Army Service Forces agencies initiated a total of 115,214 terminations, with a commitment value of over 23 billion dollars. The wartime terminations of the Army Service Forces had a commitment value of 15.4 billion dollars, as compared with the 8 billion dollars in commitments canceled after the close of hostilities.

As a result of the flood of VJ-day contract terminations, the backlog of unsettled terminations under the administration of Army Service Forces agencies jumped from 9,823 terminations on 31 July 1945, having a commitment value of 4.5 billion dollars, to 65,288 terminations on 31 August, having a value of 10.8 billion dollars. By 31 May 1946 (after adding all terminations initiated in the interim) only 3,139 unsettled terminations, having a commitment value of $3,356,000,000, remained.

The renegotiation of contracts, even more than contract termination, represented a continuing activity that must be viewed over the entire period of the war as well as the immediate postwar years. As early as April 1942, Congress passed the first of a series of Renegotiation Acts designed to limit wartime profits. A total of about 70,000 contracts had been assigned to the Technical Services for renegotiation under this legislation by 31 May 1946. This work resulted in the recovery of excessive profits amounting to $6,278,000,000, of which Army Service Forces agencies recovered $3,974,000,000 and the Army Air Forces, $2,303,000,000. It is estimated that about 70 percent of the recoveries of excessive profits under statutory renegotiation would

CHART 39. ASF TERMINATION SETTLEMENTS, RELATIVE TO WORKLOAD*

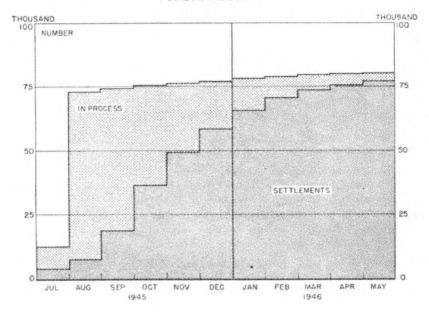

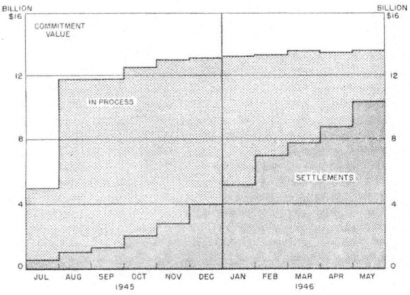

*WORKLOAD IS TERMINATIONS IN PROCESS ON 1 JULY 1945 PLUS SUBSEQUENT NET INITIATIONS.

have come to the Treasury in the form of income taxes in any case. However, the salutary effect of a program that held profits within reasonable limits was incalculable. Many contractors preferred to return excessive profits voluntarily rather than to submit to statutory renegotiation. Voluntary recoveries of excessive profits from 28 April 1942 to 31 May 1946 amounted to $4,254,000,000, bringing aggregate recoveries of all types for that period to about $10,532,000,000.

Property Disposition

Between 1943 and 1945, Government policies for the disposal of surplus property and the termination of contracts, two of the most important factors in demobilization, were in a constant state of flux. In 1943, Army surpluses were turned over to the Procurement Division of the Treasury for disposal. As a result of the Baruch-Hancock Report early in 1944, a Surplus War Property Administration in the Office of War Mobilization was set up with jurisdiction over both surplus matériel and contract terminations. The Contract Settlement Act of 1944 in August created the Office of Contract Settlements under the Office of War Mobilization.[3] The Surplus Property Act in October provided for a Surplus Property Board of three members. Appointments were not completed until January 1945, and regulations prescribed by the Board were not available to the Army Service Forces until April 1945. The Board was abolished in September, and a single administrator was established. Surplus war matériel in oversea Theaters was originally disposed of by the Foreign Economic Administration. In December 1944 responsibility for surplus in Theaters of Operations was transferred to the Office of Foreign Liquidation, and in September 1945 to the State Department. In volume of work, property disposition dominated the postwar matériel activities of the Army Service Forces as well as of the Army. By June 1944 various aspects of property disposition had become sufficiently important to warrant the establishment of a reporting system and the publication of a section in the Monthly Progress Report to record its progress.

Prior to VE-day, disposition activities were concerned primarily with attempts to put salvageable materials back into war production and with the redistribution of excess serviceable equipment. Between VE-day and VJ-day the emphasis was upon a new "supply balance" designed to meet the quantitative needs of the one-front war and the changed character of operations concentrated wholly against Japan.

---

[3] After 3 October 1944, Office of War Mobilization and Reconversion.

Revised war plans, for example, called for more infantry, more amphibious vehicles, and for fewer of the heavier tanks that had been used in Europe. These, and similar changes in strategic and tactical plans, required a reorientation of property disposition policy in order to clear depots and supply lines of matériel that was no longer needed either in the Pacific campaigns or for the postwar Army.

The defeat of Japan left the Army with vast quantities of matériel in the hands of troops, in oversea reserves, and also in supply pipe lines extending all the way back to manufacturing establishments. During the period of hostilities, for example, tanks were produced in quantities sufficient to make replacements available months later at the battle fronts. At the same time, additional tanks of new types were being produced to replace older types. The latter were no longer desired by the Army, but remained in use until better equipment became available. Because of the 2- to 5-month period between the acceptance by the Army of supplies from manufacturers and the arrival of these supplies at battle stations throughout the world, large quantities were in pipe lines when the war ended. Detailed studies of probable needs had been made long before the defeat of Germany, but at the end of the war it was necessary to reappraise needs in terms of occupation requirements, postwar reserves, and the requirements of the postwar Army in the United States. Property disposition absorbed a large proportion of the energies of the Army Service Forces following VJ-day, and upon the dissolution of the Command the following June, it was perhaps the major problem passed on to the successors of that agency.

In the handling of excess and surplus property a broad distinction was made between "principal" items (those most important for military purposes, by dollar value or in terms of the production problems involved) and other types of items. The former category was by far the most significant from the standpoint of volume and dollar value. Many of the more common civilian-type items, such as nails, shoes, and clothing but excluding certain types of motor vehicles, belonged to the second category. For principal items, it was important to establish a disposal level that would insure that all foreseeable needs would be met. Future requirements were determined, item by item, for the occupation forces, the postwar Army, and various war reserves. The quantities remaining after these needs had been met were available for disposal.

Other than principal items were declared excess to existing and anticipated needs within successively broadening circles. Thus, a given stock of matériel that was "excess" at a post or depot might be declared excess successively within a Service Command or Technical Service installation within a Technical Service, within the Army Service Forces, and finally, within the War Department. It then would be declared "surplus" and made available to the disposal agency for disposition to priority purchasers, or, if not saleable, it might be salvaged, destroyed, or abandoned, depending upon its nature, the location, or other circumstances. The Army liberalized the original procedure by reducing the amount of circularization required and by permitting, and even encouraging, the local disposition of selected categories and quantities of matériel. In some instances items urgently needed by the civilian economy were released even though the Army had foreseeable needs in the relatively near future.

The Army Service Forces was particularly desirous of declaring large quantities of civilian-type items surplus in order to assist the civilian economy at a time of acute shortage. The Supply Division, War Department General Staff, feared that property would be released that might have some future usefulness to the War Department. A board of officers was appointed by the Chief of Staff to review policies governing postwar reserves. Questions concerning the size and nature of the various reserves that should be established before surplus quantities could be released were settled on the basis of the Board's report. By 31 March 1946 the redistribution activities of the War Department had already shifted property valued at more than 3.5 billion dollars from one command to another or from overseas to the United States. This redistribution of assets did much to alleviate local Army shortages and to make Theater surpluses needed in the civilian economy available for disposition.

Disposal Agency Backlogs

Huge stocks of surplus property accumulated in the Zone of the Interior and overseas. These stocks had been declared to the disposal agencies, but remained in Army possession awaiting disposition instructions. This backlog grew from a value of less than 2 billion dollars on 30 September 1945 to 6.3 billion dollars by 31 May 1946. Of this total, 3.1 billion dollars was in oversea areas, and 3.2 billion was in the United States. Although a number of disposal agencies were involved, the disposal of 97 percent of the matériel was the responsibility of the two principal agencies: the War Assets Administration, for property in the United States, the territories, and possessions; and the Office of Foreign Liquidation, for property in oversea Theaters.

The disposal agencies encountered their greatest difficulty in the disposition of military-type property. Contractor inventory and nonmilitary types of property were disposed of without much trouble, and the Defense Plant Corporation and the Foreign Economic Administration took complete aircraft off Army hands almost immediately after declaration. Army Air Forces matériel, other than aircraft, and Army Service Forces military-type property both were difficult to sell. The growing backlog each month included more and more of the harder-to-move property. By 31 May 1946, the 3.2 billion dollar backlog in the Continental United States contained one billion dollars' worth of Army Air Forces property, less than eight million dollars of which represented aircraft. Of the Army Service Forces backlog on 31 May, 2.1 billion dollars' worth was military-type property, and less than 200 million dollars was for contractor inventory and nonmilitary-type property.

The main impact of the growing backlog upon the Army was felt in storage operations within the United States. Ordinary depot supply activities declined steadily after the end of hostilities because of the diminution of both oversea and continental requisitioning. As the quantities of supplies to be moved through the depots dwindled, the quantities to be stored mounted rapidly. The problem of storing the incoming matériel was partially solved by more efficient utilization of the space available and by increasing the use of open, unimproved storage areas wherever possible. By the end of May 1946 the occupancy of the latter amounted to over 77 million square feet. This was three times the amount occupied on VJ-day. The figures themselves do not reflect the full impact upon storage operations, because some entire Army installations were turned over to the disposal agencies for their use. The Army space maintained actually represented an increase in total storage area, over and above the increase in the use of open, unimproved area. Each month saw an increase, or at best a very small decrease, in the area utilized for storing surplus property awaiting disposition instructions. Throughout this period the space thus occupied represented the difference between a fluid and a congested condition in most depots.

Because of its nature, ammunition presented a special storage problem. The amount of ammunition in storage increased almost two and one-half times in 1945, with the greatest increase occurring during the period between VE-day and VJ-day. At the end of 1945, 85.4 percent of the space in igloos and magazines was occupied, and the occupancy of open ammunition storage sites was 83.5 percent of capacity. It appeared in December that it would be necessary either to stop the flow of ammunition from theaters or to expand ammunition storage facilities. During the ensuing months efforts were concentrated on the latter. Igloo and magazine space was almost fully utilized at the end of December, and a small margin remained from which usable space might be recovered. The total amount of open ammunition space, however, could be expanded almost indefinitely at a low cost.

Between May 1945 and the end of May 1946, open ammunition space was increased from 8.5 million to 25 million square feet. Even with this increase in total space, occupancy rose from the 83.5 noted above to 89.3 percent. This resulted largely from the return of ammunition from overseas, because production on all except a very few items had been stopped as soon as Japan surrendered. Ammunition, unlike most other types of property, was not susceptible to handling and disposition by the disposal agencies. After training and war reserves had been set aside, the remainder had to be broken down into component parts and some of these converted before disposal could be accomplished.

The storage problem created by the growing backlog of matériel awaiting disposition instructions could be solved only by a radical acceleration of out-shipments. This depended upon the receipt of disposition instructions from the disposal agencies. Out-shipments of surplus property from Army Service Forces depots increased steadily after October 1945 and rapidly after February 1946. March shipments reached 192,000 short tons. In April, shipments reached a peak of 235,000 tons, from which they receded slightly in May. The March, April, and May shipments were encouraging, but the quantities were small when compared with the total backlog. They were no greater for the period than incoming shipments. At the end of April, Army Service Forces depots contained more than 3 million tons of matériel declared to the disposal agencies, but still on hand awaiting disposition instructions. This was a quantity that would require more than a year for disposition at the April rate of movement, without allowing for additional declarations of surplus. Moreover, these quantities did not include the ammunition noted earlier, which, though not declared surplus, was in fact surplus to Army needs. During May there were signs that the generation of surplus by the Army had reached or passed its peak, and there was the prospect that the disposal agencies would begin to reduce the huge backlog.

Direct Disposition by the War Department

In contrast to the relative slowness of the disposal agencies in disposing of surplus property, the War Department made steady progress in moving excess and surplus property. The redistribution of more than 3.5 billion dollars in excess property has already been mentioned. In addition to this redistribution, the Army disposed of surplus personal property (both military and civilian types) valued at 6.8 billion dollars by 31 May 1946, of which 2.4 billion dollars represented disposals by the Army Service Forces. This latter sum included 1.5 billion dollars in sales to contractors, 150 million dollars in transfers to other agencies, 600 million in salvage turn-ins, and 100 million in donations, destructions, abandonments, and other disposals. In destructions and abandonments (representing the greatest degree of loss on the original cost of the property concerned) the proportion of the total value of disposals was considerably less for Army Service Forces property than for the War Department as a whole. With minor exceptions both the Army Service Forces and the Army Air Forces kept abreast of the disposal problem.

The fastest progress was made in the handling of contractor inventories. By 31 May 1946 the backlog awaiting action was less than 2 million dollars. Substantial progress was also made in disposing of nonmilitary property which consisted mainly of property at arsenals, proving grounds, and at Government-owned privately-operated and privately-owned Government-operated manufacturing or modification establishments. On 31 May this backlog was less than 200 million dollars, of which the Army Service Forces was responsible for 150 million.

Military property was more difficult of disposition because of its size and also because of its complexity. At the time of the dissolution of the Army Service Forces, there was no firm policy regarding types of quantities of military property that should be determined excess or declared surplus. There were also numerous limitations on the demilitarization of certain types of military property prior to disposition. Fortunately, the disposal of military property was not subject to the same pressures as were other types that were vitally important to the readjustment of the Nation's economy. Military property included a certain proportion of items adaptable to civilian use. These were usually disposed of quickly. The ratio of military property to the total amount of dispositions each month increased rather suddenly in March to about 60 percent, after running at a fairly uniform 43 to 47 percent since September 1945. This increase, which leveled off during the next three months, offset the declines registered in other types of property, and was also accompanied by an appreciable increase in the backlog of military excess and surplus awaiting action at the end of each month. Military property was the core of the surplus property problem at the time of the dissolution of the Army Service Forces.

Disposition of Army Service Forces Property Overseas

In oversea Theaters the backlog of property awaiting disposal agency action at the end of April 1946 was valued at almost three billion dollars, of which over 75 percent was Army Air Forces property. The growth in the Theater backlog was more spectacular than that in the Zone of the Interior, having risen from only about 200 million dollars in September 1945. By the end of March 1946, however, there were indications that the generation of excess by the oversea Theaters was slowing down. Determinations of excess in March were only 570 million, as compared with 1.6 billion dollars for February. The backlog of property awaiting disposal action increased only slightly in April.

In addition to approximately 2.2 billion dollars of Army Service Forces surplus in the Theaters awaiting disposition instructions, the inventory of all other Army Service Forces matériel in overseas Theaters on 30 April 1946 was valued at 11.3 billion dollars. Class II and IV supplies represented 93.3 percent of this property. This was because expendable supplies were destined for the most part for consumption in the Theaters, and ammunition items had no civilian application. Slightly over one-half of the oversea Army Service Forces inventory was in the Pacific, and almost all the remainder in the European Theater. Only insignificant quantities were in the Mediterranean, China, and India-Burma Theaters. Of the disposal agency backlog overseas, 67 percent was concentrated in the European Theater and 24 percent in the Pacific.

Theater plans for the utilization or disposition of Army Service Forces supplies overseas provided that over half of the total be retained for use in the Theaters. Of the remaining 5.27 billion dollars' worth, 1.6 billion dollars was to be turned over to disposal agencies, 1.5 billion to be salvaged, abandoned, or destroyed, and 2.2 billion returned to the United States. Of the 2.2 billion, only 319 million represented civilian-type items that would probably be declared surplus upon arrival in the United States. Noteworthy, also, was the high proportion of the total destined for abandonment or disposition as salvage. On 28 February 1946 the Theaters had estimated that about 8 percent of the total inventory would be abandoned, destroyed, or turned in as salvage. Their 30 April estimate increased the proportion to 13 percent of the total. With relation to the quantity for which the Theaters foresaw no local use, the proportion of property thus to be disposed of rose from an estimate of 16 percent to one of 30 percent. Up to that time the proportion of direct disposals accounted for by salvage, turn-ins, and "other" disposals (destruction, abandonment, donations) had fluctuated steadily between 50 and 54 percent. The percentage rose abruptly to 73 in April 1946. Indications were that this was not an isolated development, but one that could be expected to continue, because of the increasing pressure to dispose of surplus quickly and the failure of other methods of disposal.

Assisting the Civilian Economy

Property disposition activities received their greatest impetus from the needs of the civilian economy that during the war years had been denied the lumber diverted to the war effort for construction, boxing, crating, and dunnage; the steel, copper, and aluminum consumed in the manufacture of munitions; the textiles, cigarettes, and foodstuffs needed for the troops. Countless industrial plants had been diverted from civilian production and had been engaged in the manufacture of munitions. Contractor inventories had to be cleared out, machine tools and molds readapted, and innumerable other changes made in order to speed the reconversion to civilian production. The whole policy of surplus property disposition was geared to this general need, and there were certain fields in which immediate action could be taken. The Army possessed large stores of building materials, blankets, pajamas, and other articles sorely needed in the civilian economy that could be made available quickly. Efforts in this direction were pushed by the War Department Surplus Property Clearance Subcommittee, which was organized on 10 December 1945. It included representatives of the disposal agencies and other agencies interested in rapid reconversion. By 30 April 1946 the work of the subcommittee was virtually completed. Some 75 million dollars worth of property had received special handling, and about 68 million dollars of this had already been turned over to disposal agencies. This was a modest amount when compared to the total quantities of surplus property involved. The real achievement consisted in releasing to civilian markets significant amounts of items that were badly needed and could be rapidly absorbed.

Paralleling the efforts of the subcommittee was the acceleration in the return of civilian items from the Pacific Theaters. Late in 1945 members of the Mead Committee visiting in the Pacific noted that a number of vessels originally loaded in the United States were anchored in various harbors awaiting a decision respecting the disposition of their cargoes. The Mead Committee recommeded that these ships be returned to the United States and that their cargoes be made available for disposal as surplus as soon as possible. Until this was done, not only the cargo but the ships were immobilized. This recommendation led to a series of conferences between Headquarters, ASF, and the Theaters that resulted in the transfer of some of the cargoes to the United Nations Relief and Rehabilitation Administration, the unloading of some of them in the Theaters, and the return of a selected group under special procedures to the United States. A few ships that had been loaded in the Theater with "roll-up" (base evacuation) cargo were also added to those returned. On 23 February 1946 the War Department ordered the Ports of Embarkation and the Technical Services to give priority handling to these shipments and to submit periodic reports on progress.

The cargo was segregated into three categories. "H" items were construction materials urgently needed in the civilian economy and required by the Federal Public Housing Authority; "R" items were issue items required by the Army that were to be returned to stock through selected depots; and "S" items were surplus to both the Army and the Housing Authority. The special procedures called for the immediate transfer of "H" items to the Federal Public Housing Authority, the immediate declaration as surplus of "S" items, and the application of standing procedures to "R" items. As finally worked out, the procedure applied to 31 selected ships. The first berthing occurred on 16 February 1946, and the last two ships berthed 6 April. On 23 April all ships except one had been unloaded, and all cargo except small quantities from four ships had been shipped from ports to depots.

In a further effort to expedite the return and release of excess civilian-type property from the Pacific, the War Department on 18 April 1946 made special arrangements for a second program, and appropriate directives were issued. It was expected that the processing of between 110 and 120 ships during the remainder of the year would be involved. Whereas the 23 February procedure had attempted to earmark the cargoes while employing normal channels and methods for processing surplus, the new arrangement established an entirely new set of procedures and contemplated the use of four ports and eight selected depots. Arrangements were made for the War Assets Administration to review the manifests and to decide to which port and depot each cargo should be routed. Except for scrap, the entire civilian-type cargo aboard a particular vessel was directed to a single depot, where it would be declared surplus and turned over to the War Assets Administration. Incidental items of military property in a cargo were excepted from the procedure. By 23 May 12 ships were under the orders of the 18 April directives. Three had reached port, and their cargoes were on their way to the designated depots.

Demobilization of Installations

The War Department's need for such facilities as ports, depots, training centers, and manufacturing plants depended upon its matériel and personnel programs. Although some command installations were declared surplus, many were maintained in an inactive status for use during redeployment and demobilization. In March and April 1945 all contracts were cancelled for the construction of industrial facilities that would not be in full production by September 1945. Construction of command facilities was stopped, except the program for additional hospital and separation center capacity.

By 31 January 1946, 200 Army Service Forces industrial facilities, valued at 764 million dollars and owned or sponsored by the War Department, had been relinquished. Another 182 such facilities valued at 3.7 billion dollars were placed in the standby, excess, or surplus categories. Only 77 Army Service Forces industrial facilities, worth less than 1.2 billion dollars, were still in operation. The latter group included 68 War Department-owned facilities costing 1.1 billion dollars. The majority of these were part of our permanent system of arsenals.

From 1 September 1945 through 31 May 1946, 103,526 plant clearance requests were made to the War Department by war contractors who had on hand either War Department-owned equipment or inventories of raw materials, parts, and components. On 31 May only 1,934 of these remained to be handled. The backlog of cases to be handled had decreased rapidly from the peak in November of 22,360.

The Army Service Forces and the Army Ground Forces occupied about 1,500 command installations, exclusive of rented office space, in the United States during the war. The total troop capacity of the posts, camps, and stations was approximately 2,450,000 men. By 31 May 1946 active troop capacity had been reduced to 995,000 men; capacity for 660,000 was in inactive status; and capacity for 795,000 had been declared surplus. Thirty-five general hospitals, 26 port installations, and 45 separate prisoner of war camps had also been placed in the category of surplus. The necessity for storing War Department reserves and handling surplus property prior to disposal made it impossible to eliminate warehouses and depots at this stage of the demobilization program. By 31 August 1945 the total value of command and industrial real estate of the War Department that had been certified to the War Assets Administration for disposal was valued, on a cost basis, at $142,386,000. By 31 May 1946 the real property of the War Department certified to the War Assets Administration for disposal had increased to $2,025,370,000. Between these two dates the number of active real estate leases held by the War Department had declined by 3,163, and annual rentals for active leases had decreased from 48 million dollars to 32 million. Annual rentals for Army Service Forces leases had diminished from 33 million to 23 million dollars during this period.

Transportation

A brief but severe crisis in the movement of troops in the United States occurred during the latter part of December 1945 and the early part of January 1946. Actually, the peak month for troop movements of all kinds was August 1945, when almost 1.2 million men were transported in organized groups. In December, although the aggregate movements declined to slightly more than a million, the number of returnees using rail transport (which had been only about 550,000 in August) increased to over 800,000. The bulk of this traffic, moreover, was concentrated on the west coast. Debarking veterans from the Pacific numbered less than 50,000 in August, but 4 months later over 400,000 of them poured into ports and staging areas. In all, some 828,000 returning troops passed through the Ports of Embarkation during December. In the latter part of the month, so many men were arriving on the west coast that staging and other areas opened for the emergency were unable to handle the load. Many troops had to be held on board ship. Around Christmas time almost 99,000 had to be held on the west coast for over two days because of the lack of transportation. In December almost 84,000 men who were entitled to Pullman service for rail trips in excess of 48 hours were deprived of it. The situation was eased by the assignment of additional transportation facilities to the Army. Three-fourths of the Nation's Pullman capacity was made available for troop service, and additional troop sleepers were delivered by manufacturers. By mid-January the pressure was relieved, mainly because of the rapid diminution in the number of troops arriving from overseas.

The end of hostilities naturally tended to reverse the ratio between supplies flowing overseas and those returning to this country. The flow of outbound shipments dwindled and more and more matériel was returned from oversea Theaters, until inbound cargo received at the ports (1,086,000 measurement tons) for the first time exceeded the volume of outbound cargo (630,000 measurement tons) in December 1945. This was because of a rapid increase in the volume of cargo returned from the Pacific. Shipments from the Pacific amounted to more than half the total volume in March. The total cargo traffic declined after January. The Army, consequently, reduced the number of ships under its control. The number had fallen to 546 at the end of May from a total of over 1,700 ships under Army control at the end of hostilities.

Civilian Supply

The War Department's civilian supply program for the areas occupied by our troops was carried on in the midst of a growing world food crisis. The task of administering this program was the responsibility of the International Division, ASF, and became its major acvitity after the termination of the Lend-lease program in the fall of 1945.

The need for relief supplies for Italy had become more acute after

VE-day. As a stopgap measure, even though the military justification no longer existed, the War Department supported the Foreign Economic Administration by the procurement of supplies valued at 100 million dollars through December 1945. This measure had been endorsed by the President in July. Finally, in August, the United Nations Relief and Rehabilitation Administration included Italy in its program. This terminated combined military responsibility for liberated areas in Europe; the provinces of Venezia-Giulia and Udine in northeast Italy continued to be a combined military responsibility, however, because of the border dispute between Yugoslavia and Italy, and because the area dominated the supply line from the Adriatic to Austria. The last Army shipments to Italy and the liberated areas, totaling 17,000 tons, arrived in November. Thereafter, the War Department's civilian supply program in Europe involved only Venezia-Giulia and Udine, and the United States Zones of Germany and Austria.

The continuation of military responsibility for a limited degree of civilian supply in occupied territories was necessary to safeguard troops against disease and unrest. The policy governing this responsibility was complicated by various political factors. In Italy the long period of military operations had required the continuance of military responsibility for the supply of the rear areas through which the supply lines passed. In July 1945 attention was abruptly focused upon civilian supply in Austria and Germany, because joint Anglo-American responsibility for supply was continued in these areas without combined responsibility for administration. At the dissolution of Supreme Headquarters, Allied Expeditionary Forces, the American forces assumed the task of supplying the French occupation zones in both Germany and Austria. Combined supply responsibility for occupied areas was formally terminated with the completion of October loadings, and the flow of civilian supplies under combined responsibility gradually tapered off during the first 2 months of 1946. The first important shipments of civilian supplies under United States unilateral responsibility were delivered to Europe in January 1946.

Early in November 1944 the State-War-Navy Coordinating Committee was organized to insure coordination of the military, naval, and foreign policies of the United States. The following March the Joint Chiefs of Staff created a Joint Civil Affairs Committee to advise it respecting joint occupation policies. The Director of the International Division, ASF, was designated as a member of the Committee. The directive governing the American occupation zone of Germany required that sufficient civilian supply imports be furnished to prevent starvation, disease, and unrest, but that no supply be permitted which would support basic living standards in Germany on a higher level than the average existing in the neighboring United Nations. Imports, moreover, were not to include scarce food items, except wheat and flour.

This policy was impracticable. Aside from the difficulty of determining how much supply would maintain living conditions at precisely the same level as that of neighboring areas, the growing world shortage of all food items, including wheat and flour, made a revision of the policy necessary. By the end of 1945, conditions in Germany were becoming intolerable, and it was decided that Theater requests should be handled essentially on the same basis as during military operations.

The supply of the occupied areas was complicated by the Presidential directive of 29 July 1945 which placed upon the War Department responsibility for the procurement and initial financing of all imports into Germany for which the Government of the United States might assume responsibility. This involved the War Department in world trade and finance, and extended its responsibilities beyond anything previously envisaged. The new financial responsibilities, moreover, embraced liabilities over which the War Department had no control and against which it could expect no offsetting credits for German exports.

American military responsibility in the Pacific for the civilian supply of the Netherlands East Indies was automatically terminated by transferring these islands from the Southwest Pacific Area to the Southeast Asia Command in July 1945. The War Department assured the Netherlands Purchasing Commission, however, that those items in the latter's program that had been certified as militarily necessary for procurement in the United States would not be affected by the transfer. In the Philippines the War Department's supply responsibility was terminated upon the completion of August loadings, and the Philippine Commonwealth Government assumed full civil supply responsibility thereafter. The Foreign Economic Administration, through the United Commercial Company, undertook to support the Commonwealth relief program by purchasing supplies in the United States.

The surrender of Japan in September 1945 occurred before plans for the occupation had been fully developed. All civilian supply estimates for the Japanese islands had been based upon operational assumptions, and the extent of civilian supply requirements under occupational conditions was not clear for several months. Civilian supply program developed in connection with projected operations had called for the provision of 1,500 calories per person per day, as opposed to the 2,000 calorie scale adopted in the European occupied areas. By the end of the year, however, it was apparent that substantial additional quantities of food would be required, as had been the case in Europe. As in Germany, the question of payment for imports was closely related to the expansion of exports. It appeared that the War Department might be called upon to supply large quantities of raw materials to Japan in order to stimulate exports.

A budget drawn up in March 1945 for the Fiscal Year 1946, based upon the assumption that operations would continue on two fronts through the calendar year 1946, called for a total expenditure of $1,365,000,000 for the administration of occupied areas. When revised and presented to Congress in June 1945, this item in the budget was reduced to about 294 million dollars to provide for occupied areas in Western Germany, Austria, and the Far East. Sufficient information had been received from the Theaters by 30 November 1945 to indicate that food requirements alone for Germany, Austria, and Japan might run well in excess of 400 million dollars. Accordingly, a revised 1946 bulget amounting to over 650 million dollars was presented to Congress in December. By the end of the year preliminary estimates indicated that 1947 budget needs might exceed 800 million dollars.

Measured quantitatively, deliveries of civilian supplies to Europe declined sharply from the peak month of August 1945 (almost one million long tons) through the balance of the year. Deliveries in December totaled only 66,214 tons. In January and February 1946 a sharp rise occurred, with shipments delivered in the latter month totaling over 190,000 tons. This marked the peak in deliveries during the post-hostilities. During the remaining months of Army Service Forces existence, the intensified world food crisis reduced deliveries of civilian supplies to Europe to an average well below the 100,000-ton mark. Even though requirements were successively reduced in light of estimated availability, the backlog of unfilled requisitions increased from month to month, reaching a total of almost 290,000 tons at the end of April. Although reduced slightly at the end of May, the backlog amounted to three times the average monthly deliveries for the previous 6 months. The backlog of requisitions for the United States Zone in Germany (three-fourths of the total) was six times greater than the volume of deliveries to Germany in May.

Civilian supply shipments to the Pacific amounted to no more than a few hundred tons until the spring of 1946. A program was submitted to the War Department in January to implement the policy of preventing disease and civil unrest in Japan. The program contemplated the shipment of 1,816,000 long tons during the first half of 1946, and an additional 1,477,000 long tons during the second half. Foodstuffs made up 89 percent of the total tonnage. This program, which was 69 percent larger than the total tonnage of civilian supply shipped from January through June 1945, was to be augmented by additional requirements for "accomplishing the objectives of the occupation," and by additional quantities requested by the Japanese Government. The first large deliveries under this program were made in April 1946 and totaled almost 123,000 tons, most of which was foodstuffs. Deliveries in May fell to 69,800 tons. Even though requirements through June had been reduced by the Department of Agriculture to about 600,000 tons, it was obvious that deliveries would fall far short of this total.

In an effort to ease the food emergency by increasing the productivity of distressed areas, the War Department inaugurated a program of fertilizer production. This involved resumption of the operation of ammunition plants having a total monthly capacity of 88,000 tons of ammonium nitrate. These plants, however, would not come into full production for from 9 to 12 months after the initiation of the project, and it appeared that a world deficit in phosphates and nitrogen was inevitable during 1947.

Food Conservation

Part of the War Department's share in the Government's battle against world famine was a special program undertaken in response to the President's appeal to the Nation to "tighten its belt." In the United States the master menus for all military personnel for February 1946 and succeeding months reduced the bread ration from 15 to 12 pounds per 100 men. This represented a saving of over 10 million pounds of wheat in 1946. By increasing the extraction of flour to 80 percent after 1 April, another 8.9 million pounds of wheat were saved. Savings of various other food items included 76,000 pounds of sugar each month, 50,000 gallons of syrup, 84,000 pounds of flour, and one million pounds of bread. These and similar measures were part of the conservation program administered by the Quartermaster Corps.

Repatriation of United States Dead

The President signed Public Law 383 on 16 May 1946, which provided for the evacuation and return of World War II dead, if desired by the next of kin. The program was made the responsibility of the Quartermaster General, who was also Chief of the American Graves Registration Service. The official sanction thus given merely crystallized the objectives of a program for which the Army Service Forces had long been actively preparing.

Oversea Graves Registration Commands had been active since VJ-day locating missing remains, identifying unknown dead, and concentrating isolated remains in temporary American military cemeteries.

Some 396 temporary cemeteries containing over 250,000 graves were established by the Army throughout the world. An additional 18,000 isloated burials were located and reported. It was estimated in May 1946 that unlocated remains in oversea areas numbered 19,650, giving an estimated total of remains to be handled of over 292,000. Legislation was under consideration to provide for the establishment of one or more national cemeteries in each State and in Alaska, Hawaii, and Panama. On the basis of the experience of the First World War, it had been anticipated that not more than one-sixth of the repatriated dead would be finally interred in national cemeteries in this country.

The appropriation of a 92.5 million dollar fund initiating the repatriation program was passed by the House of Representatives on 29 May. This was the initial appropriation for a program that would cost approximately 200 million dollars. Senate action on the appropriation was expected at an early date.

In the oversea Theaters, graves registration personnel had encountered numerous obstacles in their search for missing remains. Searching operations in China were seriously hampered by the fact that the maintenance of roads, bridges, and airfields formerly performed by American personnel had been abandoned or turned over to the Chinese Government. The two planes that had been used by searching detachments were no longer available after 1 May 1946. In the India-Burma Theater natural impediments, such as thick jungles and monsoons, combined with political unrest and banditry, hindered operations. In Europe the entire area controlled by Russia was closed to search and exhumation teams. In Japan it was discovered in some cases that the dead had been cremated and interred in communal graves. Identification frequently required a long and tedious tracing of personal effects or other painstaking research, such as the matching of fingerprints and tooth charts.

Although legislation had been approved, it was estimated that the program had been delayed as much as six months or more because of the difficulties encountered in procuring suitable caskets and shipping cases. The shortage of steel caused by coal and steel strikes in the spring of 1946 was the principal obstacle to casket procurement. Schedules for the initial contracts for 20,000 caskets indicated that first deliveries could not be made until early 1947. The exhumation program was revised, and the first remains were expected to be returned in mid-1947.

Dissolution of the Army Service Forces

The demobilization affected all fields of Army Service Forces activity. Immediate steps were taken to reduce the Army Service Forces staff to proportions commensurate with the new mission of the Army. The entire structure of the Command was reexamined, and its Staff Divisions and the Technical Services were directed to consolidate and eliminate functions which, though perhaps useful, were no longer essential. Between 31 August 1945 and 31 May 1946 the personnel of the Army Service Forces was reduced 50 percent, or from about 1,227,000 to 638,000 persons.

During the war the Army Service Forces had submitted to the Chief of Staff several proposals that contemplated the retention of a single administrative and supply agency for the War Department. Immediately after the end of the war, however, the Assistant Deputy Chief of Staff announced the creation of a board of officers, headed by Lieutenant General Alexander M. Patch, to study organizational matters. The report of the Board was submitted to the Chief of Staff on 18 October 1945. It outlined the organization finally put into effect in June 1946, although the plan was modified in certain details by the Board that later functioned under the chairmanship of Lieutenant General William H. Simpson.

On 11 June 1946 at 0001 hours, the Army Service Forces ceased to exist. The major functions of Headquarters, ASF, were decentralized or returned to the War Department General and Special Staffs, and the Chiefs of the Technical and Administrative Services regained their prewar status, reporting to the Chief of Staff through the appropriate General Staff Divisions.

An outstanding feature of the Patch-Simpson Board plan was the distribution of most Army Service Forces functions between two new agencies. All service, supply, and procurement activities were combined with those of the G-4 or Supply Division of the War Department General Staff. The new Division thus formed, the Service, Supply and Procurement Division, was to supervise the performance of these activities throughout the Army, by whatever agency or command. In addition, the Director of this Division reported directly to the Under Secretary of War on procurement and industrial matters. This provision was designed to prevent the growth of two supervisory organizations, one under the Chief of Staff and one under the Under Secretary of War. The second principal successor agency to the Army Service Forces was the Personnel and Administration Division of the War Department General Staff. This organization assumed the responsibilities of the former G-1 Division of the General Staff and the various personnel and administrative responsibilities of the Army Service Forces.

The six agencies comprising the new War Department General Staff were: The Personnel and Administration Division; the Intelligence Division; the Organization and Training Division; the Service, Supply, and Procurement Division; the Plans and Operations Division; and the Research and Development Division. The heads of General Staff divisions were called Directors, rather than Assistant Chiefs of Staff as in the prewar organization, giving them a greater measure of independent authority. The responsibility for logistic planning was vested in the new Service, Supply, and Procurement Division. The Technical Services retained control of their own special field installations. Post organizations in the Zone of the Interior were taken over by the Army Ground Forces and Army Air Forces, and the Service Commands, as such, disappeared. The field structure of the War Department consisted of six Army Areas, the Military District of Washington, and certain exempted installations. The six Army Areas were under the command of the Army Ground Forces, and the six coterminous Air Defense Areas under the Army Air Forces.

Certain details of the distribution of former Army Service Forces functions may be noted. The new Personnel and Administration Division of the General Staff inherited the functions of the Military Personnel Division, ASF, and assumed jurisdiction over the Adjutant General's Office (to which were added the functions of the Personal Affairs Division). The civilian personnel functions of the former Industrial Personnel Division, ASF, had been transferred to the Office of the Secretary of War. Labor supply and industrial relations activities were transferred to the Service, Supply, and Procurement Division as part of its procurement responsibility. One important personnel function had been shifted from the Army Service Forces before the reorganization. The Information and Education Division had, with the Public Relations Division and the Legislative and Liaison Division, been placed for coordination under a Chief of Public Information, who reported to the Deputy Chief of Staff. The Special Services Division, ASF, became an Administrative Service. The military training activities of the Army Service Forces were placed under the supervision of the new Organization and Training Division. The intelligence activities of the Command were placed under the Intelligence Division, and the Research and Development Division, ASF, was absorbed by the new Research and Development Division of the General Staff.

The reorganization of the War Department provided no clearcut solution to the problem of the duplicating supply and administrative activities of the Army Air Forces, although the announced policy of increased autonomy for the Army Air Forces made the reservation that duplication and overlapping in administrative and service activities were to be avoided. The establishment of a separate field structure for the Army Air Forces in the Zone of the Interior gave that arm an additional measure of independence.

CHART 40. MEASURES OF SELECTED ASF ACTIVITIES THROUGH 31 MAY 1946

PROCUREMENT OF MUNITIONS
ASF TOTAL*..................................... $69,626,000,000
    Ordnance Department.............. 34,213,000,000
    Quartermaster Corps................ 21,951,000,000
    Corps of Engineers................. 4,880,000,000
    Signal Corps...................... 3,972,000,000
    Transportation Corps............... 2,115,000,000
    Chemical Warfare Service........... 1,700,000,000
    Medical Department................ 795,000,000
Lend-Lease transfers to all countries (thru Dec 45)...... 15,700,000,000
Civilian supply shipments (thru Apr 46) (long tons)...... 7,873,000
Value of equipment repaired (peak) (Sep 44).......... 476,000,000

EXCESS AND SURPLUS PROPERTY
    Excess property transferred to other agencies..... 154,900,000
    Excess property sold to war contractors.......... 1,504,800,000
    Other disposals of excess property.............. 673,200,000
Surplus property declared to disposal agencies
    ASF—Total 4,362,500,000
        Ordnance 1,499,600,000
        Signal 567,800,000
        Engineers 800,100,000
        Chemical Warfare............ 121,200,000
        Medical 93,400,000
        Quartermaster 636,500,000
        Transportation 260,400,000
        Service Commands............ 383,600,000
    Surplus disposals by disposal agencies.......... 2,113,500,000
    Receipts from sale of salvage.................. 174,100,000
    Plant clearance requests received.............. 103,526
    Plant clearance requests completed............ 101,592

STORAGE AND ISSUE
    Total storage space occupied (peak) (May 46)
    (sq. ft.)................................ 259,211,000
        Warehouse and shed space occupied (peak) (Feb. 46) (sq. ft.) 69,524,000

*Above procurement totals include actual deliveries to 31 December 1945 and estimated deliveries from 1 January to 31 May 1946.

STORAGE AND ISSUE—Continued
 Total storage space occupied—Continued
  Igloo and magazine space occupied (peak) (May 46) (sq. ft.) 28,523,000
  Open-hardstanding space occupied (peak) (Mar. 46) (sq. ft.) 65,696,000
  Other types (peak) (May 46) (sq. ft.) 99,990,000
 Depot receipts (short tons).................... $92,700,000
 Depot shipments (short tons).................... 74,643,000
 Requisition line items shipped from depots...... 118,400,000

TRANSPORTATION (thru 31 May 46)
 Cargo capacity of ships in Army service (peak Dec. 44) (ship tons).................... 17,700,000
 Cargo shipped overseas (ship tons)............. 135,000,000
  Atlantic Theaters (ship tons).... 82,000,000
  Pacific Theaters (ship tons)..... 53,000,000
 Cargo received from oversea (ship tons)........ 15,495,000
 Passenger capacity of ships in Army service (peak Aug. 45).................... 666,000
 Troops and other passengers embarked for oversea 8,300,000
  Atlantic Theaters............. 5,300,000
  Pacific Theaters............... 3,000,000
 Troops and other passengers debarked from oversea 7,222,000
 Patients debarked from oversea............... 644,000
 Rail freight (ton-miles).................... 229,000,000,000
 Tonnage handled by Army-Navy consolidated car service s/t (thru Jan. 46)................ 2,389,000
 Troops moved in organized groups by rail...... 40,000,000

Chapter 11

LOGISTIC LESSONS OF WORLD WAR II

The full logistic implications of World War II must await a complete assaying of our experience. The chief lessons, however, are already apparent. The roles played by strategy and tactics, by military leadership, and by the man in combat are well known. Important and decisive as they were, they were completely dependent upon adequate logistic support. Moreover, logistic limitations in many cases dictated our strategy, as well as the type of campaign to be fought and the timing of its initiation.

Our strategy, in general, was to hold the enemy at bay while gathering our strength for offensive action and then, because we were unable, either from the standpoint of human or material logistics, to attack both at once, to give priority to the destruction of the most formidable—Germany. The holding phase of our strategy included the provision of all possible material logistic assistance to our Allies, the securing of lines of communications, and a preliminary offensive against the enemy's logistic potential by bombing his industrial plant, disrupting his lines of communications, and depriving him of raw materials. The second phase of our strategy was implemented only when our men were trained and we were able to bring to bear preponderant weight in material. We then launched the all-out assault and offensive, first in Africa and Europe, and later in the Pacific.

Ultimate victory in each Theater was assured when the quantity and quality of our weapons and equipment surpassed those of the enemy. If any indisputable logistic lesson can be drawn from World War II, it is that in any major war involving industrial powers no nation can hereafter emerge victorious without substantial and sustained superiority over its enemy in the quality and quantity of its weapons and supporting equipment.

World War II compelled the United States to utilize its resources on a greater scale than ever before. Labor, industry, agriculture, transport, science, the military—all were essential to victory. All civilian activities were affected by, and most of them in varying degrees contributed to, the war effort.

Before World War II, it had been customary to consider the potential resources of the United States as practically unlimited and sufficient for any war in which this country might become involved. The demands of World War II in some respects reached the limits of our resources. There were at all times practical limitations of one kind or another upon the production of essential items of munitions. It was always necessary to balance imperatives and to readjust requirements to available resources. It is generally true that the Armed Forces were adequately supplied, but it is also true that there were many critical shortages of important items.

The controls imposed for the purpose of directing the resources of the Nation into war channels were neither as complete nor as severe as those of our Allies or the enemy. Conservation measures and many restrictions on materials and facilities for nonessential production were voluntary or only partially effective. Except by a few indirect and rather ineffective devices, we had no means of controlling industrial and agricultural manpower. Production for civilian use continued at a considerably higher level than that of either the enemy or our Allies. That we could have increased the production of munitions by means of more stringent Government controls is a certainty.

Any future major war, regardless of the weapons and tactics employed, will be even more "total" than World War II. Great quantities of old, as well as new and more intricate types of munitions, and faster and faster means for transporting military forces over great distances will be required. Measures for the protection of the United States itself against guided missiles, radioactivity, and chemical and bacteriological warfare will require huge additional expenditures of manpower and materials. **Our logistic potential will be taxed to the** utmost. Only the fullest utilization of our resources will assure us the best possible chance for victory.

Perhaps the most significant lesson of World War II is that the military potential of a nation is directly proportional to the Nation's logistic potential. That our resources are not unlimited is the first hard fact faced in applying that lesson. Next is that the slightest delay or inefficiency in harnessing our logistic resources may cost us victory.

America's contribution to victory in World War II was decisive because: its raw materials were relatively abundant; its basic industry was larger and more productive than the enemy's; its productive plant was beyond enemy striking power; there was time in which to produce munitions, to train our military forces, to organize our Government and economy for war. In both World Wars, we had advance warning and a period of protection by our Allies in which to mobilize our strength. No enemy will make the same mistake a third time. Our military forces, Government, and economy must be carefully and skillfully prepared for instant, complete mobilization in defense of the Nation.

Time is the most precious element in logistic preparations for security. Measures must be prepared in advance for the all-out logistic mobilization that must be completed between the time when danger threatens and the time that war actually strikes. Our intelligence must give us adequate forewarning. Reserves of supplies and equipment, of machine tools, of munitions plants, of strategic materials, and of trained manpower must be maintained to bridge the gap between peacetime operations at the time of the warning of danger and full conversion to meet aggression. Mobilization must be rapid, efficient, and automatic so that fully trained and equipped forces, supported by the full-blast production of munitions, will be available the moment the United States is attacked. The alternative would be to create and maintain a large, active military establishment with its vast stores of munitions, and constantly to supplant, in quantity, older weapons and equipment with the latest types. This would be contrary to our national tradition, and the cost prohibitive.

It is imperative that advance plans provide for more effective organization encompassing the civilian war agencies. Most serious duplications, wasteful methods, and complex procedures existed during World War II, when the organization of these agencies was largely improvised. Their very multiplicity impeded the accomplishment of essential activities. Many of their charters were drawn in such general terms that it was difficult for the Army and Navy, and even for the agencies themselves, to determine exactly what their responsibilities were. The War and Navy Departments found it necessary to maintain large staffs merely for conducting business with the maze of Washington agencies, and too much time and energy was uselessly expended. Although it is not the business of the military establishment to control or interfere with the civilian agencies necessary for the conduct of war, the Armed Forces have a most vital interest in their efficiency. The organization of the Executive Branch of the Government for war must be examined, and careful plans developed, in order that the benefits of all possible improvements, simplifications, and economies in directing and controlling the Nation's effort in the event of another emergency may be derived.

World War II disclosed other important lessons. Earlier wars were confined to a few well-defined combat areas. The divisions of responsibility and spheres of action between our land and sea forces were clear-cut. World War II marked a radical change in the manner of waging war. World War II covered the globe; weapons became more numerous, interchangeable, and varied; airpower developed into a major offensive force; armed forces grew larger and infinitely more complex; joint operations were the rule. Future security demands that we anticipate a global war, in which all combat elements engage, in every Theater, under a single command controlling all forces—land, sea, and air. We must be able to employ all three major arms in appropriate balance and force the instant war strikes. Only the most complete of the entire logistic mechanism will assure our ability to concentrate the full logistic strength of the Nation where it is needed, regardless of the fighting force served. Such integration must be accomplished in peace—it is too late to attempt it in war.

Logistic organization and procedures within and between the military forces were far from perfect during the recent war. Too much of our success was accompanied by inefficient practices. Too much was accomplished only by placing terrific strain upon the energies of our logistic leadership. Not enough can be attributed to sound organization and efficient procedures. The many self-contained procurement and supply agencies, eight in the War Department and eight in the Navy Department, had an adverse effect upon both industrial mobilization and the supply of combat forces. Duplicating supply lines and different standards of service among the Army, the Navy, and the Air Forces complicated and slowed logistic operations. Within the War Department itself two logistic organizations developed, one for supporting the Army Ground Forces and another for the Army Air Forces.

Complex organizational structures for Army administration, services, and supply existed in each oversea Theater. No two were alike, and no entirely satisfactory organization was developed during the war. Large headquarters with ill-defined and duplicating functions were the rule and achieved only partial success in coordinating supply. It was War Department policy to give complete autonomy to Theater Commanders in organizational matters. Recommendations made by the Commanding General, ASF, for standardizing oversea logistic organizations throughout the world in the interest of facilitating supply and improving administration and services were rejected. The importance of proper logistic organization in Theaters of Operations was not understood. It had received too little attention in peacetime.

The importance of logistic organization and functions in Theaters of Operation was not understood within the Army. The subject had received little attention in peacetime. Lack of doctrine governing logistic activities complicated relationships between Theaters and supporting supply agencies. Each Theater Commander was free to set up whatever type of logistic organization he desired, with the result that no two were alike. Differing systems, procedures, forms, and nomenclature constituted barriers that made coordination difficult.

Efforts of Theater Commanders to coordinate Army, Navy, Marine, and Air logistics were difficult and left much to be desired, because of inherent differences in the basic organization and systems employed by the three Services. Single operational command over land, sea, and air forces could not fully coordinate and unify logistic operations because logistic support was drawn from separate and independent organizations.

A fully satisfactory organization within tactical units of the Army for performing logistic functions in the field was not developed during the war. The number of types of service units, over 150 at the end of the war, is one indication of the confusion in this field. In addition, special units or units with special equipment were continuously created. There was an unnecessary overspecialization in types of service troops, thereby making it difficult to secure maximum flexibility in the utilization of service personnel. There was some experimentation with combined service units, but this type of organization, which had much to recommend it, was not pushed vigorously nor fully exploited.

At the beginning of the war, the War Department had been ill-prepared for handling large-scale logistic activities. No adequate methods existed for calculating supply requirements, balancing them against resources, or for controlling procurement. Peacetime stock accounting procedures, primarily designed to determine and charge losses, impeded rather than facilitated supply operations. The establishment of the Army Service Forces early in the war placed a great many of the logistic functions performed in the Zone of the Interior under a single Command that devoted much of its energy to the improvement and simplification of supply, administrative, service, and procurement systems and procedures. The new Command brought to bear the most advanced managerial experience in industry and Government, and made tremendous progress in developing uniform, efficient procedures. The Army Supply Program, the Supply Control System, the War Department Shipping Document, the Army Service Forces Personnel Control System, and the systems for domestic and overseas requisitions are examples of the logistic techniques developed. Standard, simple techniques for systematizing all recurring operations were also created. During the war the Army Service Forces sought the best key personnel, proper organization, and a framework of practical, well-understood procedures. These are practices that have been neglected by the Armed Forces as a whole. When compared with private enterprise, our Armed Forces have been backward, except under the impulsion of war, in utilizing modern managerial methods. The gains of the war must not be lost. Managerial improvements must be continuously and vigorously sought and applied.

Throughout the war, troop bases authorizing the numbers and types of troops to be activitated, trained, and deployed were unsatisfactory for logistic purposes. In 1943 at least 9 different War Department Troop Bases governed logistic planning and action at any given time. The Army Service Forces was compelled to anticipate the plans and decisions of the Combined Chiefs of Staff, the Joint Chiefs of Staff, and the War Department General Staff in order to have sufficient lead time to implement them. War is unpredictable and does not lend itself readily to precise long-range planning; however, a better system must be developed for estimating troop requirements and anticipating the deployment of units—one that will provide the logistician time and a firm basis for producing munitions and equipping the forces needed to implement strategic and operational plans.

Throughout the war insufficient numbers of service troops were provided in the War Department Troop Bases, which governed the number of service personnel trained and units activated. The needs of Theater Commanders were never completely filled; nor was the quality of service units as high as desired, because sufficient time was seldom provided for their training, and the need for the assignment of able individuals to service activities was not fully recognized. It is clear that in the future service troops will be increasingly vital to operations, that they must be carefully trained, and that they must be provided in adequate numbers both in the Zone of the Interior and in the Theaters of Operations.

Faulty military personnel administration was the source of a great many problems encountered in logistic operations, and the handling of military personnel was less efficient, in general, than other activities. Personnel policies and procedures governing the flow of individuals through induction, processing, training, assignment, and shipment overseas were complex and wasteful. Although the Army Service Forces made substantial progress in controlling and utilizing its own personnel, progress was not satisfactory throughout the War Department or in the oversea commands. No accurate statistics exist, but it is safe to say that the time lost because of unnecessary processing and delays in assignment was enormous. Methods of estimating personnel requirements in specific categories and of controlling assignments to such categories were inefficient. Personnel is the heart of any enterprise. Certainly it is basic to warfare. We were scraping the bottom of the barrel before World War II ended. Inefficiency in the utilization of the Nation's manpower will be unsafe in a future war.

Training in logistic planning and operations had been seriously neglected by the educational system of the Armed Forces. The Army War College and the Army Industrial College before the war gave some attention to certain phases of these subjects, but the overwhelming emphasis in officer training was upon tactics. The curricula of the Service Schools and the Command and General Staff School seldom included the handling of units larger than division or corps. Nowhere in an officer's training was there a comprehensive treatment of the logistic problems of the War Department or Theaters of Operations. Extensive knowledge of purchasing, production, distribution, storage, transportation, construction, communications, hospitalization, and finance was possessed by too few persons within the Armed Services. No captain of industry or commerce, regardless of his ability, was qualified to deal with the large and complex problems of Theaters of Operations, of the Technical Services, or of the War Department. This was also true of some of the officers who were made responsible for large and important commands. Few had training or experience in the management of large enterprises or the broader aspects of logistics. Granting the fundamental importance of logistics in modern war, it follows that military leaders must have a thorough appreciation and knowledge of the subject as a prerequisite to top command.

World War II demonstrated the importance of scientific research in the most spectacular manner. Never in the history of warfare were there more rapid and far-reaching scientific and technological developments in weapons. This was achieved through the unprecedented teamwork of science, industry, and the military. A most important logistic lesson is that our safety depends upon the continuation of this close collaboration in the development of new instruments of war. Scientific research is never static, nor is the secrecy surrounding weapons and production processes ever permanent. Our present superiority cannot be retained without a comprehensive, long-range research and development program designed to assure full scientific, industrial, and military participation. Such a program will be costly, but we dare not let penny-pinching or neglect endanger our security.

Victory in World War II was fashioned of superior munitions, of mobility, and of the skill, cooperation, and courage of our fighting forces. The exact nature of any future war cannot be foreseen. That it will be different from World War II is a certainty. Technological advances already have made obsolete many of the weapons and tactics of the last war. Self-propelled and guided missiles may eventually replace artillery and aircraft as major weapons. It is uncertain whether or not new applications of atomic energy will render battleships and carriers ineffectual and reduce the role of infantry and armored divisions to that of security and occupational duty. No one knows what offensive or defensive weapons electronics may provide. If new developments prove to be as revolutionary as it appears they may, it is entirely possible that contemporary concepts of naval, air, and ground warfare will be outmoded. It is already clear that different strategy, different tactics, and different methods of organizing the combat elements will be employed in a future war. Warfare will become more mobile, more mechanical, more destructive, more dependent upon science and technology. War will tend to involve more and more of the world's population and to spread to every corner of the globe.

It is inescapable that logistics will play a predominant role in any future conflict. Provision still must be made for the maintenance and comfort of the combat forces, regardless of their mission, and regardless of how they are organized and deployed. The rapid movement of troops and equipment to threatened points throughout the world will be of the utmost importance. Rapid mass production of new and improved weapons and all types of military equipment will be imperative. The destruction of logistic potentials will be the primary objective of warfare, the defeat of combat forces in the field becoming a secondary consideration.

The security of the United States presents a complex problem in logistic preparedness. How should we plan, and how can we organize for national security? What should be the place of logistics in the organization? What should be the relationship of logistic agencies to the combat arms and to other Government agencies? What is the best internal organization for accomplishing logistic functions? How shall we provide for the continuous research and development of new weapons; for adequate quantities of equipment and sufficient numbers of trained forces to meet sudden attack; for rapid manpower, industrial, and Governmental mobilization?

These are questions for which we must find satisfactory answers. They must be approached objectively, intelligently, and with courage. It is inevitable that the human tendencies to revert to old habits of thought and action, to promote segmentary interest, to protect the established order, to resist change, to be swayed by sentiment, will exert powerful influences. These tendencies have no place in our efforts to insure our Nation's security. Realism demands that we rise above lesser motivations and loyalties and work always for the highest good of the Nation.

Our future security depends upon the application of the logistic lessons of World War II. If the United States should again be attacked at a time when we are logistically unprepared, the result will be disaster.

Summary

Wars cannot be won without logistic superiority. The major logistic axiom of any war is: *"Get there first with the most."* Our inability to support the Philippines lost them. Skill, courage, and guts are not enough.

The outcome of the next war may very well be decided by what we have at the moment war strikes. The United States will be the first target next time, and we cannot count on Allies powerful enough to rescue us, once overcome.

The logistic organization with which we will fight must be in being and capable of immediate expansion. Our 1941–42 logistic organization had to be radically changed and a logistic command created. There will be no time for reorganization if war strikes again.

Military effectiveness must govern, but *logistic supportability is the first prerequisite.* Our resources are limited. The utmost economy within the framework of military effectiveness is imperative. Whether or not we use our resources efficiently is apt to mean the difference between victory and defeat.

We must be able to strike with full force and to *maintain that force until victory is won.* The Germans unquestionably had logistic superiority at the start of the war. They lost the war because they were unable to maintain that superiority.

Industrial and Governmental mobilization planning must be complete, precise, and capable of instant execution. We shall not have time, by trial and error, to improvise war agencies in the future. Nor can we expect to survive duplication or inefficiency.

Our research and development must secure and maintain, and our intelligence must confirm, *unquestionable superiority in weapons and military equipment.* The best possible balance between superiority in quality and superiority in quantity is imperative, and must be in being at all times.

Appendix I

LIST OF IMPORTANT MANAGEMENT IMPROVEMENTS ACHIEVED IN ASF TO 11 JUNE 1946

1. The Supply Control System. — A method of determining procurement requirements based upon ready comparison of estimated demands, stocks on hand, and post issue experience was all shown on one form. It introduced great improvements in and more ready control of procurement programs.

2. Procedure for Oversea Movement. — A standard procedure defining responsibilities of Technical Services, home ports, and staging areas in moving troops overseas was provided. This greatly improved all troop movements.

3. Procedure for Oversea Replacements. — Similar procedure for individual replacements.

4. Stock Control for Posts. — Standard procedure for fixing quantities of supplies to be held at Army posts, reduced stocks on hand, insured careful management of all supplies, and fixed requisitioning procedures to avoid overburdening depots.

5. Depot Missions. — A program which carefully defined the type of supplies to be stocked in all depots and gave stockage information to all interested parties, thus avoiding confusion in routing supply requisitions.

6. Identification of Individual Shipments. — A standard method of marking all cargo shipped overseas to identify shipper, receiver, and contents.

7. Procurement Assignment Board. — An agency for centralizing procurement of like items in a single service, reducing procurement and storage quantities.

8. Food Service Program. — A program to improve messing operations and menus, to reduce food requirements, and to cut food wastage.

9. Army Conservation Program. — A program to make all military personnel conscious of the need for careful maintenance of equipment and clothes, as well as to save electricity and other consumption.

10. Publications Control.	Required all ASF originated publications to have approval of review board, consolidated field printing plants, and reduced volume of field and contract printing through budgetary restrictions.
11. Standard Publications Program.	Rapid reproduction of necessary publications, by having 4 categories and procedures whereby plates were flown to various cities for printing near central points of distribution. Cut distribution time for manuals from 90 to 25 days, for orders from 25 to 9 days.
12. Company Pricing Program.	Procedure for review of company-pricing policies and financial position as a general guide on individual contract negotiation, thus providing broader and fairer basis for finding lower prices.
13. Consolidation of Training Centers.	Concentration of training in fewer locations as load declined—19 replacement training centers and 11 unit training centers concentrated into 13 ASF training centers.
14. Preactivation Training Program.	Advance designation of personnel for units while still being trained as individuals, thus hastening unit training.
15. Decentralization of Assignment Procedures.	Fixed responsibility for personnel assignments in ASF upon training centers and service commands, rather than Headquarters ASF, thus cutting number of field centers reporting to Washington from 1,900 to 36, and the types of installations for assignment from 65 to 37.
16. Pretermination Planning Program.	Advance agreements on methods of fixing the costs of settling termination contracts, thus hastening settlements.
17. Troop Movements Scheduling.	Exact time of troop movements within a 1-week range fixed by Chief of Transportation, thus insuring maximum utilization of railway equipment. At one time, seven divisions were moved throughout the United States with one set of rail equipment.
18. Consolidating Station Operations.	Less than carload lots of freight consolidated into carload lots to reduce freight charges and car demands.
19. Shipping Period Cycle System.	Each month divided into two shipping periods—convoys formed, ships loaded, supplies brought from depots on a standard, prearranged basis, saving manpower, and insuring full loading.
20. Block-Release System.	Method of preventing congestion in ports, requiring a release on all freight moving from depots and plants to ports.
21. Improved Loading Program.	Palletized loads and deck loading insured utilization of all space, saving need for additional ships.
22. Cost Accounting on Utilities and Repairs.	A means developed to check expenditures at posts to insure reduction of high cost operations.

23. Records Management Program.	Provision for the periodic retirement of files as accumulated, destruction of useless papers, microfilming to lessen volume of essential files—official files reduced 50 percent and essential files reduced another 50 percent by weeding out and microfilming.
24. Reports Control.	Nonessential reports were eliminated and a review of all existing and new reports made to insure usefulness—at beginning eliminated some 2,900 reports.
25. Work Simplification Program.	A program for careful analysis of clerical and materials handling operations developed to equalize load among existing personnel and to reduce waste motion and unnecessary operations.
26. War Department Shipping Document.	A single form developed to cover all operations in the shipment of supplies from depots to posts or overseas, thereby eliminating the preparation of some 6,000,000 shipping tickets a month, the preparation and mailing of 2,500,000, acknowledgments of receipt, and property accountability procedures at depots—this last alone saving the need for 500 clerks at ports.
27. Procedures for Discharge of Patients from Hospitals.	Required forms were reduced from 54 to 19 and the number of copies from 110 to 56. This reduced time required from 3 weeks to 3 days, and saved 20,000 beds a year in hospitals.
28. Sales Commissary Procedure.	Standardized procedures for issue of foodstuffs to sales commissaries provided, eliminating each year the preparation of some 15,000,000 issue slips, 1,350,000 requisition and inventory forms, and 750,000 copies of report of cash collections.
29. Physical Reclassification of Officers.	A new procedure reduced the average hospitalization of an officer being physically reclassified by approximately 29 days, with an annual savings of $5,000,000.
30. Payment of Telephone and Telegraph Bills.	A study of this activity resulted in a "Manual of Administrative Procedures for Communications Services" prescribing procedures that resulted in a 30 percent saving in personnel.
31. Officer Promotion Procedures.	A standard procedure for preparing and processing officer promotions was developed which resulted in an estimated annual savings of 550,000 man-hours and 2,500,000 sheets of paper. This procedure was also adopted by the Army Air Forces.
32. Tonnage Carried by Railroad Cars.	By means of a continuous analysis of freight moving on Government bills of lading, heavier loadings per car resulted in an annual saving equivalent to 150,000 cars.
33. Freight Rates.	Through informal negotiations with the railroads, and by formal cases presented to ICC an annual savings in freight cost of some 39 million dollars were obtained.

34. Use of Inland Waterways.	A program of routing Army freight via inland waterways whenever practicable resulted in a yearly saving in transportation costs of approximately $1,000,000.
35. Standard Procedure for Armed Forces Induction Stations.	Simplified procedures made the medical worksheet a basic form for induction processing, eliminating three forms, and saved an estimated 6,000,000 documents a year.
36. Regular Monthly Army Pay Rolls and Army Discharge Pay Rolls.	"Remarks" entries required on all regular monthly Army pay rolls and all Army discharge pay rolls were reduced and standardized in the fall of 1944. "Remarks" data were reduced 30 percent on the monthly Army pay rolls and 50 percent on the discharge pay rolls. Preparation, consulting, and checking time was reduced 30 percent. A new final payment pay roll for discharges was developed permitting the insertion of several names on one pay roll. Previously a separate pay roll was prepared for each enlisted man being discharged. As a result, the time required for preparation, computing and checking of these pay rolls was reduced 50 percent. The estimated savings for this procedure were some 600,000 man-days per year eliminated in preparation of pay rolls and over 350,000 copies of documents eliminated per year.
37. Retirement of Enlisted Personnel.	Simplified procedures to accomplish retirement of enlisted personnel reduced the number of forms from 31 to 15 and expedited the verification of length of service. Previously, retirement from hospitals required from 50 to 60 days. This was reduced to 17 days and an estimated savings per year on the procedure were about 62,000 copies of documents eliminated and some 1,800 hospital beds made available.
38. Service Record Form.	The extract from service record form was redesigned to facilitate preparation and reduce the information required. Approximately one-half of the data for which space was provided on the old form was eliminated from the revised form and the time required for preparation was reduced approximately 60 percent.
39. Hospital Admission Records.	The basic forms used for hospital admission records were simplified. Where formerly six basic admission forms had been prepared on the typewriter in six separate operations, the separate operations were eliminated by one typing of the constant information on a mimeographed stencil and the reproduction of the information on the six forms.
40. Individual Clothing and Equipment Records.	A consolidated form was developed early in 1945 to replace the individual clothing and equipment record, the individual equipment record, and the individual clothing and equipment record—quar-

	termaster property account. This consolidation resulted in an estimated yearly savings of over 11 million documents.
41. Personnel File Practices.	Standard procedures were established whereby the 201 file traveled with the enlisted man or officer, and when discharge or release from active duty occurred, the file was forwarded to the Office of The Adjutant General. Formerly each station at which an enlisted man or officer was assigned established and maintained a permanent 201 file covering his period of service at that post. Under the new procedure, the retention for each type of paper was specified and approximately 75 percent of the papers normally filed were destroyed at the end of the specified period. Some 15,000 file cabinets were made available for use through the destruction of these nonessential papers.
42. Reception Center Operations Procedures.	A processing schedule was developed that reduced the stay at reception centers by 1 day for over half of the enlisted men. A 1-page form for enlisted men's initial family allowance pay roll was subsituated for a 3-page form and an initial issue slip form for recording issues for up to 15 men was substituted for a copy of the individual clothing and equipment record prepared for each man. As a result of the simplified procedure, it was estimated that over 900,000 documents per year were eliminated.
43. Separation Centers.	A simplified procedure reduced the number of basic forms prepared for each enlisted man and officer from 32 to 6, cutting clerical work 30 percent. The original War Department plan had allowed 5 days for separation center processing. ASF reduced it to 2 days. The estimated savings were computed as some 500,000,000 documents eliminated from the entire demobilization job.
44. Processing Shipping Documents at Ports of Embarkation.	Early in 1945, procedures for processing shipping documents at ports of embarkation were revised and the copies of documents required by the port reduced by six on each oversea shipment. Over 16 million copies of documents per year were eliminated.
45. Depot Supply Procedures.	Depot supply procedures were standardized for all depots operated by Technical Services of the ASF, simplifying the receipt and issue of supplies, the processing of reports of survey and inventory adjustments, local purchases, and the receipt of excess supplies returned from stations and ports of embarkation.
46. Repairs and Utilities Materials.	Each Service Command established a repairs and utilities supply warehouse and a system whereby excess repairs and utilities materials at posts

257

	were reported to Service Command headquarters and, if desired, shipped to the Service Command warehouse for use in filling requisitions. Each Service Command also stored all stand-by supplies except minimum essentials required at each station for emergency purposes.
47. Preparation of Legal Opinions.	Formerly legal opinions of The Judge Advocate General's Office were several pages in length and recited history of legislation behind particular statute involved, and precedents upon which the opinion was based. Under a new procedure a supporting memorandum was prepared, but the opinion dispatched was a condensed form, usually only one or two short paragraphs, giving only the answer to the problem. A savings in typing personnel was made possible by the new procedure.
48. Civilian Pay Roll System.	A new procedure, later prescribed by the General Accounting Office for all Government agencies, simplified the preparation of the semimonthly pay rolls to show simply name and amount, and preserved the complete details of the payment on an annual card. Formerly, a card had to be submitted with each pay roll justifying individual changes. The annual card was audited quarterly which dovetailing with the pay roll periods considerably reduces the work load involved and levels out the peak load periods. Payments to civilian employees separating from Federal service were simplified by local payments of terminal leave in a lump sum and by local refund of civil-service retirement deductions.
49. Official Travel.	A new procedure prescribed a per diem in lieu of the mileage method of reimbursement to officer personnel for expenses incident to the performance of official travel on a temporary basis, thus reducing the expenditure of public funds and vastly simplifying the computation and payment of such travel accounts. Under the mileage system, an official trip of 5 days might return for instance $200 to an officer making an inspection of 1 day at some distant installation (round trip of 4,000 miles). Under the per diem system only $35 ($7 per day) would be allowed for this duty. The monetary advantages of brief trips covering long distances were nullified, and the per-diem standard of $7 per day for expenses resulted in more careful planning of official travel.
50. Coordination of Field Auditing.	Field audit coordination committees were established to avoid duplication of auditing when a contractor dealt with more than one agency of the War Department or with the War and Navy Departments. Also, the principle of selective

auditing was adopted in place of the previous policy of a 100 percent detailed audit of all transactions.

51. Office Services and Supplies. In 1943 a survey was made of the space and personnel engaged in office supply and service activities within the entire Army Service Forces. The survey disclosed that some 130,000 square feet of space was being used to house office supplies, and approximately 300 people were engaged in office supply functions in the ASF. As a result of the survey these functions were centralized in The Adjutant General's Office resulting in a savings of about 80,000 square feet of space, 85 persons, and $100,000 per month in operating costs.

52. Forms Standardization. At one time it was estimated that there were 200,000 different forms in ASF. A program was inaugurated to standardize and reduce the number of forms used, and Forms Design and Standardization Sections were established in the headquarters of staff divisions, Technical Services, and Service Commands. These headquarters decentralized the activity to the field for more effective administration. A forms inventory taken as of 1 April 1944 indicated that there were 179,524 forms in use in ASF. As of 1 May 1945, there were only 136,875 forms in use, a reduction of 42,649 or 23.8 percent. There were more forms than this actually eliminated as a survey showed that an average of 3,308 different forms were created each month because of new directives and changes in procedures. The objective of the forms program was to reduce all ASF forms to an inventory of 50,000. Economies were obtained by controls exercised over manifolding or special forms. One of these forms in the Transportation Corps was replaced by a style better suited to the job, and a savings of $22,000 was made on the first order.

53. General Hospital System. Because of the scarcity of outstanding medical specialists the functions of particular general hospitals were specialized as amputation centers, neurological centers, etc. Accordingly, the relatively few top-flight specialists in each field were placed in a few large institutions where they could reach and help the greatest number of patients needing the particular type of care in which each excelled. By this method special care was given to more than twice the number of patients for which the general hospital system was originally equipped to care, and this was done in spite of a reduction in the number of specialists engaged in the work.

54. Hospital Reports to Washington.	A revision in the procedure for submitting medical reports to the office of the Surgeon General eliminated the need for 80 full-time clerks in Washington and made it possible for medical installations in the field to omit the preparation of 250,000 report cards for 1944 alone.
55. Reciprocal Hospitalization of Army and Navy Personnel, and Bills for Out-Patient Treatment.	The office of the Surgeon General initiated and arranged with the Navy for reciprocal hospitalization of Army and Navy personnel without the necessity of billing for such service. Effected by an agreement between the two Secretaries, the new procedure eliminated a large amount of reporting, billing, bookkeeping, payment and auditing procedures, not only in both Departments but also in the hospitals, finance offices, and the General Accounting Office.
56. Supply of Ammunition.	The adoption of a credit system for the supply of ammunition under lend-lease and for training permitted either direct shipments from loading plants or from depots nearest the port of export. This procedure resulted in the elimination of many cross-hauls and back-hauls, and a savings of an estimated $500,000 per month.
57. Signal Corps Message Book.	A new message book was developed as a modification of Message Book 210-A which not only increased its usefulness, but cost about 45 percent less for each of the new books. Since there are approximately 30,000,000 message books used a year, an annual savings of about $1,300,000 was attained.
58. War Department Signal Center.	When the traffic load in the War Department Signal Center quadrupled during the first year of the war, it became apparent that ordinary methods of direct teletypewriter operation of circuits were wasteful, and that only through more efficient procedures could the immense volume of traffic yet to come be handled satisfactorily. Early in 1943, the installation of the most modern type of semi-automatic tape relay equipment was started. This equipment permitted the relay of equipment messages with a minimum of delay and manual handling. From January 1943 to January 1945, the number of personnel in the War Department Signal Center only increased from 722 to 790 while the words handled per day increased from 780,000 to 8,250,000 a 9 percent increase in personnel as against a 1,100 percent increase in traffic load.
59. Monthly Progress Report.	ASF developed a Monthly Progress Report of 27 sections providing a complete statistical record of progress made in the performance of various activities. This enabled the Commanding General and Staff Divisions to check on favorable or unfavorable trends.

60. Civilian Personnel Organization. Immediately after its creation, ASF built up civilian personnel staff units at each level of command and developed a civilian personnel program with primary emphasis upon proper placement, in-service training, employee welfare activities, employee counseling, and employee evaluation. This program resulted in better utilization of employee skills and a smaller civilian turn-over.

61. Consolidation of Fiscal and Finance Activities. ASF consolidated in one budgetary fiscal service, accounting, and disbursing activities with most operations decentralized to the field and emphasis in Washington upon proper staff planning. This resulted in greatly improved fiscal operations and the elimination of the need for a large central staff.

62. Improved Investigative Procedure. All necessary investigative operations were decentralized to field offices and the Washington office was reduced from 26 officers and 118 civilians to 10 officers and 9 civilians. A complicated 8-page personnel investigation form was reduced to a single page and clerical operations were cut 1,640,000 man-hours a year. Nearly 400 clerical workers were released in Service Command headquarters.

63. Service Command Reorganization. The Army Corps Areas, shorn of tactical authority and assigned to ASF, were reorganized into Service Commands and given responsibility for field performance of all ASF activities except procurement, storage, transportation, and construction. This program promoted improved coordination in the field of all interrelated activities.

64. Mail Handling. A mail manual was published to standardize practices for handling military mail at all Army installations, regular postal inspection of Army mail service was introduced and other practices modified to insure prompt distribution of all military mail.

65. Petroleum Organization. The responsibility for determining requirements for petroleum products for testing, for purchasing, for storage, and for supervising local procurement was vested in a single organization—the Fuels and Lubricants Division of the Office of the Quartermaster General. This brought about a centralized responsibility for all phases of petroleum procurement and effected savings in testing, purchasing, and storage.

66. Wage Administration. Authority was delegated to all Service Commands to make wage surveys for civilian employees subject to final approval by Headquarters, ASF, in accordance with delegation of responsibility from the National War Labor Board. Vigorous prosecution of wage surveys resulted in equalizing salaries among employees in various areas.

67. Army Travel Bureau.	ASF established central offices for the issuance of travel orders, travel requests, and the making of travel reservations. This resulted in speeding up the time required and eliminating much paper work in official travel, and insured adequate accommodations for official travel.
68. Program for More Effective Utilization of Personnel.	Between March and September 1943 a systematic effort was made to eliminate unnecessary activities by requiring all field installations to review their work and to submit recommendations for elimination of any activities regarded as unnecessary. Altogether, 3,547 recommendations were acted upon, of which 1,900 were approved. As a result, 891 nonessential activities and 682 nonessential records were eliminated and in another 457 cases authority for final action was decentralized to the field.
69. Handling of Excess and Surplus Property.	Procedures for the determination of excess and salvageable property were greatly simplified to bring about speedy action. Centralization of excess property was cut to types of items in which other agencies were interested in order to avoid unnecessary paperwork and time-consuming activity.
70. Standard Nomenclature.	A program was begun in 1944 to bring about standard nomenclature of identical spare parts to promote interchangeability and reduce spare parts procurement. By 30 June 1945 some 520,000 spare parts had been reviewed with a 30 percent reduction in catalog numbers.
71. Personnel Control System.	A standard system of personnel authorization was introduced by the ASF in June 1943, whereby bulk authorizations of personnel were made to Technical Services and service commands for allotment in turn to field installations. The personnel reporting followed the system of personnel authorization and brought all personnel needs under careful review by ASF headquarters.
72. Utilization of Electrical Accounting Machines.	Systematic inspection was introduced of all machine record units in ASF to bring about centralization of equipment, standardized instructions on their use, and the elimination of projects for which machine tabulation was not economical. In addition, a training program insuring competent operation of electrical accounting machines was introduced. The result was elimination of many units and a sizeable curtailment in the types of machine tabulating work done in the ASF.
73. Stockage of Forms and Publications.	The publication and storage of commonly used forms was centralized in The Adjutant General's Office and Service Command depots. Centralized forms and publications distribution warehouses were

established at posts. A modified stock control system on publications was introduced which eliminated many obsolete forms and redistributed excess supplies. In a 6-month period over 5,000 tons of obsolete forms were salvaged.

74. Cancelation of Allotments by Military Personnel. — A simplified procedure was introduced whereby soldiers and officers could terminate all allotments of pay. One form replaced 16 previously in existence with corresponding savings and paperwork. Field checks revealed that the new procedure prevented many errors in issuing checks for military personnel.

75. Officer Assignment Program. — Between November 1943 and April 1944 a full scale review was made of the classification and assignment of officer personnel in ASF. This program promoted better utilization of officer skills and raised the percentage of proper assignments to 97 percent of all officer personnel.

76. Care of Deceased Personnel Within the United States. — A study of the administrative procedures involved resulted in the issuance of a training manual furnishing for the first time in one book complete instructions for handling of deceased personnel. Under the new procedure the elapsed time for handling the deceased was shortened, and 22 forms and 75 copies of the forms were eliminated.

77. Discharges and Release From Active Duty. — A new procedure was developed and published in a War Department manual. This standardized procedures affecting discharges or releases from active duty at all installations other than separation centers. Yearly savings were estimated at 17,000 hospital beds made available, over 6 million man-days of enlisted personnel stay at hospitals eliminated, and over 22 million copies of documents eliminated.

78. Hospital Admission Records. — Basic forms were revised and standardized procedures were prescribed for all general and regional type hospitals in the continental United States. Where formerly six basic admission forms had been prepared on the typewriter in six separate operations the separate operations were eliminated by one typing of the constant information on a mimeographed stencil and the reproduction of the information on the six forms.

79. Immunization Register and Medical Data Form. — A revision of the form and a revised procedure of preparation resulted in an estimated yearly elimination of over 6½ million documents.

80. Individual Clothing Slip Form. — By extending usage of the existing property slip to requesting clothing, separate printing and stocking of two forms to provide for field usage of approximately 2,100,000 copies annually were eliminated and procedures simplified.

81. Return, Processing, and Disposition of Liberated American Prisoners of War From Europe.	Basic standardized procedures were developed and published in an ASF directive defining the responsibilities of ASF staff divisions, Technical Services, and Service Commands. Prior to this there had been numerous directives covering some phases of the activity, and other phases had not been covered at all.
82. Pay Data Card for Enlisted Personnel.	Under a new procedure this form was filled out only when a soldier was alerted for oversea duty, and was not maintained while the soldier was performing service within the United States. Over 100,000 man-days per year formerly utilized in the preparation of the form were saved.
83. Physical Reclassification and Retirement of Officers.	The procedures were simplified and standardized. Authority to issue orders was decentralized to station commanders of medical facilities authorized to reclassify officers and conduct retirement procedures. Unnecessary reviews were eliminated, officer stays in hospitals were reduced by an average of 29 days and transportation costs were reduced materially by increasing the number of disposition and retirement boards at hospitals. An estimated 1,000 hospital beds a year were made available and over 360,000 man-days of officer stays at hospitals eliminated.
84. Reception Stations Processing of Enlisted Personnel and Officers Returned From Overseas Under the Rotation Plan.	New procedures speeded up the processing of records by the use of mechanical office equipment. Time schedules were established for processing and provisions made to process many records prior to the actual arrival of returning personnel. Paying facilities were included in the processing line and pay tables prescribed to expedite computation of partial pay. A simple pay-roll form was substituted to cover five types of pay rolls formerly handled on four different forms. The preparation of certain forms was simplified and other forms were completely eliminated.
85. Service Records.	The preparation of service records was simplified and the numbering of required entries reduced to a minimum. The revised procedures eliminated 23 general classifications of information and some 34 million entries per year.
86. Purchasing Procedure for Procurement Offices.	The procedure in each technical service in ASF was simplified, standardized, and for the first time published in one volume. The revised procedures reduced the range of purchase orders and contracts distributed by Technical Services which had formerly been from 7 to 90 copies to from 7 to 26 copies. This, together with other simplifications in documentation, resulted in an estimated yearly savings of 18 million copies of documents eliminated.

87. Information Furnished Oversea Theaters on Army Shipments. A manual covering War Department practices was revised and expanded to a joint Army-Navy manual which established standard procedures for the flow of information covering movement of supplies, personnel, and baggage for both Army and the Navy from the United States to Theaters of Operations, between Theaters of Operations and from Theaters of Operations, back to the United States. Among the improvements obtained was the facilitation of the advance planning of supply programs by the oversea theaters. A more effective and prompt disposition of supplies upon arrival was possible and quicker turn-around of ships resulted.

88. Organizational Structure for Supply Depots. A standard organizational structure was published for all supply depots operated by the technical services of the ASF in order to increase the efficiency of administration.

89. Processing Domestic Requisitions. Development of simplified procedures expedited station supply operations and facilitated planning by establishing specific time limits for the completion of each supply action and by furnishing prompt information to stations on the status of their requisitions.

90. Laundry and Dry Cleaning. Standard procedures were developed for receiving, returning, and accounting for laundry and dry-cleaning bundles and for supplies and payments in fixed quartermaster laundries and dry-cleaning plants located in the United States. Savings under the new procedure were estimated at some 400,000 copies of documents and 70 million clerical operations eliminated.

91. Subsistence Supplies at Sales Commissaries in the United States. Standardized and simplified procedures were developed for the requisition, purchase, receipt, issue, shipment, and accounting for subsistence supplies at all sales commissaries located in the United States. The triple posting of over 2 million vouchers per year was reduced to one posting and the processing and filing of one additional copy of each of these 2 million vouchers was eliminated. Accounting for charge sales was simplified and the closing of sales officers' accounts at the end of the month was speeded up by approximately 15 days. The procedure eliminated the preparation of some 300,000 separate documents per year; posting of 4,300,000 vouchers and filing of 2,150,000 vouchers were eliminated.

92. Supplies at Posts, Camps, and Stations Directly Supplying Troops in the United States. Procedures were developed for the issue of supplies by posts, camps, and stations of the ASF and extended to all posts, camps, and stations in the continental United States. Army-wide uniform and simplified methods were thus established for the requisition, purchase, receipt, issue shipment,

and accounting for matériel and supplies (except subsistence supplies, blank forms, publications and harbor defense property) at posts, camps, stations, Army Air Forces bases and fields, and other War Department installations directly supplying troops in the United States.

93. Depot Inventories. Standard inventory procedures and specified mandatory frequencies for taking depot inventories were developed which prescribed that periodic inventories were to be taken and the most practical method to be employed for taking the actual physical count was specified. The accuracy of depot stock records made the stock record system of the ASF more reliable and resulted in more effective supply operations.

94. Oversea Supply. As a result of a study of the problems involved of the time required to effect oversea supply, it was decided that by eliminating schedules for west coast ports the current staggered initial and limiting dates, the over-all order and shipping time to the theater might be reduced. The west coast shipping period schedules were shortened 10 days to an over-all total of 65 days as a result of this schedule.

95. The Army Supply System. A study was made of the procedural directives issued in connection with the various phases of the Army Supply System. The study revealed that these directives covered almost 3,800 printed pages and contained about 1,300,000 words. Recommendations of the study to reduce these directives to a series of flow charts and manuals were approved. The new procedure when completed standardized operations within the Technical Services and coordinated the activities of the staff divisions.

96. Equipment for Kitchen Cars. Standardized lists of equipment for kitchen cars were developed and standardized, kit specifications were worked out. A manual was prepared illustrating not only what equipment should be included and how a car should be set up, but also how the equipment should be cleaned, packed, and delivered to a transportation officer for return to originating station. The use of the manual promoted the rapid assembly of supplies and equipment for departing troop trains and enabled the prompt return of equipment in condition for immediate reissue.

97. Subsisting Persons Traveling With Group Movements of Patients From Debarkation Hospitals. A simplified procedure was established for subsisting persons traveling in connection with group movements of patients from debarkation hospitals which completely clarified former procedures. A simplified accounting system was established in connection with the procedure for the

operating of messes and the subsisting of persons when no Army messing facilities were available. The system substantially reduced the burden of handling hospital trains. The accounting system was developed in detail, forms were designed and published, and the administrative detail formerly required of train ration officers was reduced.

98. Linen Control in General Hospitals. — Standard procedures for linen control were developed and established in all general hospitals in the United States except the Army Medical Center. These resulted in the elimination of all intermediate stocking between the laundry and the ward, and all counting and checking except at the laundry. From a multiplicity of forms the new procedure used one daily requisition and one quota sheet for each ward.

99. Daily Sick Report. — A procedure was established for the maintenance of the Daily Sick Report (WD AGO Form 5) which eliminated $16/18$ of all entries required by the existing sick report procedure. It was estimated that over 380,000 man-days per year was saved by the revised procedure in Zone of the Interior alone, and that over 215,000 man-days per year saved in oversea communications zones.

100. Processing Oversea Requisitions. — Standard procedures were developed for processing oversea requisitions which expedited oversea supply by establishing specific processing time limits and by eliminating uncontrolled extracting of oversea requisitions from one source of supply to another. Information on supply availability was provided to ports of embarkation for cargo planning and standard information on supply availability was furnished to the oversea Theaters. Later improvements in the original procedure effected substantial savings in the preparation and distribution of papers.

101. American Prisoner of War Information Bureau. — The use of automatic typewriters, form letters, and master flexoline lists of all American prisoners of war permitted one typing operation to serve more than one purpose. The maximum use of microfilm and photostat for reproduction of letters, documents, and lists and an addressograph system used for rapid addressing of parcel labels sent to next of kin of American prisoners of war and interned civilians also achieved many economies in operation.

102. "Master Inspection Responsibility List" and "List of Approved Commercial Reproducers of Classified Materials." — Maintenance of these lists on flexoline strips, and reproduction of lists by photographic methods instead of typing and mimeographing, reduced by almost 80 percent the clerical work involved and eliminated the possibility of error in reproduction.

103. Fiscal Pay Voucher for Officer.	A new fiscal pay voucher for officers and other military personnel who certified their own vouchers was developed which made possible the compiling of a final pay and mileage as well as mustering-out pay on a single voucher.
104. Typing of Constant Data on Forms.	Typing of constant data on forms, particularly names, army serial numbers, etc., was reduced to a minimum.
105. Transmittal Sheets and Memo Routing Slips.	Standard WD AGO forms for transmittal sheets and memo routing slips were developed which replaced hundreds of forms formerly used by the Headquarters, Army Service Forces, and subordinate offices in Washington.
106. Form for Oaths of Office.	Various forms for oath of office were combined into one form.
107. AGO Central Microfilming Plant.	A central plant was established, combining three separate plants in Washington; the number of employees was reduced from 349 to 220 within six months with 10 percent increase in production.
108. Mail and Telegraph Messages.	A message form was designed and introduced to encourage the sending of brief messages by mail as well as telegraph as a measure to reduce traffic by electrical means.
109. Decorations and Awards.	The entire list of forms used in connection with decorations and awards were redesigned and specialized forms were developed with the maximum data printed on the form. Cards were also used as the last copy of each form making it unnecessary to prepare a folder for filing since the name of the individual appears in the left-hand corner of the card. Machines were procured which would imprint the names of recipients of medals on the medals thereby eliminating hand engraving.
110. Reports of Casualties.	At first individual reports and telegrams were prepared on each Army casualty and distributed to the various interested agencies and next of kin. Under a new procedure one standard form was developed on document paper and from it were reproduced reports for next of kin. The new system was used for reporting deaths, missing in action, interned, prisoners of war, and in appropriate cases return to duty. A form was also developed for preparing in one operation reports on wounded, injured, and seriously ill and return to duty. The reporting of domestic deaths was simplified by handling this on a documat and producing the necessary copies therefrom. The new procedures resulted in a reduction in the cost of operation, materials used, reporting operations and the time required in preparation of reports.
111. Morning Report.	As a result of a study of the Company Morning Report, the Headquarters Morning Report, and the

Report of Change, the Company and the Headquarters morning reports were consolidated and the Report of Change was eliminated. Revised morning reports were prepared and forwarded in triplicate to Machine Records Units. One entire procedure was thus eliminated and the procedure was transferred from typewriter preparation to machine preparation.

112. Hospital Inspection. Formerly, inspection visits to hospitals were made independently by various representatives of the Surgeon General's Office and service command headquarters with little or no coordination. A new coordinated type of inspection, after testing, was put into effect in April 1944. The new inspections, taking one day or at most two days, were predicated on taking the maximum amount of corrective action on the spot, and thus avoiding correspondence and indorsements, covering both professional and administrative matters.

113. Housekeeping and Administration Services in the Signal Corps. In 1943 steps were initiated to consolidate the services and function common to two or more Signal field installations at the same general location. These included utility services, performance of local housekeeping and administration services, the processing of military and civilian personnel activities, writing of travel orders, handling of fiscal and legal functions, and other miscellaneous services. The program resulted in considerable centralization and saving of personnel, equipment, space, and reports. It also provided for uniformity of procedures and operations, and for simplification of staff supervision by headquarters. It was estimated that at least 500 additional personnel would be required if these services had been performed by each individual installation.

114. Delivery of Messages by Signal Corps. The use of pneumatic tubes and conveyor belts within the Signal Center expedited the transfer of messages to various locations and eliminated the need for messenger service.

115. Message Center of Chemical Warfare Service. A survey of the CWS message center resulted in the adoption of new procedures and a reduction in the number of employees from 145 in September 1942, to 86 in March 1943, and 53 in April 1945. A follow-up study reduced the number of personnel from 53 to 39 in July 1945.

116. Control of Nonappropriated Funds. AR 210–50, 210–65, and 210–70, with War Department Circulars 218 and 219 set up guiding principles on financial operations of Army exchanges, Army motion picture theaters, and messes. These revenue-producing activities were to be kept solvent at all times, the profits were to be

used for the benefit of the post where accumulated except that above specified limits the income was to go to the Army Exchange Fund and an Army Central Welfare Fund. Dividends of exchanges were fixed so that excess capital would be paid out during the war. These provisions prevented the accumulation of large funds at posts which might be used for building construction or other improvements, and gave support to exchange activities at small posts.

Appendix II

KEY PERSONNEL

Key Personnel
9 March 1942
Services of Supply

Commanding General	Major General Brehon Somervell.
Chief of Staff	Colonel W. D. Styer.

Office of the Commanding General

Deputy Chief of Staff for Requirements and Resources.	Colonel Lucius D. Clay.
Director of Procurement and Distribution.	Colonel Charles D. Young.
Deputy Director of Procurement and Distribution.	Mr. Douglas C. MacKeachie.
Assistant for Production	Major General T. J. Hayes.
Assistant	Mr. A. R. Glancy.
Assistant for Purchases	Mr. Albert J. Browning.
Assistant for Distribution	Colonel F. A. Heileman, Acting.
Army Member, Executive Committee, Army-Navy Munitions Board.	Brigadier General Charles Hines.

Functional Staff

Administrative Assistant	Colonel Joe N. Dalton.
Public Relations and Information	Colonel A. Robert Ginsburgh.
Control	Colonel C. F. Robinson.
Operations	Brigadier General LeR. Lutes.
Training	Brigadier General Clarence R. Huebner.
Personnel	Colonel James E. Wharton.
Budget and Financial	Brigadier General Arthur H. Carter.
Requirements	Colonel Cyrus H. Searcy.
Defense Aid	Brigadier General Henry S. Aurand.
Resources	Brigadier General Charles Hines.

Chiefs of Operating Divisions
(Supply and Administrative Services)

Quartermaster General	Major General Edmund B. Gregory.
Chief of Engineers	Major General Eugene Reybold.
Chief of Ordnance	Major General Charles M. Wesson.

Surgeon General	Major General James C. Magee.
Chief Signal Officer	Major General Dawson Olmstead.
Chief of Chemical Warfare Service	Major General William N. Porter.
Chief of Transportation	Colonel Charles P. Gross.
Chief of General Depots	Colonel Frederick S. Strong, Jr., Acting.
Chief of Administrative Services	Major General John P. Smith.
The Adjutant General	Major General James A. Ulio.
Provost Marshal General	Major General Allen W. Gullion.
Chief of Special Services	Brigadier General F. H. Osborn.
Chief of Finance	Major General Howard K. Loughry.
Judge Advocate General	Major General Myron C. Cramer.
Chief of Statistical Services	Brigadier General Leonard P. Ayres.
Chief of Chaplains	Brigadier General William R. Arnold.

Corps Areas

I	Major General Sherman Miles.
II	Major General Irving J. Phillipson.
III	Major General Milton C. Reckord.
IV	Major General William Bryden.
V	Major General Daniel L. Van Voorhis.
VI	Major General Joseph M. Cummins.
VII	Major General Frederick E. Uhl.
VIII	Major General Richard Donovan.
IX	Major General Jay L. Benedict.

Key Personnel
30 June 1943
Army Service Forces

Commanding General	Lieutenant General Brehon Somervell.
Chief of Staff	Major General W. D. Styer.

Office of the Commanding General

Deputy Chief of Staff for Service Commands.	Major General George Grunert.
Executive for Service Commands	Brigadier General Philip Hayes.
Control Division	Brigadier General C. F. Robinson.
Technical Information Division	Mr. Harry M. Shackleford.
Intelligence Division	Colonel James M. Roamer.

Staff Divisions

Director of Personnel	Brigadier General Joe N. Dalton.
Military Personnel Division	Brigadier General R. B. Reynolds.
Industrial Personnel Division	Mr. James P. Mitchell.
Director, Women's Army Auxiliary Corps.	Colonel Oveta Culp Hobby.
Officer Procurement Service	Brigadier General C. H. Danielson.
Chief of Chaplains	Brigadier General William R. Arnold.

Director of Personnel—Continued
- Special Services Division — Brigadier General F. H. Osborn.
- Army Specialized Training Division. — Colonel Herman Beukema.

Director of Military Training — Brigadier General Walter L. Weible.
Director of Operations — Major General LeR. Lutes.
- Deputy Director — Brigadier General F. A. Heileman.
- Planning Division — Colonel C. B. Magruder.
- Stock Control Division — Colonel Robert A. Case.
- Storage Division — Colonel Albert B. Drake.
- Maintenance Division — Colonel William S. Conrow.
- Mobilization Division — Colonel Charles E. Dissinger.

Director of Matériel — Major General Lucius D. Clay.
- Requirements Division — Brigadier General Walter A. Wood, Jr.
- Purchases Division — Brigadier General Albert J. Browning.
- Production Division — Brigadier General Hugh C. Minton.
- International Aid Division — Brigadier General Boykin C. Wright.

Fiscal Director — Major General Arthur H. Carter.
- Chief of Finance — Major General Howard K. Loughry.

Director of Administration — Major General James L. Collins.
- Deputy Director — Brigadier General Madison Pearson.
- The Adjutant General — Major General James A. Ulio.
- Judge Advocate General — Major General Myron C. Cramer.
- Provost Marshal General — Major General Allen W. Gullion.
- Army Exchange Service — Brigadier General Joseph W. Byron.
- National Guard Bureau — Major General John F. Williams.
- Executive for Reserve and ROTC Affairs. — Brigadier General E. W. Smith.

Technical Services

- Quartermaster General — Major General Edmund B. Gregory.
- Chief of Ordnance — Major General Levin H. Campbell, Jr.
- Chief of Engineers — Major General Eugene Reybold.
- Chief of Chemical Warfare Service — Major General William N. Porter.
- Chief Signal Officer — Major General Harry C. Ingles, Acting.
- Surgeon General — Major General Norman T. Kirk.

Service Commands

- First — Major General Sherman Miles.
- Second — Major General Thomas A. Terry.
- Third — Major General Milton C. Reckord.
- Fourth — Major General William Bryden.
- Fifth — Major General Fred C. Wallace.
- Sixth — Major General Henry S. Aurand.
- Seventh — Major General Frederick E. Uhl.
- Eighth — Major General Richard Donovan.
- Ninth — Major General Kenyon A. Joyce.
- Northwest — Brigadier General James A. O'Connor.
- Military District of Washington — Major General John T. Lewis.

Key Personnel
30 June 1944
Army Service Forces

Commanding General	Lieutenant General Brehon Somervell.
Chief of Staff	Major General W. D. Styer.

Office of the Commanding General

Director of Plans and Operations	Major General LeR. Lutes.
Deputy Director	Brigadier General Walter A. Wood.
Deputy Director for Demobilization.	Brigadier General Stanley L. Scott.
Special Assistant	Brigadier General William A. Borden.
Special Advisor	Mr. Howard Bruce.
Requirements and Stock Control.	Colonel H. M. Reedall.
Planning Division	Colonel C. B. Magruder.
Mobilization Division	Colonel Charles E. Dissinger.
Control Division	Brigadier General C. F. Robinson.
Deputy Chief of Staff for Service Commands.	Brigadier General J. F. Battley.
Provost Marshal General	Major General Archer L. Lerch.
National Guard Bureau	Major General John F. Williams.
Intelligence Division	Colonel James M. Roamer.

Staff Divisions

The Adjutant General	Major General James A. Ulio.
Judge Advocate General	Major General Myron C. Cramer.
Director of Personnel	Major General Joe N. Dalton.
Deputy Director	Colonel Charles E. Hixon.
Military Personnel Division	Brigadier General R. B. Reynolds.
Industrial Personnel Division	Mr. William A. Hughes.
Special Services Division	Brigadier General Joseph W. Byron.
Officer Procurement Service	Colonel E. G. Welsh.
Chief of Chaplains	Brigadier General William R. Arnold.
Personal Affairs Division	Colonel F. G. Munson.
Morale Services	Major General F. H. Osborn.
Executive for Reserve and ROTC Affairs.	Brigadier General E. W. Smith.
Director of Military Training	Major General Walter L. Weible.
Deputy Director	Colonel Arthur G. Trudeau.
Army Specialized Training Division.	Colonel A. W. Chilton.
Military Training Division	Colonel R. T. Beurket.
Director of Supply	Brigadier General F. A. Heileman.
Distribution Division	Colonel Robert A. Case.
Storage Division	Colonel A. B. Drake.
Maintenance Division	Colonel William S. Conrow.
Director of Matériel	Major General Lucius D. Clay.
Purchases Division	Brigadier General Albert J. Browning.

Director of Matériel—Continued
- Production Division — Brigadier General Hugh C. Minton.
- Research and Development Division. — Colonel R. M. Osborne.
- International Division — Major General G. E. Edgerton.
- Renegotiation Division — Mr. J. M. Dodge.
- Readjustment Division — Colonel David N. Hauseman.

Fiscal Director — Major General Arthur H. Carter.
- Chief of Finance — Major General Howard K. Loughry.
- Audit Division — Colonel J. W. McEachren.
- Accounts Division — Colonel H. W. H. Burrows.
- Pay Allotments Division — Lt. Colonel D. H. Tyson.
- Receipts and Disbursements Division. — Colonel H. F. Chrisman.
- Special Financial Services Division — Colonel John C. Mechem.
- Administrative Division — Colonel D. T. Nelson.

Technical Services

- Quartermaster General — Major General Edmund B. Gregory.
- Chief of Ordnance — Major General Levin H Campbell, Jr.
- Chief of Engineers — Major General Eugene Reybold.
- Chief of Chemical Warfare Service — Major General William N. Porter.
- Chief Signal Officer — Major General Harry C. Ingles.
- Surgeon General — Major General Norman T. Kirk.
- Chief of Transportation — Major General Charles P. Gross.

Service Commands

- First — Major General Sherman Miles.
- Second — Major General Thomas A. Terry.
- Third — Major General Philip Hayes.
- Fourth — Major General Frederick E. Uhl.
- Fifth — Major General James L. Collins.
- Sixth — Major General Henry S. Aurand.
- Seventh — Major General C. H. Danielson.
- Eighth — Major General Richard Donovan.
- Ninth — Major General David McCoach, Jr.
- Northwest — Colonel Frederick S. Strong, Jr.
- Military District of Washington — Major General John T. Lewis.

Key Personnel
30 June 1945
Army Service Forces

- Commanding General — General Brehon Somervell.
- Chief of Staff — Lieutenant General LeR. Lutes.

Office of the Commanding General

- Deputy Chief of Staff for Service Commands. — Major General Richard Donovan.

Director of Plans and Operations	Major General Daniel Noce.
Deputy Director	Major General Stanley L. Scott.
Requirements and Stock Control Division.	Brigadier General T. M. Osborne.
Planning Division	Major General Stanley L. Scott.
Mobilization Division	Brigadier General Charles E. Dissinger.
Control Division	Major General C. F. Robinson.

Staff Divisions

The Adjutant General	Major General James A. Ulio.
Judge Advocate General	Major General Myron C. Cramer.
Provost Marshal General	Major General Archer L. Lerch.
Director of Personnel	Major General V. L. Peterson.
Deputy Director	Major General Joe N. Dalton.
Military Personnel Division	Colonel Charles E. Hixon.
Industrial Personnel Division	Colonel R. F. Gow.
Special Services Division	Major General Joseph W. Byron.
Information and Education Division.	Major General F. H. Osborn.
Chief of Chaplains	Brigadier General Luther D. Miller, Acting.
Personal Affairs Division	Colonel F. G. Munson.
Director of Military Training	Brigadier General Arthur G. Trudeau.
Training Requirements Division	Colonel W. L. Bennett.
School Division	Colonel A. W. Chilton.
Troop Training Division	Colonel R. T. Beurket.
Director of Supply	Major General F. A. Heileman.
Deputy Director	Brigadier General N. H. McKay.
Distribution Division	Colonel Robert A. Case.
Storage Division	Brigadier General H. W. Beyette.
Maintenance Division	Colonel Morris K. Barroll, Jr.
Director of Matériel	Mr. Howard Bruce.
Deputy Director	Major General G. E. Edgerton.
Purchases Division	Colonel F. C. Foy.
Production Division	Brigadier General Hugh C. Minton.
Research and Development Division.	Brigadier General E. A. Regnier.
International Division	Brigadier General Don G. Shingler.
Renegotiation Division	Colonel Maurice Hirsch.
Readjustment Division	Brigadier General David N. Hauseman.
Fiscal Director	Major General Arthur H. Carter.
Chief of Finance	Major General Howard K. Loughry.
Intelligence Division	Colonel James M. Roamer.

Technical Services

Quartermaster General	Lieutenant General Edmund B. Gregory.
Chief of Ordnance	Lieutenant General Levin H. Campbell, Jr.
Chief of Engineers	Lieutenant General Eugene Reybold.
Chief of Chemical Warfare Service	Major General William N. Porter.
Surgeon General	Major General Norman T. Kirk.

Chief Signal Officer	Major General Harry C. Ingles.
Chief of Transportation	Major General Charles P. Gross.

Service Commands

First	Major General Sherman Miles.
Second	Major General Thomas A. Terry.
Third	Major General Philip Hayes.
Fourth	Major General Edward H. Brooks.
Fifth	Major General James L. Collins.
Sixth	Major General David McCoach, Jr.
Seventh	Major General C. H. Danielson.
Eighth	Lieutenant General Walton H. Walker.
Ninth	Major General W. E. Shedd.
Military District of Washington	Major General C. F. Thompson.

Key Personnel
10 June 1946
Army Service Forces

Commanding General	Lieutenant General LeR. Lutes.*
Chief of Staff	Major General Daniel Noce.

Office of the Commanding General

Deputy Chief of Staff for Service Commands	Major General Richard Donovan.
Director of Plans and Policy	Brigadier General Aaron Bradshaw, Jr., Acting.
Assistant Director (Surplus Disposals)	Brigadier General T. M. Osborne.
Management Branch	Colonel Robert C. Kyser.
Planning Branch	Colonel James F. Torrence, Jr.
Current Branch	Colonel Thomas H. Harvey.
Program Analysis Branch	Colonel Frank A. Bogart.

Staff Divisions

Director of Personnel	Major General Joe N. Dalton.
Deputy Director	Brigadier General Thomas F. Hickey.
Military Personnel Division	Colonel Charles E. Hixon.
Civilian Personnel Division	Mr. Dudley Frank.
Personal Affairs Division	Colonel M. J. Marques.
Director of Military Training	Major General Paul W. Baade.
School Division	Colonel F. Moylan Fitts.
Troop Training Division	Colonel William C. Fisher.
Director of Supply	Colonel Arthur V. Winton, Acting.
Supply Control Branch	Colonel Edmund K. Daley.
Maintenance Branch	Colonel Morris K. Barroll, Jr.
Distribution Branch	Colonel Frank A. Henning.

*Deputy Commanding General 18 April 1945 to 31 December 1945, Commanding General 1 January 1946 to 11 June 1946.

Director of Supply—Continued
    Storage Branch — Colonel H. Spencer Struble.
    Nomenclature and Cataloging Branch. — Lieutenant Colonel Elbert M. Sleeker.

Director of Procurement — Brigadier General Don G. Shingler.
    Procurement Judge Advocate — Colonel Ernest M. Brannon.
    Current Procurement Branch — Colonel Phillips W. Smith.
    Procurement Planning Branch — Colonel Phillips W. Smith.
    Readjustment Branch — Mr. Malcolm R. White.
    Renegotiation Branch — Brigadier General Maurice Hirsch.
    Research and Development Branch — Colonel M. M. Irvine, Acting.
    International Branch — Brigadier General Don G. Shingler.

Director of Services — Major General Richard Donovan.
    Troop Units Branch — Lieutenant Colonel Robert V. Murphy, Acting.
    Movements Branch — Lieutenant Colonel Richard L. McKee.
    Installations Branch — Colonel F. Russel Lyons.
    Specialized Services Branch — Colonel John Nash.

Intelligence Division — Colonel James M. Roamer.

Administrative Services

The Adjutant General — Major General Edward F. Witsell.
Judge Advocate General — Major General Thomas H. Green.
Provost Marshal General — Brigadier General Blackshear M. Bryan, Jr.
Chief of Chaplains — Major General Luther D. Miller.
Director, Special Services Division — Major General Russel B. Reynolds.

Technical Services

Quartermaster General — Major General Thomas B. Larkin.
Chief of Ordnance — Major General Everett S. Hughes.
Chief of Engineers — Lieutenant General Raymond A. Wheeler.
Chief of Chemical Warfare Service — Major General Alden H. Waitt.
Chief Signal Officer — Major General Harry C. Ingles.
Surgeon General — Major General Norman T. Kirk.
Chief of Transportation — Major General Edmund H. Leavey.
Chief of Finance — Major General William H. Kasten.

Service Commands

First — Major General Ira T. Wyche.
Second — Major General James A. Van Fleet.
Third — Major General Manton S. Eddy.
Fourth — Major General Edward H. Brooks.
Fifth — Major General Robert S. Beightler.
Sixth — Lieutenant General Walton H. Walker.
Seventh — Major General William G. Livesay.
Eighth — Major General Kearie L. Berry.
Ninth — Colonel William M. Cravens, Acting.
Military District of Washington — Brigadier General Claude B. Ferenbaugh.

Made in the USA
Monee, IL
17 September 2019